CONTENTS

ACKNOWLEDGMENTS

I began this project over a decade ago and think of this book as an installment rather than a conclusion. I have in that time accumulated more debts than can be recorded in a page or two of acknowledgments and shall list here only the more directly relevant of them. The John Simon Guggenheim Memorial Foundation made possible a year's leave, without which I would surely not have completed even an installment. At an earlier stage of the project, the National Endowment for the Humanities provided a Summer Stipend that made possible sustained reading in the British Library, a period of study having a formative influence on my thinking about this topic. The invaluable resources of the Houghton Library of Harvard University were available to me during several periods of leave granted by the University of California, Santa Barbara, and the collections of the William Andrews Clark Memorial Library of the University of California, Los Angeles have been equally useful. Funds for assistance in preparing the manuscript for publication were assigned by the Research Committee of the Academic Senate of the University of California, Santa Barbara.

The sponsorship of the National Endowment for the Humanities enabled me to present a Summer Seminar for College Teachers on the topic of historiography and fiction. I am grateful for the opportunity I had to discuss many of the concerns of this book with twelve seminar participants who admirably combined intelligence, learning, and good humor. And over the years during which this study was developing, sometimes festering, conversation with Garrett Stewart stimulated laughter as well as encouraged thought. I am grateful for his incisive readings of several portions of the manuscript. I have profited from Porter Abbott's and Robert Mayer's helpful comments on some thorny problems in the first two chapters. Andrew Zimmerman and Muriel Zimmerman read the entire manuscript in late stages with a care that I deeply appreciate. Their comments led to improvements in each chapter.

The publisher's readers, Carol Kay and Melvyn New, read the manuscript meticulously and with a sympathetic as well as a critical eye. Their valuable suggestions shaped many aspects of the final version of the manuscript and saved me from numerous errors and confusions. They are, of course, not responsible for remaining faults, especially as in a very few cases I persisted in the error of my ways. In later stages of the manuscript's preparation, I benefited from the careful assistance of Lorna Clymer, Emily Allen, Noel Williams, and Patricia Marby. Cornell University Press and its Executive Editor, Bernhard Kendler, have as always responded with the courtesy, efficiency, and insight that lighten even the more onerous burdens of bringing a manuscript to publication.

Large portions of three formerly published essays are included in Chapters 3 and 5 and are here reprinted with the permission of their first publishers: Everett Zimmerman, "A Tale of a Tub and Clarissa: A Battling of Books," excerpted with permission of G. K. Hall, an imprint of Simon & Schuster Macmillan, from Critical Essays on Jonathan Swift, edited by Frank Palmeri, pp. 143–63; "Fragments of History and The Man of Feeling: From Richard Bentley to Walter Scott," from Eighteenth-Century Studies 23 (1990): 283–300, reprinted with permission of Johns Hopkins University Press; "Tristram Shandy and Narrative Representation," The Eighteenth Century: Theory and Interpretation 28 (1987): 127–46, reprinted with permission of the Texas Tech University Press.

And finally, I record names of some of those to whom I am now no longer able to present a copy of this book as even a minimal token of my esteem and gratitude: Elisabeth Schneider, John Carroll, William Frost, Vivian Mercier, Benjamin Sankey.

E. Z.

INTRODUCTION

"Historical Faith"

In a letter to William Warburton, Samuel Richardson protests Warburton's open reference to *Clarissa*'s fictionality and asks that the "Historical Faith which Fiction itself is generally read with" not be undermined.[1] He is not attempting to have his collection mistaken for historical letters (*Clarissa* is not a hoax), yet he is unwilling to sanction Warburton's explicit separation of *Clarissa* from the historical. Other writers of eighteenth-century fiction indicate a similar reluctance to have their fictions definitively separated from history. Readers then and now have on occasion expressed contempt for, or alarm at, the notion that fiction is in any serious way connected to history. But the alternative presupposition—that these writers of what we now know as the eighteenth-century novel were asking for nothing more than a suspension of disbelief—is not itself entirely plausible. Their various pleas for some kind of historical faith imply cumulatively (although not in the same degree or manner in each) a commitment to the historical as a relevant category for understanding their fictional achievements. I do not argue that these novelists insist that their writings be taken *as* authentic histories. They appear rather to be demanding that the relationship of their fictions to history he considered seriously. The novel thus raises questions about the verifiably referential, which had become a normative standard for history: does a rigorous application of that standard not leave gaps in our knowledge of the past that seriously compromise history's meaningfulness? The novel implies that it is a needed supplement to history, its

---

[1] *Selected Letters of Samuel Richardson*, ed. John Carroll (Oxford: Clarendon Press, 1964), 19 April 1748, p. 85. Warburton had provided a preface for *Clarissa*.

probabilistic truths adding an essential dimension to historical understanding even if they are not verifiably referential.[2]

The term "novel" as I use it refers to our post-facto construction of a restricted eighteenth-century canon of fiction but is not used to minimize or invalidate those many studies that have analyzed a more extended and diverse body of fictional work. I focus on a relatively small group of eighteenth-century writings that appear to be consolidating a notion of what is desirable in fiction, sometimes through their own appropriation of the more diverse fictions that they marginalize.[3] Of major conceptual importance here are the influential narrative experiments of Richardson in *Clarissa*, Fielding in *Tom Jones*, and Sterne in *Tristram Shandy*, which appear to be motivated in part by each author's perception of the limitations and suppressions of prior methods of narration.[4] In the context of the historiographical issues that each of these novels evokes, these narrative experiments imply that *historical* narration is also rooted in a narrator and a narrative method and not in an ineluctible series of past events that somehow make their appearance in the narrative. In this book I emphasize historiography in the sense of the theory of the reading and writing of history and do not give detailed consideration to the large-scale histories written in the eighteenth century, such as those of Gibbon, Hume, and Catherine Macaulay. The fuller treatment of the historical consciousness revealed in eighteenth-century fiction that is possible in the context of these histories will be pursued in a later book.

The critique of history explicitly and implicitly mounted by the novel is related to empiricist assumptions that invaded all aspects of eighteenth-century thought. Seventeen- and eighteenth-century empiricism is characterized by a considerably different outlook from the later and more programmatic positivism with which it is often associated.[5] Empiricism's

[2] Barbara Foley, *Telling the Truth: The Theory and Practice of Documentary Fiction* (Ithaca: Cornell University Press, 1986), makes the ingenious suggestion that early novelistic fiction asks "to be read as one kind of discourse but [mobilizes] perceptual habits and responses routinely associated with another kind of discourse" (p. 107). She argues that later fiction has a different, less balanced or ambiguous, relation with the discourses it models itself on: "Tolstoy and Wright were not imitating chronicle and biography in anything like the way that Defoe and Richardson were imitating the rogue's confession or the set of letters" (p. 108).

[3] William B. Warner, "The Elevation of the Novel in England: Hegemony and Literary History," *ELH* 59 (1992): 577–96, discusses the absorption of earlier narrative patterns by Richardson and Fielding, and the consequent displacement of Behn, Manley, and Haywood.

[4] Howard Anderson, "Answers to the Author of *Clarissa*: Theme and Narrative Technique in *Tom Jones* and *Tristram Shandy*," *Philological Quarterly* 51 (1972): 859–873, discusses interactions among these novels and novelists.

[5] Jules David Law, *The Rhetoric of Empiricism: Language and Perception from Locke to I. A. Richards* (Ithaca: Cornell University Press, 1993), characterizes empiricism as a "highly

emphasis on experience, especially on observation, was early understood in a manner for more complex than that sometimes attributed to the empirical outlook. From its early Baconian and then Royal Society phases, empiricism had to contend with the difficulties of transmitting the information derived from experimentation. This problem had long been posed by scientific instrumentation: observation is in its most immediate sense relegated to the instrument rather than to the biased or more physically limited human. And in a communally defined enterprise like that of the Royal Society, experiments had to be described in a manner likely to convey their truths persuasively through discursive accounts, despite the evident epistemological superiority of witnessing the actual experiment. Furthermore, much about natural history, geography, and culture can be conveyed only through the eye-witness accounts of travelers. Epistemological principles and rhetorical procedures needed to be reconciled if the attempt to build structures of knowledge that derive from sources beyond the comprehension of any single witness were to be successful.[6]

History, even more than natural philosophy, had to confront the problem of an empiricism that valorized witnessing and distrusted testimony. Despite this built-in skepticism toward history, British empiricism persistently maintained the validity and importance of history. Indeed, history became the arm by which empiricism encountered the social world (including religion), which in order to be understood needed to be observed through its construc-

---

rhetorical cultural enterprise, concerned with persuasion as much as demonstration, with social vision as much as scientific inquiry, and with 'coherence' as much as 'correspondence' " (p. 12). Among its central concerns is "reflection," which Law notes is "both the most natural and the most contrived of perceptual habits; it is a way of noticing (or a quality of attention) modeled on natural optical phenomena, but it is one that . . . suggests equally the processes of passive mimesis and of critical self-scrutiny" (p. 56). Law also argues that empiricism needed to keep language and sensory evidence engaged with each other in order to "sustain a complicated and constantly shifting relationship between verbal and visual meaning" (p. 59).

[6] Steven Shapin and Simon Shaffer, *Leviathan and the Air Pump: Hobbes, Boyle, and the Experimental Life* (Princeton: Princeton University Press, 1989), discuss these issues in the experimental method that became identified with empiricism. They argue that three technologies were needed for Boyle's experimental method to succeed: "a *material technique* embedded in the construction and operation of the air pump; a *literary technology* by means of which the phenomena produced by the pump were made known to those who were not direct witnesses; and a *social technology* that incorporated the conventions experimental philosophers should use in dealing with each other and considering knowledge claims" (p. 25). They point out that "the power of new scientific instruments, the microscope and telescope as well as the air pump, resided in their capacity to enhance perception and to constitute new perceptual objects" (p. 36). Witnesses needed to be multiplied not just through the performance or replication of experiments, they suggest, but through *virtual witnessing*, "the production in a *reader's* mind of such an image of an experimental scene as obviates the necessity for either direct witness or replication" (p. 60).

tion over time. Empiricists like Hume sometimes exhibit skeptical reservations about historical knowledge but also confirm the value of history for understanding social behavior. They carefully define criteria for testimony, creating potential validations for such evidence from the past. The long conflict between antiquarian and humanist history continued in the eighteenth century despite the evident need to join the two approaches. Antiquarianism employed and further developed the tools that could facilitate a more empiricist interrogation of the past—for example, such procedures as those of the new philology and textual studies developed in the Renaissance and now expanded; an enhanced facility in the interpretation of material remains; the systematic organization of cabinets for displaying artifacts as well as the later museums—but it avoided attempts at elucidating the large issues of social and political life. Empiricism had, however, joined with humanist history in designating the understanding of such larger structures of society as the purpose and therefore justification of history.

The novel intervenes in these vexed issues of historiography and empiricism, providing a critique of historical studies as a way of making a place for itself. Early in the period that I consider, the novel mediates between figural and empiricist discourses, those founded on the biblical master narrative and those connecting themselves to the new ideology of systematic observation. This mediation exposes limitations of both discourses. But the novel commits itself to the necessity and validity of careful observation even as it refuses to find the observation in itself meaningful without further construal. The novels of midcentury—especially those of Richardson, Fielding, and Sterne—comment directly or implicitly on the process of establishing fact and finding meaning in an emplotment of human actions, placing themselves in a complementary as well as critical relationship with history. From the perspective of the developing novel, history is limited in ways that require the supplementations of fiction, while it also exhibits the same fictionality as novels in its construction of meaning through the linkages of plot. But by the time of the appearance of Scott's historical novels, fiction has separated itself from the common, but shadowy and interpenetrated, border that it claimed with history. Scott claims both historical and fictive elements and accepts their essential division even as he joins them. Baldly stated, in the late eighteenth century literature becomes associated with poetry and the aesthetic and begins gradually to exclude history. The eighteenth-century novel, however, exploited its not yet fully stable boundaries and separated itself from poetry, defining itself instead as history-like. Yet at a certain point its epistemological questioning becomes difficult to see as other than symbolic and merely verisimilitudinous. Having established itself as a distinctive form, the novel then accepts its link with poetry even while reserving the right to make occasional forays into history.[7]

Paul Ricoeur's magisterial *Time and Narrative* has provided guidance at many places in this book, possibly more guidance than is appropriately discussed in an introduction that can do little justice to the complexities of his arguments. Ricoeur's allegiance is to phenomenology and he tends to stress ontological questions, whereas I use his work to focus on epistemological applications and ignore much that is of phenomenological concern. Here I sketch only a few of the most directly relevant conceptions of *Time and Narrative*, using Ricoeur's essays, "Narrated Time," and "The Human Experience of Time and Narrative," for references.[8] For Ricoeur, fiction and history exhibit a profound commonality that their differences in reference obscure: "It is in the intersection of history and fiction in the refiguration of time that we discover or invent—it's all the same—what we might suitably call *human time*" (p. 354). History requires the mediations of fiction in its treatment of the past, "the role of the imaginary . . . clearly evident in the non-observable character of the past" (p. 352). Fiction and history are both narratives of the past that have similar but not identical responsibilities. Fiction is "quasi-historical" and history "quasi-fictional," the former approaching history in its rendition of 'unrealized' potentialities of the historical past" (p. 354). The narrative voice of fiction is presumed to be free but is in fact constrained: "Free *from* the exterior constraint of documentary proof, must not the creator still make himself free *for*—on behalf of the quasi past" (p. 354)?

The two conceptions developed by Ricoeur that most apparently connect and divide historical and fictional narrative while also having direct relevance to my epistemological concerns are those of *emplotment* and *trace*. Emplotment is a process of placing events into a meaningful sequence or

[7] Lionel Gossman, "History and Literature: Reproduction or Signification," in *The Writing of History: Literary Form and Historical Understanding*, ed. Robert H. Canary and Henry Kozicki (Madison: University of Wisconsin Press, 1978), pp. 3–39, discusses these changing allegiances of history and literature. This important essay may also be found in Lionel Gossman, *Between History and Literature* (Cambridge: Harvard University Press, 1990).

[8] These essays give summary versions of materials treated much more extensively in *Time and Narrative*, which is cited elsewhere in this book. References in the introduction are to the essays collected in *A Ricoeur Reader: Reflection and Imagination*, ed. Mario J. Valdes (Toronto: University of Toronto Press, 1991). I admire Ricoeur's achievement, yet I must also note two areas of reservation. Ricoeur appears to have little knowledge of eighteenth-century fiction, which he associates with consistently reliable narration. It is possible that this misapprehension of the multitudes of narrative experiments in the century derives too from a rather limited view of narrational perspectives. Ricoeur's dismissive reading of Hume also appears to be inadequately responsive to the complexities in Hume's apparent historical uniformitarianism.

configuration, making the "succession of events into significant wholes which are the correlate of the act of grouping together" (p. 109). Whether fictional or historical, such an emplotment of events as a whole enables the movement from an end to a beginning, a reversal of the "so-called natural order of time," placing actions within memory as well as within time (p. 110).[9] The conception of *trace* is particularly linked to history because of history's "recourse to documents and monuments" (p. 344). The trace as a remnant of the past has a double nature: it is here now, part of our present, "while the past context of the trace—people, institution, actions, passions—no longer exists" (p. 345). The trace thus exists as trace "only for one who can deal with the mark as a present sign of an absent thing, or better, as the present vestige of a passage that exists no longer." Thus "to follow a trace is to effect the mediation between the *no-longer* of the passage and the *still* of the mark." The palpability of the trace insists on the reality of the past from which it is severed, yet its reference as trace is to something itself impermanent.

I have used Ricoeur's conceptions as a way of formulating eighteenth-century fiction's critique and simulation of historical narrative. If history is an emplotment of traces with the purpose of creating an absent past, its fictionality is apparent even if its intent is markedly different from novelistic fiction. The fictionality of history may construct only a virtual, or may reconstruct a real, past depending on our judgment of its powers of managing the foundational traces. Yet the reality of the traces is always a compromised one; they may be authentic enough, but as traces they exist only in the mediation that connects past and present. Eighteenth-century fiction's exploitations of the fictions of history locate themselves in this ambiguous area of the trace, an area where novelistic fiction can claim the virtuality that is all that history might perhaps claim.

But of course this book is itself a history of a certain portion of the novel, which is then itself a trace, an undeniable remnant of a past that is a passing, however full we may believe our contexts are. We study the novel for signs of the purposes, the cause-and-effect relationships, that it betrays, for it is itself a trace that also implicitly and sometimes explicitly scrutinizes the uses of traces. We must of course follow our common sense in insisting that the traces *within* novels are made-up (even though sometimes they aren't), and that the traces of histories exist outside their narratives (although sometimes they don't, or don't to our knowledge, or no longer do). Yet the novel on

[9] For those preferring an account of the process of emplotment from the perspective of analytic philosophy, Arthur C. Danto, *Narration and Knowledge* (New York: Columbia University Press, 1985), chap. 8, "Narrative Sentences," provides a cogent account (see especially pp. 167–69).

occasion puts our common sense to the test, challenging use to differentiate the basis of novelistic foolhardiness from history's convictions. As E. L. Doctorow's narrator in *The Waterworks*, a newspaper editor, put it: "If journalism were a philosophy rather than a trade, it would say there is no order in the universe, no discernible meaning, without . . . the daily paper."[10] After the day's stories are set, this editor regularly goes to a bar where he is able to read his "construed news" as "the objective thing-in-itself from heaven-poured type" (p. 26).

The history of eighteenth-century fiction as rendered here in the context of historiography does not reveal a systematic line of development in any usual sense, although novels share a nexus of concerns that appear to become increasingly urgent and then to some degree lose their urgency with the rise of the properly historical novel. The novels of midcentury and after that are central to my study, principally *Clarissa*, *Tom Jones*, and *Tristram Shandy*, appear to be responsive to one another, exploring narrative possibilities that arise as a consequence of a predecessor's triumphant but always demonstrably limited achievement. Such interaction fosters a shared set of issues but cannot easily be construed as development in a large sense. As a way of showing these shared concerns without implying a continuous pattern or direction, I have generally organized each chapter around two novels that speak to each other, although I have occasionally included briefer analyses of additional novels.

The first and second chapters function as introductory in several different ways. The opening chapter includes extended consideration of an eighteenth-century philosophical and historiographical context for the novel, and it is mainly focused on skeptical tendencies in eighteenth-century empiricism as well as on the attendant arguments for controlling and limiting such skepticism. Biblical interpretation, historiography, and philosophy are closely interconnected in the eighteenth-century intellectual world, and all share in the problems and possibilities posed by an empirical outlook. The second chapter deals with the transition from a figural discourse to the markedly different empirical discourse that eventually comes to characterize the novel. *Robinson Crusoe* illustrates some of the conflicts engendered by this shift of discourses, a shift that is further explored through extended analyses of *The Pilgrim's Progress* and *A Journal of the Plague Year*. I place the particular concerns of this present historiographical study in relation to recent work by Michael McKeon and John Bender and use Michel Foucault's earlier books *The Order of Things* and *The Archeology of Knowledge* to describe the shift in discourses.

---

[10] E. L. Doctorow, *The Waterworks* (New York: Penguin, 1994), p. 25.

In Chapters 3 through 5 I concentrate on extended analyses of paired texts, each chapter devoted to a somewhat different historiographical issue. I use Swift's *A Tale of a Tub* and Richardson's *Clarissa* to explore the ancients and moderns controversy, with concern for the nature of the novel's modernity as exhibited in *Clarissa*. I examine the differing conceptions of history adopted by ancients and moderns through an analysis of William Wotton's *Reflections on Ancient and Modern Learning*, with its extolling of modern information management as opposed to the very different responses of Temple and Swift to the proliferation of books and indexes. I analyze *Clarissa* as an archive, an exemplar of information management, and also as an exploration of the possibilities of connecting various versions of text and of self.

Tom Jones and *Caleb Williams* are paired in Chapter 4, which is a study of possibilities in emplotment. Rather than taking the archive as represented by *Clarissa* to be a self-evident artifact, Fielding exposes the need for, and dangers of, a strong narrative manager, who must produce a configuration, a meaningful concatenation of events that may not be apparent without such a manager's direct assistance. *Caleb Williams* installs such a manager as a first-person narrator who constructs detailed narratives about himself and Falkland, yet must conclude at the end that his careful narrative has missed the point, derailed by the assumptions of a corrupt society. Fielding shows that history demands the freedom from individual bias that is to be found in consensus. His narrator and reader examine all aspects of his construction and arrive at a narrative construal that represents the values of a community, not the needs of an individual. William Godwin shows that the narrative a community underwrites may still be corrupted. History itself may be a record construed by means of mistaken values no matter how communally persuasive the emplotment.

In Chapter 5 I pair *Tristram Shandy* and *The Man of Feeling*, novels that extol individuality as embodied in Tristram's powers as author and Harley's exemplarity as man of feeling yet also expose and concede the materiality, thus reduction to undifferentiation, of body and book. Both confront the textuality that is the basis of history and is linked to death. Richard Bentley, the great eighteenth-century scholar, saw textual scholarship as the guarantor of life for books and the perpetuator of history; Sterne and Mackenzie show texts degenerating into fragments of dubious provenience and indeterminate meaning despite the administrations of textual physic. The chapter ends with a brief consideration of Scott and the turn from historicized fiction to historical fiction. Scott draws on the eighteenth-century satirical and novelistic traditions in festooning his fictions with the detritus of learning—prefaces and notes by Scriblerian editors and amateur pedants. Yet he conducts a serious engagement with the novel and with history while also signaling a turn away from the earlier eighteenth-century contestation of their borders, acknowledging essential differences between the two categories.

Chapter 6 brings together several seventeenth- and eighteenth-century summaries of received wisdom about historiography (which, nevertheless, have their own emphases and interests) with Hume's conceptions of history. The earlier historiographical writings struggle with the conflict between the assumption that history has a pattern in its events and the acknowledgment that there is a recommended rhetoric of history, a way of writing that makes this pattern appear immanent in the events, not imposed by the writing. Hume's later analysis of history in relation to other forms of literature—epic, tragedy, and biography—reveals his open acceptance of narrative emplotment as a device for creating meaningfulness and persuasiveness. Significance must be found; it does not simply impose itself. Yet history is not thereby denigrated but remains central to the effort to comprehend society.[11] Although Hume decisively separates the historical from the fictional on the basis of reference, his method of analysis yields a description that applies to much of the project of the eighteenth-century novel, not just to eighteenth-century history. Both Hume and eighteenth-century fiction engage in significant exploration and critique of society's master narratives.

[11] Donald W. Livingston's *Hume's Philosophy of Common Life* (Chicago: University of Chicago Press, 1984), has heavily influenced my understanding of the scope of history in Hume's thought.

CHAPTER I

Skeptical Historiography and
the Constitution of the Novel

I

Eighteenth-century British fiction insistently claims a relationship with history. Such markedly differing novelists as Defoe, Richardson, Fielding, and Sterne call their fictions histories and adopt a narrative stance that, they urge, has affinities with the role of the historian. Their novels simulate the more private forms of history—for example, biography (*Tom Jones*), autobiography (*Robinson Crusoe*), or family history (*Clarissa* and *Tristram Shandy*)—and also sometimes include sustained references to public historical events, such as the Jacobite rebellion of 1745 in *Tom Jones* or King William's War and the War of the Spanish Succession in *Tristram Shandy*. Although the references these writers make to history have been regarded as mere question-begging devices of verisimilitude, their books form a consequential commentary on issues related to the writing of history. Eighteenth-century novels explore the basis of narrative authority, raising questions about the evaluation of evidence contained in writing.[1]

[1] Among the many studies bearing on these contentions, the following are directly relevant. J. Hillis Miller, "Narrative and History," *ELH* 41 (1974): 455–73, discusses the frequent claim of the novel to be history and the concomitant questioning of history when narrative is subverted by the novel. John A. Dussinger, *The Discourse of Mind in Eighteenth-Century Fiction* (The Hague: Mouton, 1974), takes as his topic "how eighteenth-century narrative fiction sets forth the problem of knowledge for narrator, character, and reader alike" (p. 13). Jerry C. Beasley, *Novels of the 1740s* (Athens: University of Georgia Press, 1982), analyzes the "very serious interest in the historical functions of prose fiction" that is exhibited by Richardson, Fielding, and Smollett (p. 74), suggesting that "members of the eighteenth-century audience would have read the novels in the context of popular historical biographies" (pp. 78–79). Hamilton Beck, "The

Studying narrative fiction and history together has a meritorious rationale without any necessary connection to a specific historical period. Both forms emplot events, actual or putative, and give them a narrative structure that orders and emphasizes narrated details in the interests of a larger conceptual unity. This commonality permits the use of similar analytical procedures for understanding both, as Hayden White has repeatedly demonstrated and as Hume illustrated in his analysis of cause and effect plots in history, biography, and epic.[2] Nevertheless as Paul Ricoeur has cogently argued in *Time and Narrative*, significant and irreducible differences remain, differences that can be summed up as history's responsibility to a past.[3]

Novel between 1740 and 1780: Parody and Historiography," *Journal of the History of Ideas* 46 (1985), argues that "the eighteenth-century novel was in part an imitation of historical writing, an imitation which was then parodied, leading finally to a return to historical techniques" (p. 405). J. Paul Hunter, *Before Novels: The Cultural Contexts of Eighteenth-Century English Fiction* (New York: W. W. Norton, 1990), finds that "characteristic of the [novel] from the first was the desire to define something essential in the historical moment, a need to record the crucial interactions of its time and represent the cultural consciousness" (p. 338).

[2] This analysis can be found in "Of the Association of Ideas," a chapter Hume cut sharply in the last edition of the *Treatise of Human Nature*, presumably because its length and complexity disperse the central point he is pursuing. Most twentieth-century editions follow this last edition of Hume's lifetime, thus omitting a statement important to understanding Hume's conception of history. Hayden White analyzes the similar structures in fiction and history in numerous discussions, including "The Fictions of Factual Representation," where he asserts that the "techniques or strategies that [historians and writers of fiction] use in the composition of their discourses can be shown to be substantially the same, however different they may appear on a purely surface, or dictional, level of their texts" (in *Tropics of Discourse: Essays in Cultural Criticism* [Baltimore: Johns Hopkins University Press, 1978], p. 121). Leo Braudy, *Narrative Form in History and Fiction: Hume, Fielding, and Gibbon* (Princeton: Princeton University Press, 1970), gives specific attention to the similarities of narrative technique in eighteenth-century examples of fiction and history, discussing the efforts of novelists (especially Fielding) and historians "to form time, to discover its plot, and to give a compelling and convincing narrative shape to the facts of human life" (p. 3). Roland Barthes, "The Discourse of History," trans. Stephen Bann, *Comparative Criticism* 3 (1981), an essay that first appeared in French in 1967, begins by asking "whether it is fully legitimate to make a constant opposition between the discourses of poetry and the novel, the fictional narrative and the historical narrative" (p. 7). He subsequently erodes the referential as a criterion for history, thus questioning a factor conventionally used to distinguish history from novel: "In 'objective' history, the 'real' is never more than an unformulated signified, sheltering behind the apparently all-powerful referent. This situation characterizes what we might call the *realistic effect*" (p. 17).

[3] Paul Ricoeur, *Time and Narrative*, vol. 3, trans. Kathleen Blamey and David Pellauer (Chicago: University of Chicago Press, 1988). Ricoeur's project reveals many interconnections of history and fiction, yet Ricoeur insists that their difference must not be elided. Of particular relevance to this question are two chapters: chapter 6, "The Reality of the Past," and chapter 8, "The Interweaving of History and Fiction." Leopold Damrosch Jr., *Fictions of Reality in the Age of Hume and Johnson* (Madison: University of Wisconsin Press, 1989), suggests that "in recovering a sense of the epistemological stakes that Hume, Johnson, and Gibbon saw as

Studying both history and fiction together facilitates the examination of important concepts, to include referentiality, adequacy, and verifiability. The presumed reference of historical writing to actual events has been the dominant method of separating fiction from history, although fiction that refers both to actual events and to merely plausible ones complicates this picture, as does ancient history's reporting of speeches that were apparently created by the historian. Verifiability is often also taken as a standard for history, as history is presumably able to survive an evidentiary test of its assertions and even courts such testing through footnotes. Yet much past history has relatively little verification, its own assertions being prominent among the little evidence that has survived. And eyewitness accounts, as well as the private documents often used as sources, sometimes have no more external verification than fiction does. Further, history that reports only the substantially verifiable and omits the merely plausible often appears to be inadequate, unable to place its assertions within a context that would make them meaningful. The divisions between the two antithetical forms are eroded, in some circumstances, from one direction or the other: history is sometimes enticed to resort to the techniques associated with realistic fiction, and fiction often simulates some of the techniques of historical writing, including the use of footnotes.

The limitation of this study primarily to the history and fiction of the eighteenth-century is not intended to be arbitrary. Michael McKeon has argued plausibly in *The Origins of the English Novel* that the English novel was constituted as a distinct category in the middle of the eighteenth century, despite earlier appearances of fiction with similar features.[4] Although the novels considered here differ sharply from one another, they also exhibit

---

fundamental to their work, it is often helpful to turn not to literary theory but to current arguments about the nature of historical writing, for which the problem of a reality independent of the text remains inescapable" (p. 10). As many eighteenth-century writers of fiction make their claims in the same arena as the writers of history do, they too profit from the considerations of historiography.

[4] Michael McKeon, *The Origins of the English Novel, 1600–1740* (Baltimore: Johns Hopkins University Press, 1987): "The genre of the novel can be understood comprehensively as an early modern cultural instrument designed to confront, on the level of narrative form and content, both intellectual and social crisis simultaneously. The novel emerges into public consciousness when this conflation can be made with complete confidence. The conflict then comes to be embodied in a controversy between Richardson and Fielding" (p. 22). Ralph Rader, "The Emergence of the Novel in England: Genre in History vs. History of Genre," *Narrative* 1 (1993): 69–83, argues that McKeon's analysis ignores the actual characteristics of the genre of the novel because McKeon focuses on the continuities that culminate in the novel without paying adequate attention to the formal differences between, for example, *Pamela* and earlier fiction. It appears to me that Rader is right to call attention to a formal organization that distinguishes the

the features of a shared enterprise, a gradually emerging genre. And among the common elements that permit the constitution of a category at this time is fiction's oppositional collaboration with history, each form defining a trajectory of development for itself that separates it from the other, despite also retaining similar features.

The limited number of fictions that I have chosen to analyze are perhaps justified by this notion of a shared enterprise. As William Warner has argued, the two novelists who became dominant in the 1740s—Richardson and Fielding—have been seen as founders of the genre because they in fact incorporated earlier fictional patterns characteristic of writers such as Behn and Haywood, making these patterns part of their so-called new works, which although held to be distinct from the earlier "romance" reproduce many of its features.[5] I emphasize this second wave of canonical novels, *Clarissa*, *Tom Jones*, and *Tristram Shandy*, not because these replace the full range of the early novel, but because they conveniently encompass much of the earlier novel's narrative complexity and its self-conscious claims.[6]

Any historical consideration of the relationship of history and fiction must deal with both the innate complexity and the mutability over time of the two terms of comparison: what is taken as the norm for history and for fiction is not persistent. Furthermore, what at any given time history takes for fiction or fiction for history may bear little relationship to the practices then current. In *Poetics of the New History*, Philippe Carrard suggests that many theorists of the boundaries of history and fiction tend to take some version of positivist

novel as later understood from the earlier "novel" or proto-novel. I am, however, uneasy with the sharp distinction that he makes between *Pamela* and *Moll Flanders* in subsequent stages of the debate with McKeon: "The readerly imagination never constructs the letters in *Pamela* as genuine documents but as manifest elements of the author's story . . . whereas in *Moll Flanders* . . . the implicit claim of the invisible author is indeed that the book is an historical document" ("The Novel and History Once More," *Narrative* 1 [1993]: 177). I suggest that the reading being asked for by both Defoe and Richardson erodes the distinction between history and fiction without eliminating it. Rader's view of these early novels is developed more fully in "Defoe, Richardson, Joyce, and the Concept of Form in the Novel," in *Autobiography, Biography, and the Novel* (Los Angeles: William Andrews Clark Memorial Library, 1973).

[5] William B. Warner, "The Elevation of the Novel in England: Hegemony and Literary History," *ELH* 59 (1992), argues that "modern attempts to tell the novel's rise follow in the wake of Richardson's and Fielding's efforts to introduce 'new species' of English novels by displacing the popular novels written, in the six decades before 1740, by Aphra Behn, Delariviere Manley, and Eliza Haywood" (p. 577). Warner then suggests that the novels of Richardson and Fielding use the features of the "old discredited novel" to "help bring popularity" to their own books (p. 583).

[6] My neglect of Tobias Smollett does not reflect a negative judgment on his value or general relevance but a recognition that much of my argument is based on metanarrative comment and narrative experiment to which Smollett's undeniable virtues would add little.

history as "a fixed point against which the literariness of fictional texts can, so to speak, be measured," whereas "any analysis of the relations between history and literature must assume that both domains are subject to change."[7]

William Nelson's useful *Fact or Fiction* traces the entanglements of the categories of history and fiction in the Renaissance, summarizing the medieval and ancient backgrounds for Renaissance defenses of poetry and fiction. He notes that the writers of antiquity had a rather tolerant attitude toward admixtures of the fabulous in works of history and biography and attributes the sharpened opposition of the two categories, at least in part, to Christianity, with its "Hebraic tradition," which "surely gave force to the idea that it was important to distinguish the veritable past from falsehood and fiction."[8] During the Renaissance and the seventeenth century historians persisted in their attempts to sharpen the distinctions between the fictional and the historical, including in this program an increased concern for the authenticity of sources and a concomitant support for abandoning the "classical license to invent speeches and descriptions" as well as "improbable traditions, however venerable" (p. 41). But "when history was understood as historians practiced it, rather than as the naked truth they professed it to be" (p. 93), the distinctions blurred, especially when writers dealt with eras and cultures about which there was very limited evidence. Violating the available evidence was, of course, condemned, but there was a considerably more toler-

---

[7] Philippe Carrard, *Poetics of the New History: French Historical Discourse from Braudel to Chartier* (Baltimore: Johns Hopkins University Press, 1992), p. 117. The changes in historiography over time make it difficult to define the boundaries of history and fiction narratologically, except with reference to a particular time. Even so seemingly unexceptional a statement as that by Dorrit Cohn on psychological ascriptions in history does not describe common historical practice in every period: "And it is indeed only when such privately revealing sources as memoirs, diaries, and letters *are* available to him that a scrupulous historian will feel free to cast those of his statements touching on psychological motives and reactions into the past-indicative tense. In the absence of reference, he will have to make do with inference (and its grammar)" ("Signposts of Fictionality: A Narratological Perspective," *Poetics Today* 11 [1990]: 785).

[8] William Nelson, *Fact or Fiction* (Cambridge: Harvard University Press, 1973), p. 7. Nicholas Lenglet-Dufresnoy, *A New Method of Studying History . . .* , 2 vols., trans. Richard Rawlinson (London: Charles Davis, 1730), advances a view not unusual in the eighteenth century when he remarks that "the History of *Greece*, the finest for its great events, is also the most fabulous in some parts" (p. 51). It is perhaps best not to ascribe what we regard as fabulous in the content of ancient history to any widespread theoretical neglect of the criteria of truth among the ancients. George H. Nadel, "Philosophy of History before Historicism," in *Studies in the Philosophy of History: Selected Essays from History and Theory*, ed. Nadel (New York: Harper, 1965), pp. 49–73, defines a classical historiography that does not so much condone laxity about truth as attempt to link truth to civic needs, a tradition that lasted through the eighteenth century. This prevalent rhetorical tradition in ancient historical writing is regarded by Lucian, among others, as productive of bias (p. 61).

ant attitude about filling in the hiatuses. Nelson states that by the seventeenth century, however, "the gap between [the historians'] métier and that of the 'poets' had widened to the point where one could no longer mix the two genres without qualms" (p. 105).

In the eighteenth century, growing scrupulousness about historical evidence led to developments in historiography that ultimately encouraged the aspirations of nineteenth-century German scholarship to scientific history. As Joseph M. Levine shows, Richard Bentley and other successors to the humanist scholarship of the Renaissance developed philological procedures in classical and biblical scholarship that eventually produced a picture of the ancient world markedly different from that held by their contemporaries, such as William Temple and Jonathan Swift.[9] And these same textual and archeological procedures that altered the view of the ancient world were used to extend historical knowledge into little-known cultures such as that of Anglo-Saxon England and eventually also to transform the historiographical practices of those concerned with less remote eras. The Ossian controversy, generated by James Macpherson's claim to have discovered and translated the texts of an ancient Gaelic poet, attested to the hunger of the time for firsthand documentary evidence of seemingly lost cultures. This hoax revealed general scholarly sophistication as well as naïveté; even only moderately informed intellectuals often saw the difficulties with Macpherson's claims, asking him for the kind of information about the transmission and provenience of the manuscripts that is required for any historical document.[10]

[9] Joseph M. Levine, *The Battle of the Books: History and Literature in the Augustan Age* (Ithaca: Cornell University Press, 1991), is the fullest and most authoritative survey of the historiographical implications of the ancients and moderns controversy in England. Unfortunately, the section of this comprehensive book devoted to Swift is not fully responsive to the complexities of Swift's attitude to Temple and the controversy. R. C. Jebb, *Bentley* (London: Macmillan, 1909), is a readable survey of Bentley's life and achievements.

[10] Ian Haywood, *The Making of History: A Study of the Literary Forgeries of James Macpherson and Thomas Chatterton in Relation to Eighteenth-Century Ideas of History and Fiction* (London and Toronto: Associated University Presses, 1986), places these forgeries in the context of eighteenth-century discussion of connections of history to fiction, finding the forgeries to be significant instantiations of contemporary historiographical concerns, as well as precursors to the historical novel in the mode of Scott. Haywood points out that the novel borrowed the new authority of the manuscript and thus often appears as a historical document (p. 63). Anthony Grafton, *Defenders of the Text: The Traditions of Scholarship in an Age of Science, 1450–1800* (Cambridge: Harvard University Press, 1991), discusses the somewhat parallel case of scholarly advances precipitated by the forgeries of Annius of Viterbo, who "insinuated, into both his forgeries and his commentaries, a set of rules for the choice of reliable sources" (p. 90). Yet, Grafton suggests, these rules represent a systematization of principles long held; thus the question is raised about whether there were any sharp changes from humanist historical practice during the seventeenth and eighteenth centuries. Grafton endorses the view of Levine (in *Dr.*

The very successful antiquarian enterprise recovered more and more of the past history of Roman Britain and extended its researches into the seemingly dark reaches of pre-Roman times, using and contributing to the techniques of philological and archeological analysis that had been devoted to the understanding of classical and biblical antiquity. These researches did not, however, have the satisfying narrative scope expected of humanist history, a history intended to educate those needing to understand public issues. The norm for antiquarians was the sustained analysis of details that might appear unimportant in themselves rather than the sweeping narrative easily convertible into moral or practical instruction. For example, Levine describes George Hickes's *Linguarum Vett. Septentrionalium Thesaurus Grammatico-Criticus et Archaeologicus* (1703, 1705), which was intended to include "every scrap of available evidence for Saxon England" (p. 356), as "the capstone of the antiquarian enterprise, the most remarkable work of modern scholarship in its time" (p. 367), yet also notes that it was "sprawling and badly organized," needing a *Conspectus brevis* (1708) by William Wotton, later translated as *Wotton's Short View of George Hickes's Grammatico-critical and Archaeological Treasure of the Northern Languages* (1735), to make the material stuffed into the work accessible (*Battle of the Books*, p. 356). The two traditions of historical scholarship remained detached from each other until they reached something of an accommodation in Gibbon's great history.[11]

In "The Rise of Antiquarian Research," Arnaldo Momigliano shows that this double tradition of studies of the past had existed since classical antiquity.[12] He suggests that the powerful influence of Thucydides, who emphasized political and military history, was responsible for this separation of antiquarianism from a seemingly central historical tradition. But, he suggests further, the skepticism of the seventeenth century gave an increased prestige

---

Woodward's Shield: History, Science, and Satire in Augustan England [Berkeley: University of California Press, 1977]) and others that "the simple accumulation of data, generation after generation, did more than method could to catalyze the fixing of a modern canon of classic texts and objects" (p. 79). The distance between the older philology and that of the late seventeenth and eighteenth centuries is great but appears often as altered practice based on increased knowledge, rather than as pronounced theoretical advance.

[11] Joseph M. Levine, *Humanism and History: Origins of Modern English Historiography* (Ithaca: Cornell University Press, 1987), describes Gibbon's history as "a heroic attempt to resolve the age-old quarrel at its very center by joining the views of both ancients and moderns about the nature and purpose of history, and by marrying the two methods of approaching the past that were so generally kept apart" (p. 183).

[12] In Arnaldo Momigliano, *The Classical Foundations of Modern Historiography* (Berkeley: University of California Press, 1990), pp. 54–79.

to antiquarian studies: skepticism about historical narratives was resolved by pointing toward "coins, statues, buildings, inscriptions" (p. 72), the seventeenth-century antiquarians perhaps modeling their efforts on the methods of observation derived from Galileo's work (p. 57). In eighteenth-century England the antiquarians and historians continued to maintain their separate traditions, despite the desirability of combining the two traditions as demonstrated by the recovery of Anglo-Saxon England and the restructuring of large aspects of antiquity, biblical and pagan.

The two great histories of the later eighteenth century—Hume's and Gibbon's—are sweeping narratives covering a vast ground, and as Leo Braudy has shown in *Narrative Form in History and Fiction*, they have a great deal in common with the narrative problems and solutions in the novels of Fielding.[13] Yet each of these histories also shows the impact of the skepticism associated with the philological and antiquarian traditions that resisted sustained narrativity.

Gibbon's *History of the Decline and Fall of the Roman Empire* is a "literary" history from the perspective of later, more rigorously "scientific" history, depending as it frequently does on the interpretations of previous historians and creating its impact through rhetorical skills rather more than through newly discovered, or radically reinterpreted, materials. But it also incorporates a good deal of archaeological investigation that depends on Gibbon's previously acquired antiquarian expertise in coins and measures, thus making its evidentiary basis something more than that of a history that is a summary of summaries.[14] In defending his chapters on Christianity, Gibbon emphasizes his painstaking concern for an evidentiary basis and establishes his familiarity with the technical scholarship associated with Richard Bentley and the antiquarians. In *A Vindication of Some Passages in the Fifteenth and Sixteenth Chapters of the History of the Decline and Fall of the Roman Empire*, Gibbon explains that the two chapters on Christianity to which there is so much objection "are illustrated by three hundred and

---

[13] Gibbon admired Fielding enormously, judging from his praise in his autobiography (*Memoirs of My Life*, ed. Betty Radice [London: Penguin, 1984], chap. 1): "The successors of Charles the Fifth may disdain their brethren of England: but the romance of *Tom Jones*, that exquisite picture of human manners, will outlive the palace of the Escurial and the imperial eagle of the house of Austria" (p. 42).

[14] See Arnaldo Momigliano, *Studies in Historiography* (London: Weidenfeld & Nicholson, 1966), "Gibbon's Contribution to Historical Method," pp. 40–55: "[In Gibbon] we find no trace of the new type of patient analysis of sources which his German contemporaries were just beginning to develop" (p. 40). Gibbon, however, knew his sources "extraordinarily well" and "had digested the results of innumerable dissertations on major and minor points of scholarship" (pp. 40–41). He was thus able to combine the new philosophical history associated with the *philosophes* and the erudition of the antiquarian tradition.

eighty-three Notes" with supporting quotations that "cannot amount to less than eight hundred or a thousand."[15] He asserts that "it has been my invariable practice, to consult the original; to study with attention the words, the design, the spirit, the context, the situation of the passage to which I had been referred [by a secondary source]" (p. 86). He does not, however, merely accept the available sources: "The writer . . . is obliged to consult a variety of original testimonies, each of which, taken separately, is perhaps imperfect and partial. . . . [T]heir evidence must be so intimately blended together, that as it is unreasonable to expect that each of them should vouch for the whole, so it would be impossible to define the boundaries of their respective property" (pp. 58–59). Among a number of examples of his detailed familiarity with preceding scholarship is his citation of Bentley's reply to Boyle as his authority for the dating of Suidas (p. 106). Much earlier in his *Essay on the Study of Literature*, Gibbon had distinguished among "truly great" scholars, including Richard Bentley, and "mere compilers."[16]

Hume's modernity in his *History of England* is revealed less by evidentiary scrupulosities, although there are many, than by interpretive skepticism—his attempt to avoid the blatant ideological patterning that had brought political history into disrepute. He remarks critically on the biblical typological patterns used by others to structure history and eliminates such false predictors from his own writing. Further, he attempts to remove the accretions of previous political, primarily Whig, schema from his narrative.[17]

But Hume's *History* also eschews deep investigation into the Anglo-Saxon past, thus dealing perfunctorily with the portion of England's past that

---

[15] Edward Gibbon, *A Vindication of Some Passages in the Fifteenth and Sixteenth Chapters of the History of the Decline and Fall of the Roman Empire* (London: W. Strahan & T. Cadell, 1779), p. 12.

[16] Edward Gibbon, *Essay on the Study of Literature* [trans. 1764] (printed for T. Becket and P. A. De Hondt), pp. 16–17.

[17] Richard H. Popkin, "Skepticism and the Study of History," in *David Hume: Philosophical Historian*, ed. David Fate Norton and Richard H. Popkin (Indianapolis: Bobbs-Merrill, 1965), identifies Pierre Bayle and David Hume as the culmination of the tradition of historical skepticism that he describes (p. ix). Duncan Forbes, "Introduction," in David Hume, *The History of Great Britain: The Reigns of James I and Charles I* (Harmondsworth: Penguin, 1970), describes Hume's rejection of the idea dear to some Whigs of an immemorial constitution, whose guaranteed liberties needed to be recovered in the seventeenth century: "In Hume's opinion the patriots who stood for liberty in the parliaments of James I and Charles I were putting forward a plan of liberty which was something hitherto untried and unheard of in any government, ancient or modern" (p. 34). A fuller treatment of Hume's *History* in relation to contemporary political concerns is to be found in Duncan Forbes, *Hume's Philosophical Politics* (Cambridge: Cambridge University Press, 1975), chap. 8, "The History of England: Philosophical History as Establishment History."

contemporary antiquarian history was engaged in opening. Hume neglects pre-Roman British history, in part out of his prejudice against a society he thought did not truly participate in the progress of civilization, but also out of his consequent unwillingness to grant authority to the available documentation. He nevertheless praises Robert Henry's subsequent study of Saxon England, noting that Henry added the qualifications of antiquary to that of historian and congratulating Henry for sucess in an area where he himself had been inadequate.[18] Hume's attack on Macpherson's *Ossian* too is based on a knowledge of the standards of critical history in his time: as Macpherson gives no detailed provenience but presents the work as if it were a translation of a well-known poem, Hume urges Blair to get evidence that the poem existed even five years ago if he wants to save any credit for it; and he finds anachronistic the stone houses, the boats capable of sea voyages, and wind and water mills.[19]

The new fiction of the eighteenth century was regarded by some contemporary social critics as a threat to genuine history because it substituted a more stimulating though less accurate representation of reality. James Beattie, for a not untypical example, finds that whereas fiction may be used to impart truths, a "habit of reading [romances] breeds a dislike to history, and all the substantial parts of knowledge."[20] This fiction shares with history a mode of representation that employs realistic narrative, but it erodes the standards of verifiability that history is imposing with increasing stringency. For example, the imagined speech of a major historical character, once conventional, has by the later eighteenth century disappeared from respectable history.[21] Readers of Boswell's *Journal of a Tour to the Hebrides* will recall Johnson's mockery of Dalrymple's *Memoirs of Great Britain and Ireland* for its invented speeches and even its internal views of historical personages. Late to a dinner with Dalrymple, Johnson remarks to Boswell: "I have as good a right to make *him* think and talk as he has to tell us how

[18] David Hume, "Review of Robert Henry's *History of Great Britain*," in *David Hume: Philosophical Historian*, p. 388.

[19] David Hume, "Of the Poems of Ossian," in *David Hume: Philosophical Historian*, pp. 389–400.

[20] James Beattie, *On Fable and Romance* (1783), in *Novel and Romance, 1700–1800: A Documentary Record*, ed. Ioan Williams (New York: Barnes & Noble, 1970), p. 327. See also William Warburton, "Preface to Volume III of *Clarissa Harlowe*" (1748), in *Novel and Romance*, who writes of the "barbarous *Romances*" that had come into existence because of "a jaded appetite" unable to tolerate true history (p. 123).

[21] In his *History*, Hume, however, frequently creates a sense of the evidence and issues bearing on the possible choices of a historical character at a particular historical juncture by reciting the relevant material as if it were a debate going on within the mind of this personage.

people thought and talked a hundred years ago"; "heartily laughing all the while," Johnson then mockingly narrates Dalrymple's presumed impatience at his guests' lateness: "Dinner being ready, he wondered that his guests were not yet come. . . ."[22] The disappearance of imagined speeches and of other such imaginatively compelling if unverifiable detail leaves lacunae that impair the reader's sense of full historical reality. Substitutions for these vacancies in history can then be found in the fuller emergence of the private in the new fiction. The important issue behind this eighteenth-century contest between history and fiction is not precisely that of truth (for fiction claims its kind of truth just as history claims its kind) but of verifiability and adequacy. History's claim to verifiability is not only a strength but also a limit, whereas fiction's representations are fuller and, sometimes, seemingly more adequate.[23]

In general novelistic fiction's likeness to history retains a markedly private cast—biography, autobiography, memoir, and collections of letters are the forms it tends to simulate—from Daniel Defoe and Eliza Haywood to Tobias Smollett and Frances Burney. A number of well-known histories of the seventeenth and eighteenth centuries also acknowledge a personal aspect, claiming the advantage of direct observation (Clarendon's much admired seventeenth-century *History of the Rebellion* and Burnet's later *History of His Own Time*, for examples), but the trajectory of history is toward the structure and voice of impersonal truth. Instead, however, of merely conceding defeat on that public ground where history finally chose to make its stand, fiction moved toward privacy without abandoning its critique of history. The novel exposed the limits of the verifiable and the inevitability of a narrative perspective (even in history) that is rooted in time, place, and individuality, not in abstract truth and universality. The contestations of

[22] James Boswell, *Journal of a Tour to the Hebrides*, ed. Frederick A. Pottle and Charles H. Bennett (New York: McGraw-Hill, 1961), p. 392.

[23] For example, in the often reprinted *Introduction to the Classics* (London: William Cantrell, 2d ed., 1719), Anthony Blackwall praises classical historians but also notes that many have criticized the somewhat improbably detailed and eloquent speeches represented by them. While mitigating some of the improbabilities charged, he agrees that "they might not deliver themselves in that exact Number and Collection of Words which the *Historians* have so curiously laid together" (p. 61). He then defends this perhaps invented material in language that might have been taken from the preface to a novel: "Whoever made those noble Speeches and Debates, they so naturally arise from the Posture of Affairs, and Circumstances of the Times which the *Authors* then describe, and are so rational, so pathetic and becoming, that the Pleasure and Instruction of the *Reader* is the same" (p. 63). J. Paul Hunter notes the confused borders of history in the eighteenth century, citing the "memoir" as one of the forms of history that partakes of the private while claiming public significance (*Before Novels*, pp. 342–44). It is precisely such already confused borders that the novel exploits in its campaign against history's valorization of its truthfulness in comparison to fiction.

fiction and history, in fact, join both forms as quite similar exemplars of the human need to personalize the immensities of universal time, inscribing within it representations of a human ordering process that creates a history characterizable as both individual and communal. History-like fiction places itself within a world of acknowledged history that must itself be recognized as a human construction combating the immensities of time that are, in Paul Ricoeur's phrase, "impervious to our mortality" (*Time and Narrative*, 3:123).

William Godwin's unpublished essay "Of History and Romance" is a late-eighteenth-century (1797) salvo in these contestations of history and fiction.[24] This essay, usefully for our purposes, reflects arguments made piecemeal in a multitude of prefaces to earlier eighteenth-century fiction, combining them, but also extending them in a sustained and assertive fashion. Perhaps Godwin's essay needs to be seen as an extension of tendencies existing in earlier fictional claims rather than as a precise representation of those claims. As part of its not fully consistent argument, the essay valorizes emotive aspects of history (as opposed to evidentiary requirements), whereas earlier eighteenth-century novelists tend to be somewhat more respectful of history's evidentiary claims.

Godwin maintains a limited respect for history even as he concludes that realistic fiction can best perform the functions that make history important. He argues that an understanding of people is central to any history, including the kind that focuses on "the machine of society" (p. 362), making clear his preference for ancient rather than modern history (primarily on grounds of the greater emotive power of the historians), and his disappointment in Enlightenment historians: "Read on the one hand Thucydides and Livy, and on the other Hume and Voltaire and Robertson. When we admire the personages of the former, we simply enter into the feelings with which these authors recorded them. The latter neither experience such emotions nor excite them" (pp. 365–66).

Godwin derives his preference for romance or the novel from his comparison of two kinds of history, neither of them fully satisfactory. Suggesting that "all history bears too near a resemblance to fable" (p. 367), he compares the writings of Sallust to those of modern historians: "Read Sallust. To every action he assigns a motive. Rarely an uncertainty diversifies his page. He describes his characters with preciseness and decision. He seems to enter into the hearts of his personages, and unfolds their secret thoughts. Consid-

---

[24] William Godwin, "Of History and Romance," appendix 4 in *Caleb Williams*, ed. Maurice Hindle (New York: Penguin, 1988), pp. 359–73. The essay was prepared for the *Enquirer*, to be printed should there have been demand for another volume.

ered as fable, nothing can be more perfect. But neither is this history" (p. 368). To this kind of fabulous history Godwin contrasts an equally deficient "modern kind": "In this mode, the narrator is sunk in the critic. The main body of the composition consists of a logical deduction and calculation of probabilities. This species of writing may be of use as a whetstone upon which to sharpen our faculty of discrimination, but it answers none of the legitimate purposes of history" (p. 368).

Given then the deficiencies of both kinds of history, Godwin suggests that there should be some intermediate way of achieving the ends of history. He turns to the romance or novel as the form most nearly able to fulfill history's function:

> Romance then, strictly considered, may be pronounced to be one of the species of history. The difference between romance and what ordinarily bears the denomination history, is this. The historian is confined to individual incident and individual man, and must hang upon that his invention or conjecture as he can. The writer collects his materials from all sources, experience, report, and the records of human affairs; then generalises them; and finally selects, from their elements and the various combinations they afford, those instances which he is best qualified to portray, and which he judges most calculated to impress the heart and improve the faculties of his reader. In this point of view we should be apt to pronounce that romance was a bolder species of composition than history. (p. 370)

Although Godwin does not explicitly make the point, this description of the romance serves as a unification of the two separate branches of history that he defines at the opening of the essay: "the study of mankind in a mass, of the progress, the fluctuations, the interests and the vices of society; and the study of the individual" (p. 359). What the description of the romance implies is that the understanding of society and of the individual may be brought together to show their true interconnectedness because the writer of romance may select and recombine in ways that do not depend on the evidence about an actual individual.

Godwin is acutely aware of the narrative constructedness of history, of how it inevitably represents an ordering mind, not just the speech of the traces:

> The reader will be miserably deluded if, while he reads history, he suffers himself to imagine that he is reading facts. Profound scholars are so well aware of this, that when they would study the history of any country, they pass over the historians that have adorned and decorated the facts, and

proceed at once to the naked and scattered materials, out of which the historian constructed his work. This they do, that they may investigate the story for themselves; or, more accurately speaking, that each man, instead of resting in the invention of another, may invent his history for himself, and possess his creed as he possesses his property, single and incommunicable. (pp. 370–71)

The historical skepticism evidenced here must also, if held consistently, infect the better kind of history—the romance or novel. At the very end of the essay, Godwin unexpectedly reverses the too easy triumph he has awarded the novel and gives its place to that attenuated history whose meager truths are left undisturbed by his analysis. The admittedly limited truths claimed by history may at least be valid, whereas the preferred novelistic synthesis is too demanding for human frailty:

> To sketch a few bold outlines of character is no desperate undertaking; but to tell precisely how such a person would act in a given situation, requires a sagacity scarcely less than divine. . . . Here then the historian in some degree, though imperfectly, seems to recover his advantage upon the writer of romance. He indeed does not understand the character he exhibits, but the events are taken out of his hands and determined by the system of the universe, and therefore, as far as his information extends, must be true. The romance writer, on the other hand, is continually straining at a foresight to which his faculties are incompetent, and continually fails. (p. 372)

Godwin's historical skepticism exceeds what most eighteenth-century novelists or novels will support. Eighteenth-century fiction generally implies a skeptical view of historical writings as part of its strategy to place itself within history's broadened parameters. Yet this fiction's position remains distinct from pyrrhonism, a systematically extreme skepticism: the fiction of the eighteenth century claims a kind of knowledge for itself and allows history also to claim its kind. The novel's position is, however, that the two kinds are not so distinct as history and its mongers claim. The eighteenth-century novel often displays prominently its narrative assimilation and meaningful ordering of the putative traces on which it founds itself, using such narrative display to foreground the common border that fiction and history share.

In *Joseph Andrews*, for example, Fielding reverses the meanings of historian and romancer, giving us a treatment of the reversal that contrasts to, as well as resonates with, Godwin's. He shares Godwin's faith in the powers of fiction, yet finally has a less skeptical view of the historical enterprise. The romancers of history "describe Countries and Cities, which, with the Assistance of Maps, they do pretty justly. . . . But as to the Actions and Characters of Men, their Writings are not quite so authentic."[25] This deficiency in what we call history and Fielding calls romance is crucial because it leads to "Facts being set out in a different Light," as a result of the failure of these writers to understand the historical actors. The consequent contradictions among the accounts of these romancers of history lead readers to the conclusion that all is "a happy and fertile Invention." But, Fielding suggests, the "biographer" gets the characters right, although the "Age and Country wherein [events] happened" is often mistaken (pp. 185–86). This latter kind of failure is in Fielding's view of lesser consequence, however, for the similarity of human nature from age to age and culture to culture implies truths that are not limited by the particularities of chronology and geography. Although these truths are not so precisely delimited in time and space as a detailed narrative suggests, they provide a schematic understanding of the human character that is a necessary enabling factor for any meaningful history. Thus the contribution of a successful "biographer," even if the details of topography and chronology are wrong, is foundational to history. Fielding places character in a prominent position and finds meaning in an emplotment that does not rely on contingent details to substantiate truth claims.

Yet there is a commitment to historical actuality in Fielding's fictional narration that differs markedly from Sidney's views of poetry and at least somewhat from Aristotle's. Although Fielding finds the understanding conveyed by his kind of writing to be essential to history and thus superior to any history that lacks it, he regards the true, that is, complete, historical enterprise to be what narrative aspires to. Although he rejects those implied historical claims to the actual truths of quotidian life so emphasized in Defoe and Richardson, Fielding nevertheless retains a connection between his more generalized, thus more philosophical, narrative and its embodiment in particular history. After his theoretical disquisition on fictional biography and history, he refers explicitly (although not by name) to several living people, among them Ralph Allen, and states, "These are Pictures which must be, I believe, known: I declare they are taken from the Life, and not intended to exceed it" (p. 191). These connections of the narrative to exemplary living worthies imply that abstract moral patterns transcending the particularities of history must also be specifiably referential if fiction is to be meaningful. Fielding assumes that the permutations of fictional form and substance must find their close analogies within the repetitions of history. In

[25] Henry Fielding, *Joseph Andrews*, ed. Martin Battestin (Middletown: Wesleyan University Press, 1967), p. 185. The references are to bk. III, chap. i.

the preface to his *Journal of a Voyage to Lisbon*, he gives a powerful endorsement of nonfictional history that would seem surprising if it were not remembered how his defense of fiction is substantially based on a kind of uniformitarian history that must, nevertheless, be particularizable:

> I am far from supposing, that Homer, Hesiod, and the other antient poets and mythologists, had any settled design to pervert and confuse the records of antiquity; but it is certain they have effected it; and, for my part, I must confess I should have honored and loved Homer more had he written a true history of his own times in humble prose, than these noble poems that have so justly collected the praise of all ages; for though I read these with more admiration and astonishment, I still read Herodotus, Thucydides and Xenophon, with more amusement and more satisfaction.[26]

Behind both Fielding's and Godwin's somewhat differing defenses of the historical powers of the romance or novel is a conception of truth as probable. When Fielding insists on fiction's ability to present the truths of human nature without their being linked to a specific time and place, he is implying that these truths are not necessarily verified by reference to a specifiable occurrence but by our many experiences of human behavior. Thus someone's behavior in particularized circumstances is often not known but may, nevertheless, be inferred from a preponderance of other relevant empirical evidence that is not accumulated only through scientific study but also through the ordinary experiences of life. When Godwin finds that the writer of a romance or novel can combine accumulated experience with all other sources of knowledge and thus not be confined to the verifiable aspects of a particular event, he is suggesting that probabilistic fiction can give a less limited version of truth than conventional history. Fiction can incorporate

---

[26] Henry Fielding, *The Journal of the Voyage to Lisbon*, ed. Harold E. Pagliaro (New York: Nardon Press, 1963), p. 26. Catherine Gallagher, "Nobody's Story: Gender, Property, and the Rise of the Novel," *Modern Language Quarterly* 53 (1992), interprets the narrator's point in *Joseph Andrews* as being that "because a fictional characterization refers to nobody in particular, it *indirectly* . . . refers to everybody of a certain 'species'" (p. 273). This interpretation also appears in the context of a discussion of Maria Edgeworth in *Nobody's Story: The Vanishing Acts of Women Writers in the Marketplace* (Berkeley: University of California Press, 1994), in which is described Edgeworth's view that true events are often untypical and should thus not be integrated into fictional stories (pp. 283–85). Using different passages, I suggest that Fielding puts a somewhat greater value on referentiality in narrative. Claims to universality are fully validated only if they can also be instantiated in particularized histories. In his analysis of *Tom Jones*, Leo Braudy argues compellingly that "Fielding searches for general truths about man, but he demands that these general truths be in a continually self-correcting interplay with the particulars from which they are derived" (*Narrative Form*, p. 178).

the probabilities known to general experience as well as the verifiable details of an individualized event.

During the seventeenth century, truth claims based on various degrees of probability were gradually accepted as a supplement to certainty.[27] Much empirical research was recognized as incapable of producing the kind of certainty claimed by a logic based on, or analogous to, mathematics. Barbara Shapiro describes the newer probabilistic reasoning as follows: "Knowledge in all fact-related fields was seen to fall along a continuum. The lower reaches of this continuum were characterized as 'fiction,' 'mere opinion,' and 'conjecture'; its middle and high ranges as 'probable' and 'highly probable'; and its apex as 'morally certain.' . . . The morally certain was also a form of knowledge, and the highly probable came close to being another" (p. 4).

History was influenced by the new probabilistic view of knowledge, which offered the possibility of deriving truth claims equivalent to those of the burgeoning empirical sciences from techniques "for gathering substantial evidence" rather than on requirements for the "achievement of ultimate truth" (p. 268). The mild skepticism that motivated natural science to scrutinize its epistemological foundations also motivated history to examine its evidentiary foundations in testimony and documentation, linking history to probabilistic knowledge of the kind that empirical science was seeking. The quarantining of poetry from history in this developing epistemological paradigm gave the novel the opportunity to exploit its ambiguous position between the two. It could claim historicity and even approach empiricism by opposing poetry and romance, and at the same time it could weaken history's claim to empirical truth by exposing the weaknesses in history's claims to exceed the truths of literature.[28]

---

[27] Barbara Shapiro, *Probability and Certainty in Seventeenth-Century England: A Study of the Relationships between Natural Science, Religion, History, Law, and Literature* (Princeton: Princeton University Press, 1983), studies "the modification and eventual breakdown of a centuries-old tradition that divided 'science,' 'knowledge,' 'certainty,' and 'philosophy' on the one hand, from 'opinion,' 'probability,' 'appearance,' and 'rhetoric' on the other" (p. 3). Douglas Lane Patey, *Probability and Literary Form: Philosophic Theory and Literary Practice in the Augustan Age* (Cambridge: Cambridge University Press, 1984), shows probabilistic thinking at work internally in eighteenth-century fiction: "What is distinctive about the Augustan character is that he is a reader of *probable* signs and exercises his sagacity within a narrative whose very fabric is a structure of conjectures and expectations, probable inferences by which he judges others and by which he is himself judged" (p. 213).

[28] Jules David Law, *The Rhetoric of Empiricism: Language and Perception from Locke to I. A. Richards* (Ithaca: Cornell University Press, 1993), distinguishes "classical empiricism" from "more modern, positivist philosophical movements" (p. 5). Empirical thinking in the eighteenth-century sense might include much that is not acceptable in more recent empiricist agenda. Among the terms that Law explores as centrally important to "classical empiricism" is *reflection*, which carries both its senses of passive reproduction and of active reconsideration (p. 4).

Not only, then, did the new eighteenth-century fiction opportunistically fill the gaps created in history by the demand for verifiability, but it also simulated (and sometimes parodied) the documentary concerns of history. The prominent metafictional concerns in the eighteenth-century novel focus attention on the authority of the narrator, who often in turn refers or defers to the evidentiary foundation of the narrative. Richardson's *Clarissa*, for example, attempts to evade the challenge to a narrator's authority by appearing to be a collection of the traces from which the heroine's story may be constructed and evaluated, an archive constituted by a series of editors. The collection of letters was a familiar source for historians; more generally, the presentation of the relevant documentary evidence as a substitute or foundation for the narration of history (as suggested in Godwin's essay on romance and history) had a number of analogues in eighteenth-century historiography. For example, Thomas Madox's *Formulare Anglicanum* (1702) is described as "a collection of ancient Charters and Instruments of Divers Kinds, taken from Originals, placed under several Heads, and deduced (in a Series according to Order of Time) from the Norman Conquest to the end of the Reign of Henry VIII" (Levine, *Battle of the Books*, p. 368). And Nicholas Lenglet-Dufresnoy in *A New Method of Studying History, Geography, and Chronology* writes that "besides the common Historians, I do not believe there is a more secure Method of knowing History, than from Memoirs and Letters."[29] The history of the interpretation of Richardson's archive, the aim of which appears to be to simulate an unchallengeable documentary foundation, and of Richardson's attempts through editorial intervention to control the proliferating interpretations, is an exploration and unintended critique of the possibilities of documentary self-evidence.[30]

Tristram Shandy too confronts the concerns of history by foregrounding its struggles with narrative, making explicit the sharp differences between any narrative representation and unmediated reality. Furthermore, it incorporates documents apparently foundational to the story, sometimes fictional and sometimes historical ones, subjecting them to a skeptical interrogation that questions any easy reliance on a documentable foundation. Although both Richardson's and Sterne's claims to the title of editor and historian

---

[29] Nicholas Lenglet-Dufresnoy, *A New Method of Studying History, Geography, and Chronology*, 2 vols., trans. Richard Rawlinson (London: Charles Davis, 1730), 1:221.

[30] Carol Kay, *Political Constructions: Defoe, Richardson, and Sterne in Relation to Hobbes, Hume, and Burke* (Ithaca: Cornell University Press, 1988), comments on the suspicions introduced by the very size and complexity of this archive: "The monstrous size of the collection suggests to us that . . . we should be able to come to an understanding in some way superior to [the characters' understanding]. As always in Richardson's fiction, the superabundance of evidence and explanation rouses the suspicions he had hoped to allay" (p. 185).

suggest emulation of the authority of history, that very notion of historical authority is also contested when these authors foreground their chosen narrative perspectives, making the limitations of a perspective apparent and thus questionable.

II

The attacks on the foundations of historical knowledge that are implicitly advanced by the novel were already explicit in eighteenth-century thought. Questions about the reliability of witnesses, who are often, if not inevitably, biased and also about the textualization of accounts of the past, with all the problems posed by the transmission of texts through time, were important to the thinking of philosophers, clergymen, and historical scholars. History, biblical scholarship, and fiction in the eighteenth century share the recognition that textuality undermines assumptions about presence.

Despite their reliance on the Bible, Milton and Bunyan claim an inspiration that is not subsumed by a text; their contemporaries and successors are, however, systematically skeptical of such claims. Although Milton took scripture as his authority in writing *The Christian Doctrine*, he subordinated the textual problems of the New Testament to spiritual insight: "It is difficult to conjecture the purpose of Providence in committing the writings of the New Testament to such uncertain and variable guardianship, unless it were to teach us by this very circumstance that the Spirit which is given to us is a more certain guide than Scripture, whom therefore it is our duty to follow."[31] The very extent and intensity of Milton's claims to inspiration in *Paradise Lost* suggest that for him prophecy has not ceased. Bunyan too roots his subject matter and language in scripture, but for him scripture is privately appropriated, not publically fixed. The Bible is for Bunyan and Milton the universal pattern into which all other experience is fitted, but that pattern is made private. Milton and Bunyan reconcile presence and text through an inward persuasion: contemporaries not of their dissenting views as well as later writers of the eighteenth century use the norms provided by historical scholarship as their criteria for meaning and belief.

[31] John Milton, *The Christian Doctrine*, ed. James Holly Hanford and Waldo Hilary Dunn, trans. Charles R. Sumner, in *The Works of John Milton* (New York: Columbia University Press, 1934), 16:277, 279. Richard Jacobson, "Absence, Authority, and the Text," *Glyph* 3 (1976): 137–47, describes and explores the implications of a situation similar to that presented by England's repudiation of its religious radicals, the situation in Israel after the final priestly redaction of the Pentateuch. Prophecy is antagonistic to the idea of the fixed text; the text becomes a device to define and limit unauthorized speech and action.

The verification of even universal truths is often in the eighteenth century sought through historical inquiry—not through inspiration or even insight ("genius" was sometimes their word) but through documentation. Because the scholarship of the eighteenth century left little room for belief in a presence that can be conveyed by documents, eighteenth-century historicists had to attempt to situate themselves somewhere between the extremes of presence and pyrrhonism, recognizing the pastness of the past while retaining a theoretical probability of connecting it to the present. Locke and his successors attempt the difficult task of defining an empiricist view of testimony that will both valorize direct experience and save historical knowledge. This effort culminates in Hume, whose epistemology is both skeptical and rooted in history.[32] But before surveying a range of opinion on empirical and skeptical views of testimony and textuality, we should examine the views of one writer between Locke and Hume who had a relatively unsystematic but still significantly illustrative approach to the dilemmas posed by the combinations of empiricism, skepticism, and historicism.

The strains of holding a position that is skeptical of historical knowledge yet at the same time finding such knowledge to be essential to the conduct of life are well illustrated by Henry St. John Lord Bolingbroke's *Letters on the Study and Use of History* (1752).[33] These letters produced a storm of opposition in eighteenth-century England, especially because of their dismissive view of the historical portions of the Old Testament. Nevertheless, Bolingbroke's attempt to save an efficacious history even as he incorporates a skeptical Enlightenment view of its inaccuracies is a demonstration of the uncomfortable yet largely indestructible position of historical knowledge within a society in which an empirical ideology is dominant.

---

[32] Popkin's "Skepticism and the Study of History," in *David Hume: Philosophical Historian*, discusses Bayle as a pyrrhonist who nevertheless shows in his practice how one might decide on the reliability of historical data (p. xxviii). Popkin finds that Hume used Bayle's dialectic "to decimate rational philosophy," which he wished to replace with a science of man "in which history would serve as the laboratory study" (p. xxx). David Fate Norton, "History and Philosophy in Hume's Thought," pp. xxxii–1, in the same collection, discusses Hume's efforts to form a critical historiography that would have adequate criteria of reliability despite the impossibility of complete certainty.

I use "historicist" and "historicism" to denote any theory that makes historical understanding centrally important. It is not used in the restricted sense to denote a theory that makes history predictable. Georg Iggers, *The German Conception of History: The National Tradition of Historical Thought from Herder to the Present* (Middletown: Wesleyan University Press, 1968), pp. 287–90, justifies this broader usage as opposed to continuing the distinction between "historism" and "historicism."

[33] References are to *Lord Bolingbroke: Historical Writings*, ed. Isaac Kramnick (Chicago: University of Chicago Press, 1972). Although not published until after Bolingbroke's death, the *Letters on the Study and Use of History* were written during Bolingbroke's stay in France from 1735 to 1738.

Bolingbroke finds history to be a necessary extension to the limitations of human experience: "Experience can go a very little way back in discovering causes: and effects are not the objects of experience till they happen"; whereas through history "place is enlarged, and time prolonged . . . so that the man who applies himself early to the study of history, may acquire in a few years, and before he sets his foot abroad in the world, not only a more extended knowledge of mankind, but the experience of more centuries of the world than any of the patriarchs saw" (pp. 19, 18–19). The initial claim that history is a *supplement* to experience turns into the implication that it is experience itself; history is separated from experience but then also allowed a somewhat equivocal entry into the category. Only one with "genius" can in Bolingbroke's view dispense with either history or a large personal experience (p. 11). Both experience and history are essential for ordinary humans in a world in which "the ages of prophecy, as well as miracles, are past": "We must content ourselves to guess at what will be, by what has been: we have no other means in our power, and history furnishes us with these" (p. 22).

This secondary experiential power conveyed by history is acquired through active engagement in its study, not through passive exposure, thus bolstering Bolingbroke's weak notion that history approaches the power of direct experience. He suggests (following a classical rhetorical tradition) that because history appeals through examples rather than through abstractions, it appeals to both senses and understanding (p. 9). Furthermore, as we must "frame the precept after our own experience," history's "instruction comes . . . upon our own authority." This difficult, and perhaps confused, combination of notions is apparently an attempt to make the acquisition of historical knowledge analogous to direct experience; the reader has an interactive response to history, which is less mediated than other discourses. And to supplement the view that history furthers the empirical project of rooting meaning in experience, Bolingbroke endorses the contention that the general principles needed for ethics and politics can be acquired only from a long range of experience that reveals what is "conformable to the invariable nature of things" (p. 28). In such areas immediate personal experience must be placed in a fuller context of human experience before its meaning can be evaluated.

Yet with this elevated notion of the importance of history, Bolingbroke is notably disparaging of the veracity of history, which he finds is too often extended "beyond all our memorials" (p. 30). Ancient history is in his view markedly unreliable, especially Greek history, and the Old Testament has "come down broken and confused, full of additions, interpolations, and transpositions, made we neither know when, nor by whom" (pp. 32–35, 40). Although making his strongest case against the evidentiary weaknesses of the ancient historians, Bolingbroke does not rest there but agrees that "history has been purposely and systematically falsified in all ages, and that partiality and prejudice have occasioned both voluntary and involuntary errors, even in the best" (p. 51). In his very first letter, Bolingbroke expresses a "thorough contempt for the whole business of these learned lives; for all the researches into antiquity, for all the systems of chronology and history, that we owe to the immense labors of a Scaliger, a Bochart, a Petavius, an Usher, and even a Marsham" (p. 5). In his view these worthies have created merely seemimg history out of "disjointed passages" and "broken traditions of uncertain originals" (p. 5).

We might expect that one with so austere a view of history's propensities to degenerate into fable might seek solace in the precision of the narrowest of antiquaries and chroniclers. But Bolingbroke reserves his particular scorn for these memorializers of the past, finding that they do not serve the function of history at all:

> But ten millions of such anecdotes as these, though they were true; and complete authentic volumes of Egyptian or Chaldean, of Greek or Latin, of Gallic or British, of French or Saxon records, would be of no value in my sense because of no use towards our improvement in wisdom and virtue; if they contained nothing more than dynasties and genealogies, and a bare mention of remarkable events in the order of time, like journals, chronological tables, or dry and meagre annals. (p. 63)

For Bolingbroke the educative function of history, its revelation of circumstances and causes and effects that enable analogical or direct understanding of the present, demands that true history engage itself in precisely those parts of history that are most suspect, parts difficult to demonstrate and narrate (p. 69).

Bolingbroke's emphasis on the power of history to teach by example sometimes threatens to bring it into the domains of fiction. This propensity of his didactic emphasis is taken up in the fourth letter, where he states that the force of examples depends on our believing them. But why may a powerful fiction then not produce the same effect as historical examples? Or why should a true historical example necessarily be superior to a falsified one? Bolingbroke briefly takes up "fables [that] bear an appearance of truth," disposing of them by arguing that they are given credence only as realistic fictions: "Reason dispenses, in favor of probability, with those strict rules of criticism that she has established to try the truth of fact. . . . If they pretended to be history, they would be soon subjected to another and more severe examination. What may have happened, is the matter of an ingenious fable: what has happened, is that of an authentic history" (p. 50). And that which is accepted as actual, as having happened, has a more powerful effect than the merely probable: "The impressions which one or the other makes are in proportion."

Here Bolingbroke directly confronts the sweeping form of skepticism that he calls pyrrhonism and associates with Bayle, a skepticism that regards all history as "fabulous" and thus not distinguishable from probable fictions: "The very best is nothing better than a probable tale, artfully contrived, and plausibly told, wherein truth and falsehood are indistinguishably blended together" (p. 51). Given the degree of suspicion that Bolingbroke suggests is proper in dealing with history and his emphasis on its affective powers in providing efficacious examples, he appears to be close to a position that is content to accept stories for their moral lessons even though strict accuracy cannot be assured. But the other great emphasis in his praise of history is its connection with experience, its making possible the tracing of causes and effects that often exceed any individual life. This function of history demands verified past truth as a way of enabling our understanding of present probabilities.

Despite his skepticism about large stretches of history, Bolingbroke not surprisingly firmly repudiates pyrrhonism, maintaining that historical knowledge is an adequate repository of experiential report capable of usefully guiding present understanding. He suggests that history requires degrees of assent, rather than total rejection or total belief. When "memorials" are absent, "we must be content to remain in our ignorance"; when we have only a few remaining memorials, the others having been destroyed or suppressed, we must try to establish the truth of history "on concurrent testimony" rather than on individual testimony (p. 55). Further, he finds that criticism is able to establish "from various authors a series of true history, which could not have been found entire in any one of them" (p. 56). Thus although our assent may be limited, "there is no reason to establish Pyrrhonism, that we may avoid the ridicule of credulity" (p. 55). Bolingbroke finds that pyrrhonists often support their conclusions by focusing on inessential detail, using the relatively meaningless information of antiquaries and chronologers to impeach what is on larger issues possibly sound history: "The sceptics, in modern as well as ancient history . . . triumph in the notable discovery of the ides of one month mistaken for the calends of another, or in the various dates and contradictory circumstances which they find in weekly gazettes and monthly mercuries" (pp. 70–71). Such skeptical attacks on history, Bolingbroke suggests, tend to reduce history to verifiable trivialities: "The nearer a history comes to the true idea of history, the better it informs and the more it instructs us, the more worthy to be rejected it appears to them" (p. 69).

Bolingbroke attempts to break the links between history and fiction through his repudiation of pyrrhonism, which makes history only another kind of fable. Yet in insisting that history must do much more than establish a factual base, he also indicates an alliance with the probable fictions that exceed the "memorials" of what happened. Consider, for example, Bolingbroke's expectations of the unfinished portion of Livy's admirable history:

> Would you not be glad, my Lord, to see, in one stupendous draught, the whole progress of that government from liberty to servitude? the whole series of causes and effects, apparent and real, public and private? those which all men saw, and all good men lamented and opposed at the time; and those which were so disguised to the prejudices, to the partialities of a divided people, and even to the corruption of mankind, that many did not, and that many could pretend they did not, discern them, till it was too late to resist them? (pp. 68–69)

Bolingbroke's vision of the potentialities of history implies its connection to the literary imagination, a relationship insinuated by his recurent use of analogies to literary analysis in order to explain historiographical issues. He uses Boileau's comments on the modern translation of ancient authors to explain the nature of the imitation that should be accorded to historical examples: "We must catch the spirit . . . and conform ourselves to the reason of them; but we must not affect to translate servilely into our conduct . . . the particular conduct of those good and great men, whose images history sets before us" (p. 27). The process of periodizing in order to organize the study of history efficiently is presented as an analogy to the study of the plot of drama: "Examine this period of history as you would examine a tragedy or a comedy; that is, take first the idea or a general notion of the whole, and after that examine every act and every scene apart. Consider them in them-selves, and consider them relatively to one another" (pp. 94–95). And in arguing that England should be cautious of entering into continental affairs, he cites the rule given by "Horace for the conduct of an epic or dramatic poem" that forbids the intervention of the gods except when truly necessary (p. 147).

This awareness of textualization and emplottedness in history and life coexists, however, with a determined resistance to any violation of the bor-ders between history and merely probable fiction, any abrogation there implying the victory of the pyrrhonism that will threaten empiricism itself.[34] Bolingbroke's complex (some will say confused) position is perhaps best signaled by his recommendation that historical reading should include

[34] Leo Braudy, *Narrative Form*, comments astutely on Bolingbroke's use of the "metaphor of literature" (p. 27). I cannot, however, agree with his generalization that for Bolingbroke "The

both the philosophical history that he values and the memorials on which it ought to be based: "By joining history and that which we call the *materia historica* [public acts and monuments, private letters, treaties] together in this manner, and by drawing your information from both, your lordship will acquire not only that knowledge, which many have in some degree [but also] . . . a knowledge of the true political system of Europe during this time" (p. 95).

III

The bulk of what follows consists of a survey of relevant seventeenth- and eighteenth-century views on two related topics: the validity of testimony and the hermeneutical implications of a referential view of meaning. Fiction's deficiency of reference is explored in relation to its claims to be history. Although eighteenth-century treatments of both topics—testimony and reference—appear to veer erratically from historiographical questions to applications in biblical interpretation, our twentieth-century distinctions between the two areas are often unproductively anachronistic when applied to an eighteenth-century context. Eighteenth-century commitment to the Bible as historical made it subject to the same criteria as other texts that claimed historicity. Both opponents and upholders of the dominant view of the Bible's historicity found in biblical texts and concomitant church teachings compelling materials for historiographical debate. In a text aimed at summarizing the best that had been thought and said about history—a handbook for reading history intelligently—Lenglet-Dufresnoy finds sacred history, the Bible, to be foundational: "As the History of God's people is the most certain, and serves as a rule to the others, so in it we have the comfort to see the continuation of the true religion, uninterrupted from the creation of the world, and therefore from it ought we begin our study of particular History" (*New Method*, 1:41). The validity of testimony and the nature of referential interpretation are germane to this kind of historical foundationalism.

As biblical events are known primarily or entirely through testimony, it was a matter of some importance for eighteenth-century believers to be sure

---

only superiority history has over fiction of any type, the quality that gives its examples their persuasive power, is the reader's knowledge that it really happened." This view leaves out of consideration Bolingbroke's assertions that veracious history is needed in order to understand those cause and effect patterns that are analogous to concerns of the present or that directly impinge upon the present.

that biblical testimony met the criteria established for valid testimony in any historical inquiry. The related question of reference poses important hermeneutical questions. If at least some portions of the Bible are historical, then those portions must be interpreted as referring to historical events and their meaning must be consistent with those events. Such a hermeneutic subjects the biblical text to the interpretive criteria of plausible historicity; events outside the text must support, or at least not contradict, any interpretation that claims to be authoritative. Such a procedure leads to seeing the text itself as historical, representative of a particular time and place in which its meaning must be sought. And finally what emerges from both the pursuit of valid criteria for testimony and the search for the referential meaning of the text is a seemingly paradoxical focus on the materiality of the text itself. At first both interpretive issues—the validity of testimony and the reference of documents—direct attention to various contextualizations, yet both also then turn attention to the historicity of the text itself—its language and provenience, including its material transmission.

When Locke analyzes the degree of assent demanded by the testimony of others, he is particularly concerned to diminish the assent required by hearsay: "The Being and Existence of the thing it self, is what I call the original Truth. A credible Man vouching his Knowledge of it, is a good proof; But if another equally credible, do witness it from his Report, the Testimony is weaker; and a third that attests the Hear-say of an Hear-say, is yet less considerable" (*Essay*, IV, xvi, 10).[35] He cites approvingly the legal practice of not accepting a copy of a copy: "Though the attested Copy of a Record be good Proof, yet the Copy of a Copy never so well attested, and by never so credible Witnesses, will not be admitted as a proof in Judicature." Extending the principle behind this legal application to the experience of ordinary life, he states: "He that has but ever so little examined the Citations of Writers, cannot doubt how little Credit the Quotations deserve, where the Originals are wanting; and consequently how much less Quotations of Quotations can be relied on" (11). Tradition, Locke finds, is actively corrupting, turning propositions properly unbelievable at first into "authentick Truths" merely because they have survived; tradition thus functions as an "inverted Rule of Probability" (10). Realizing that his strict standard calls into question much history, Locke states that he "would not be thought here to lessen the Credit and use of *History*," going on to assert that he thinks "nothing more valuable than the Records of Antiquity: I wish we had

---

[35] John Locke, *An Essay concerning Human Understanding*, ed. Peter H. Nidditch (Oxford: Clarendon Press, 1975), p. 664. All quotations are from pp. 663–64; citations include book, chapter, and paragraph numbers.

more of them, and more uncorrupted" (11). Locke supports the efforts of history, yet regards it as unable to surpass the quality of the documents available to it.

Locke's sometimes bumptious disciple Anthony Collins uses these comments to foreground the difficulties in claiming a religious revelation based on testimonies about the miraculous.[36] In *An Essay Concerning the Use of Reason in Propositions, the Evidence whereof depends Upon Human Testimony* (2d ed., 1709), Collins identifies much that is called revelation as testimony, and he then attempts to grapple with the problem of testimony that is in conflict with reason. He urges a hermeneutic that brings testimony within the compass of the rationally acceptable: "Endeavor to find such a sense of a suppos'd Revelation as is agreeable to the discoveries of our Reason, if the words under any kind of Construction will bear it, tho at first view they may seem repugnant to Reason, and to one another" (p. 13). In an argument adumbrating aspects of Hume's later one, he states: "If our natural Notions of other things are as certain as our natural Notions of God, then it follows, that nothing which we judg[e] repugnant to natural Notions ought to be assented to upon the highest Testimony whatever" (p. 12). He argues against accepting writing "deliver'd to us as a Revelation from God upon Human Authority" if it persistently negates our perceptions; the implications of accepting as revelation that which negates our perceptions would "bring Confusion, Disorder, and Uncertainty into all the Affairs of Mankind" (p. 11).

John Craige's curious *Theologiae Christianae Principia Mathematica* (published in 1699) is a markedly different response to the problem Locke posed. Craige attempts to evaluate mathematically the credibility of testimony about the past, trying to validate testimony on a basis more rigorous and systematic than that possible through more informal probabilistic judgments. He begins his pamphlet by stating that "Historical Probability Is Diminished From Three Sources Especially: the number of witnesses through whom the testimony is successively transmitted; the distance of the place from which the subject is reported . . . and the length of time through which the history is transmitted." He then promises that his "propositions"

---

[36] James O'Higgins, S. J., *Anthony Collins: The Man and His Works* (The Hague: Martinus Nijhoff, 1970), discusses Locke's early friendship with Collins as well as Collins's markedly different religious views, as shown in Collins's later writings. Gerard Reedy, S. J., *The Bible and Reason: Anglicans and Scripture in Late-Seventeenth-Century England* (Philadelphia: University of Pennsylvania Press, 1985), discusses the heavy commitment of Anglican theologians to the evidence of testimony in support of scriptural truth: "The divines often said that there is as much assurance of the existence and authorship of Moses as of, say, Thucydides and Euclid" (p. 52).

will demonstrate the "rate by which probability decreases."[37] He concludes (p. 70) that Christ will not return until 3150, the date beyond which testimony about Christianity cannot be credible and, therefore, the date after which "When the Son of Man returns" he will "find no faith on Earth" (cf. Luke 18:8). Craige's recent translator and commentator Richard Nash points out that despite our present perceptions of this work as bizarre, Craige achieved serious attention from a number of important figures of the eighteenth century, including Tindal, Warburton, Pope, and Hume (p. xv), and, further, "throughout the eighteenth century, mathematicians, theologians, and philosophers returned to a problem that lies at the heart of Craige's treatise: Can one develop a rigorous model for measuring the credibility of human testimony" (p. 3)?

The historiographical implications of Locke's views are taken to their pyrrhonist extreme in an astonishing pamphlet called *Christianity Not Founded on Argument* (1741). The textualizing of past testimony is here seen as an unassailable argument against its possible verification. The author is not given, although he is identified in the British Library Catalog as Henry Dodwell the younger, who was in eighteenth-century terms a "freethinker."[38] The pamphlet announces itself as a defense of Christianity against the depredations of those who would subject it to rational scrutiny, claiming instead that religious truth must be founded on an inner conviction able to survive the inevitable onslaughts of reason: "The indelible Characters stamped upon those living Tablets [our hearts] are such as are out of the Power of the Unfaithfulness or Ignorance of Transcribers to falsify or pervert" (p. 60).

Dodwell's major thrust is against those who attempt to ground Christianity in history by means of documentary evidence. He cites without criticism the view that the text of the Bible itself can be of little authority, given the need for transmission by human means and materials: "The Original itself, though penn'd like that on Mount *Sinai* by the very Finger of God himself, and engraven even on Adamant instead of Marble; must in Time come to want Repairs. . . . The very first Step therefore from this genuine Palladium into a Copy and Representation at second Hand, will . . . detract in a great Degree from its divine Authority, as this must be the Work of Man" (pp. 60–

---

[37] John Craige, *Mathematical Principles of Christian Theology*, translated and edited by Richard Nash (Carbondale: Southern Illinois University Press, 1991), p. 57.

[38] [Henry Dowell], *Christianity Not Founded on Argument; and the True Principle of Gospel-Evidence Assigned* (London: T. Cooper, 1741). Leslie Stephen, *A History of English Thought in the Eighteenth Century* (London: Smith, Elder, 1888), vol. 1, sec. 3, pars. 76–80, discusses the broader context of Henry Dodwell's pamphlet, placing it in a context of controversy supporting the view that it is a deist tract.

61). The miracles that are cited as evidence for Christianity may have been "ocular proof" to a contemporary, but "to us . . . no more than uncertain Hearsay" (p. 53). The moment an eyewitness imparts a story "it commences human Authority, and, as such, becomes the proper Subject of our free Enquiry and Debate." For us the representations of divine presence in the Bible have become just ancient and unreliable texts: "We hear no more that awful sound [the voice of God], but by Repetition and Echo, and all that commanding Force of the great original Attestation and Acknowledgement is sunk with us, into the uncertain Assertions of Fallible Men relating it after one another"(p. 52).[39]

The reader of *Christianity Not Founded on Argument* (1741) is likely to be reminded of the later and far better known work by David Hume, "Of Miracles," which was published as part of the *Enquiry Concerning Human Understanding* (1748, although written for and withdrawn from the earlier *Treatise*).[40] Like the writer of *Christianity Not Founded on Argument*, Hume regards at least some biblical documentary evidence in support of Christianity as unreliable, but unlike him, Hume also attempts to avoid the trap of historical pyrrhonism. Wittily (or maliciously, depending on one's perspective) Hume bases his onslaught on the historicity of miracles on a distinction that he attributes to Tillotson's argument against the Roman Catholic doctrine of the "real presence" in the Eucharist—the distinction between the evidence of the senses and of testimony: "It is acknowledged on all hands, says that learned prelate, that the authority, either of the scripture or of tradition, is founded merely in the testimony of the apostles, who were eyewitnesses to those miracles of our Saviour, by which he proved his divine mission" (p. 109). It is the witnessing that makes the testimony credible, a view with the consequent implication that firsthand testimony takes precedence over hearsay: "Our evidence, then, for the truth of the *Christian* religion is less than the evidence for the truth of our senses; because, even in the first authors of our religion it was no greater; and it is evident it must diminish in passing from them to their disciples; nor can any one rest such confidence in their testimony, as in the immediate object of his senses" (p. 109).

---

[39] P. Doddridge, *An Answer to a Late Pamphlet, Intitled, Christianity not founded on Argument* (London: M. Fenner, 1743), uses a comparison to general history as a *reductio ad absurdum* of Dodwell's argument: the argument that the antiquity of a document impairs its truth "will also *prove* that we can have *no rational Evidence* of any Thing that was done *before we were born*; or, indeed, of any Thing which we have not *seen with our own Eyes*" (p. 27).

[40] David Hume, "Of Miracles," sec. 10 of *An Enquiry Concerning Human Understanding*, in *Enquiries concerning Human Understanding and concerning the Principles of Morals*, ed. L. A. Selby-Bigge and revised P. H. Nidditch (Oxford: Clarendon Press, 1975), pp. 109–31.

For Hume our belief in testimony has a basis similar to that of our belief in causal reasoning about natural events, in which the consistency of one thing following another is the index to the persuasiveness of any attribution of cause: "The reason why we place any credit in witnesses and historians, is not derived from any *connexion*, which we perceive *a priori*, between testimony and reality, but because we are accustomed to find a conformity between them" (p. 113). But when we are presented with testimony that contradicts our observations of natural events, as in testimonies of miracles, we must ask whether our experiences of the truth of testimony or of the patterns of nature are the more reliable. Hume concludes that as "there must . . . be a uniform experience against every miraculous event, otherwise the event would not merit that appelation," no testimony can confirm a miracle (p. 115).

While taking the same skeptical view of hearsay testimony that Locke does, Hume also defines a perspective outside the documentary evidence, one that does not leave the past a hostage to the quality of its written documentation. Hume's aim is not alone the negative one of depriving the miracles, thought to verify Christianity, of their claims to historicity. Unlike Dodwell, he does not merely allow a total skepticism—pyrrhonism—to undermine history as well as Christianity but is also concerned to establish the possibility of veridical history even as he shows its limits. For Hume, "There is no species of reasoning more common, more useful, and even necessary to human life, than that derived from the testimony of men, and the reports of eyewitnesses and spectators" (p. 111). A substantial portion of "Of Miracles" is devoted to establishing the probabilistic kind of thinking that will enable the use of testimony from the past without a consequent commitment to its not infrequent preposterousness.

The commonplace principle that Hume establishes for empowering the historian to interpret the past is that "the objects of which we have no experience, resemble those of which we have; that what we have found to be most usual is always most probable" (p. 117).[41] To explain, then, how it is that accounts of prodigies, all outside our experience, have gained credence, in part 2 of his essay "Of Miracles," Hume examines a series of topics that expose human propensities for believing and perpetuating implausibilities: of central importance is the agreeableness of "the passion of *surprise* and

---

[41] David Wootton, "Hume's 'Of Miracles': Probability and Irreligion," in *Studies in the Philosophy of the Scottish Enlightenment*, ed. M. A. Stewart (Oxford: Clarendon Press, 1990), p. 193, states that "The 'emergence of probability' made it possible to ask, in place of 'Can the truth of Christianity be demonstrated?', or 'Is it supported by authority?', questions such as 'Is it likely that the Gospel narrative is accurate?' and 'How good is the evidence for God's existence?' Modern irreligion may be said to be born with these new questions."

wonder," which is given an almost uncontrollable urgency when connected
with the "spirit of religion" (*Enquiries*, p. 117). Even in this relatively brief
dismissal of accounts of miracles, however, Hume includes nuances of interpretation that go beyond mere rejection of the inexplicable. He narrates two
hypothetical events, both contrary to experience, yet in the face of extensive
and uncontradicted testimony in favor of both, he would accept one and
dismiss the other: he would accept the report of a period of darkness lasting
for eight days, but would reject that of Queen Elizabeth dying and then
rising a month later to resume her rule (pp. 127–28). In the one case the
decay of nature, which Hume finds probable, would make the event plausible if the "testimony be very extensive and uniform"; in the other, although
the same testimony would make him believe in the "pretended death, and of
those other public circumstances that followed it," he would, nevertheless
"only assert it to have been pretended, and that it neither was, nor possibly
could be real" (p. 128). He acknowledges that he would be astonished at the
subsequent concurrence of testimony regarding so marvelous an event as the
resurrection of the dead in relatively recent times, but concludes that his
experience not only of nature but also of the "knavery and folly of men"
would outweigh the testimony.

The textualizing of testimony is not ignored by Hume, but neither is it an
insuperable problem. In the *Treatise of Human Nature*, he discusses what
happens to historical documentation that may once have had the persuasiveness accruing to eyewitness testimony, but after many years exists only as a
copy derived from a train of copies.[42] Hume accepts neither the historical
pyrrhonism manifest in a work like *Christianity Not Founded on Argument*
nor John Craige's mathematical views of credibility. He does accept the view
that if each step in the chain of evidence, that is, each copy, is treated only
as a probability, then "there is no history or tradition, but what must in the
end lose all its force and evidence" (p. 145). But that is not the case, he
argues. A copy differs from a chain of reasoning in which each step is a
probability based on a prior probability, the difference being that the steps
represented by copies of documents are not sequential reasonings but are
identical to each other. When we understand one step of this kind, we
understand the nature of all of them and are not considering the diminishing
probability of sequential rational arguments but a question of the "fidelity of
Printers and Copists" (p. 146): "It seems contrary to common sense to think,
that if the republic of letters, and the art of printing continue on the same

---

[42] David Hume, "Of Unphilosophical Probability," in *A Treatise of Human Nature*, ed. L. A.
Selby-Bigge and revised P. H. Nidditch (Oxford: Clarendon Press, 1978), bk. I, pt. iii, sec. xiii,
143–55.

footing as at present, our posterity, even after a thousand ages, can ever doubt if there has been such a man as *Julius Caesar*" (p. 145).

Any examination of the responses of eighteenth-century fiction to this kind of philosophically sophisticated historiography must confront the issue of reference: Hume is attempting to determine what happened (although he must often settle for what might have happened), whereas apparent fiction can only claim those kinds of truth that evade direct confrontation with reference. Realistic fictions perhaps show the *nature* of things that happen, or create probable responses to probable situations, or devise analogues to a variety of actual events. But although they can thus plausibly claim to assist or even supersede history, they are not in a literal sense able to sustain the claim that they refer only to externally verifiable events (without being enlisted in the category of hoax).

Yet if we acknowledge these limitations on plausible claims for reference, we are left with the question of why eighteenth-century fiction so often persists in making not fully plausible insinuations of reference. Taking as examples the prefaces to the fiction of Defoe alone, we are presented with a disconcerting obstinacy in support of the factual basis of these narratives. In the course of writing prefaces to his fictions, Defoe never relinquishes the claim that these writings are authorized by a narrative voice responsible to the events of her or his own past. The prefaces, however, are putatively written by an editor who adopts the stance of someone presenting only what was afforded by these authoritative recounters of their own stories. That objective stance is sometimes modified by acknowledgement of some necessary editorial intervention, yet Defoe never concedes that these works' claims to factuality are implausible.[43] It is perhaps not necessary to conclude that Defoe hoped that each of these narratives would be taken as a historical, that is, biographical, account; it does, however, appear that he wished them to be read in the same way as historical accounts are read. He wants to thwart any attempt to place these works definitively in the category of fiction.

Even after the great success of the early novel, Samuel Richardson believed that a reading at least similar to the one Defoe encourages was still possible. In his novels *Pamela* and *Clarissa* he strengthens the editor's hand by appearing to present the original documents themselves, without any acknowledged intermediary or long-after-the-fact narration, a procedure that both legitimizes and increases the editor's role: the editor need not acknowledge tampering with the language of the participants—hiatuses and errors may be assimilated to the narrator's distortions in the heat of the

---

[43] Ioan Williams, *Novel and Romance*, reproduces the relevant prefaces.

moment—but does have the responsibility for ordering the documents that convey the story. Although Richardson's claim to historical factuality is considerably less insistent than Defoe's, he does not entirely abandon the claim nor is he merely perfunctory in making it.

Richardson's comments *in propria persona* to William Warburton state his unwillingness to abandon the pretense to history even when it is obviously regarded by others as somewhat creaky machinery. Warburton wrote a preface for volume 3 of *Clarissa*, published after the first two volumes were already out, which praises the work as "a faithful and chaste copy of real *Life and Manners*."[44] Warburton's remarks are of interest for their acknowledgment of the close relationship between history and fiction, especially as evidenced in his comments on the affective qualities of narration, which are similar in both cases, and his derivation of the line of romance from that of history. The knowledge of human actions, Warburton states, had been extended by "the invention of *History*. Which, by recording the principal circumstances of past facts, and laying them close together, in a continued narration, kept the mind from languishing, and gave constant exercise to its reflections." Richardson's work is praiseworthy because it superseded the "barbarous *Romances*" that had come into existence because of "a jaded appetite" unable to tolerate true history. But Warburton's praise does not conceal his identification of romance, including Richardson's writing, as a substitute for history, thus definitively separated from history, no matter how close it may come. The open acknowledgment of this separation was unacceptable to Richardson, who wrote to Warburton that he "could wish that the *Air* of Genuineness had been kept up, tho' I want not the letters to be *thought* genuine." Richardson wants to maintain their "influence" and "to avoid hurting that kind of Historical Faith which Fiction itself is generally read with, tho' we know it to be Fiction."[45] Despite Warburton's eminence, Richardson had this preface removed from the second edition.

Catherine Gallagher argues that fiction early in the eighteenth century does not clearly distinguish itself from the referential and thus leaves the "discursive practice we now call 'fiction' . . . unmapped and unarticulated."[46] Later, however, the very features of realism signal that the text is *not* referential: "But the more characters were loaded with circumstantial and even insignificant properties, the more the readers were assured that the text was at once assuming and making up for the fact that it referred to nobody

[44] Ibid., pp. 122–24.

[45] *Selected Letters of Samuel Richardson*, ed. John Carroll (Oxford: Clarendon Press, 1964), 19 April 1748, p. 85.

[46] Gallagher, "Nobody's Story," p. 265.

at all" (p. 269). I find this argument ingenious and plausible in its reference to central characters and consciousnesses; the more intimately we become acquainted with them, the less probable it is that there could be any adequately corresponding evidence outside the text. But another facet of the novel is not fully represented in this argument—the novel's manner of differentiating itself from more openly fictional forms like poetry and apologue (and some kinds of satire). Each of these forms claims to be telling a truth consistent with the realities of its time and sometimes makes historical allusions, yet such truth is effectively or fully conveyed only if its fictionality is manifest, not covert. In contrast, the novel of the mid-eighteenth century appears to be seeking a constitutive equivocation, claiming its formal realism as more than a formality. Novels like *Clarissa*, *Tom Jones*, and *Tristram Shandy* (from, roughly, the third quarter of the century) take a somewhat evasive stance toward referentiality, an evasiveness located in their explicit and implicit obtrusions of historiographical concerns. I do not mean to imply that readers commonly accepted, or were asked to accept, Richardson's, Fielding's, and Sterne's novels as descriptions of actual events. The novels of these writers do, however, constitute themselve as sharing a border with history and thus impute to themselves some kind of referentiality, even if attenuated. The later development of the historical novel is premised on an open acceptance of fictionality and its distinction from the history it may include. That story has a somewhat later center of gravity than the one told here and entails a story of changes in historical narration too. As Linda Orr puts it, "It is as if history awakes in the nineteenth century surprised and even horrified to see how closely it is coupled with fiction."[47] History too must then compensate for the shifting border with fiction and enhance that border's clarity.

In pursuing the present more limited story, I use Hans W. Frei's *Eclipse of Biblical Narrative* as a guide to the hermeneutic functions of reference that form a background to the novel and motivate it to pursue concealments and ambiguities rather than acknowledge the limits of its referentiality.[48] It may seem quixotic to attach issues of biblical hermeneutics to a popular form

[47] Linda Orr, "The Revenge of Literature: A History of History," *New Literary History* 18 (1986–87): 3. Orr revises Stephen Dedalus's aphorism to "literature is the nightmare from which history is trying to wake" (p. 2): history attempts in the nineteenth century "to widen a difference within its very self, in order not to be engulfed by that other self—and the effect is to invent the modern definition of history, to inaugurate a tradition by rewriting the history of history, and in so doing to institute that difference as science" (p. 3).

[48] Hans Frei, *The Eclipse of Biblical Narrative: A Study of Eighteenth- and Nineteenth-Century Hermeneutics* (New Haven: Yale University Press, 1974), defines the pressures for establishing reference that are created by an empiricist theory of interpretation and meaning in

like the novel, yet the novel's popularity (although recent commentary sometimes does not ackowledge this) appears to have been based on its inclusiveness rather more than on its lowness. Running throughout the canonical novels of the eighteenth century are implicit, sometimes explicit, debates about the nature of the literality claimed, debates that implicate the novel in questions about typological narrative. More specifically, three of the novels discussed in ensuing chapters invoke works of scholarship that introduce biblical interpretation into the texture of the novel: as discussed in the following chapters, *Clarissa* includes reference to Anthony Blackwall, *The Sacred Classics Defended and Illustrated*; *Tristram Shandy* to William Warburton, *The Divine Legation of Moses Demonstrated*; and *Caleb Williams* to Humphrey Prideaux, *The Old and New Testament Connected*.

The Eclipse of Biblical Narrative describes an empiricist theory of interpretation that binds meaningfulness to reference and thus motivates the eighteenth-century writer of fiction to provide some rationale for at least a deferred or oblique kind of reference. The early novel's claims to history on the basis of the similarity of its narratives to those of history allies it with what Frei calls precritical narrative interpretation. Yet the novel's simulation of reconstructions of truth, as in *Clarissa* and *Tristram Shandy*, ally it with the subsequent methods of historical verification as espoused by Bentley and others. Such divided loyalty suggests a fundamental uneasiness with either position. Both precritical "narrative" interpretation and "historical-critical" interpretation predate the eighteenth century, but the apparent process of change from one dominant perspective to the other took place in the latter half of the eighteenth century, primarily in Germany, and was prepared for in the first half of the century by the controversy over deism in England. "Narrative interpretation" deals with the realistic features of biblical narrative—characters, events, sequence—as meaningful in themselves without subordination to an external meaning. Seemingly literal depiction by the text is thus constitutive of the narrative's meaning and does not primarily point toward another meaning. Historical-critical reading, on the other hand, asks questions about the reference of the story. The shape of the story itself

<hr/>

the eighteenth century. John Drury, editor of *Critics of the Bible: 1724–1873* (Cambridge: Cambridge University Press, 1989), remarks in his introduction that not only did historicism influence the interpretation of the Bible in this era, but the Bible had also already taught many of its critics to "think historically in the first place" (p. 4). Paul J. Korshin, *Typologies in England: 1650–1820* (Princeton: Princeton University Press, 1982), discusses extensions of biblical typology into secular works, including the eighteenth-century novel (see chap. 7, "Typology and the Novel," pp. 186ff.).

is central to a narrative interpretation, whereas a historical-critical interpretation focuses on an external relationship that may in some cases establish a meaning not heavily dependent on the details of the narrative itself: "The narrative became distinguished from a separable subject matter—whether historical, ideal, or both at once—which was now taken to be its true meaning" (p. 51).

Protestant biblical interpretation was based on the primacy of the literal; however, the literal is not upon scrutiny so self-evidently unitary as it first seems. The literal is sometimes identified as the explicative meaning in which the grammatical and lexical elements of the text are read with the exactness needed to posit an original sense of the text—a sense consistent with the language of the time in which it was written. But the concept of the literal is also bound up with the historical—indeed "historical meaning" is sometimes used as if identical to the literal. After all, any concept of the literal must have the language of a time and place as a normative restraint on construal if the textual meaning is to be determinate. But why stop at the *language* of a time and place in a narrow sense? One must also deal with customs, political and social circumstances, and intellectual assumptions—in short history—as constraints on meaning. In broadly philological interpretation such factors can be included within language, yet a more divisive view of interpretation is possible: the text may be compared with the circumstances it purportedly is responsive to, with the possibility that its historical meaning may be inconsistent with its explicative meaning. Here then arises a problem for a culture that had invested religious belief in a literal *and* historical interpretation of biblical narratives; this hermeneutic tended to force a choice between narrative or explicative meanings and historical ones.

Frei describes a "great reversal" of interpretation in the eighteenth century: gradually the biblical narrative came to be fitted "into another world with another story rather than incorporating that world into the biblical story" (p. 130). The process of severing historical from explicative meaning resulted in the use of verifiable, or at least plausible, historical events as a guide to the meaning of, and eventually to the value of, biblical narrative. Whereas the identity of the explicative with the historical meaning was assumed in precritical interpretation, in the eighteenth century a linguistic theory of reference was increasingly used to define meaning. In the empiricist scheme of things, it was reasonable to think "of nouns naming and thereby standing in the conceptual place of the things they refer to, things of which one would have an independent, language-neutral apprehension" (p. 24). The notion of narrative as presenting an immediately meaningful world was vanishing and being replaced by the notion that "the connection between language and its context is the reality of the author on the one hand and of the single, external reference of the words on the other" (p. 79). In the kind of interpretation that Anthony Collins and like-minded others espoused, meaning must be related to the intention of the author. Writings then make sense only in the context of what that author could conceivably have meant in particular historical circumstances. Collins took the position that for a christological figural interpretation to be plausible, the writer of the relevant passage had to have intended to refer to Christ. Yet actual examination of such passages often suggests a more immediate and historically plausible reference. Furthermore, Collins envisions the possibility of an intention that governs the words even though not clear and explicit in them.

Frei's generalizations about empiricist historical interpretation in the eighteenth century can be briefly illustrated here in relation to a series of influential, sometimes notorious, statements and controversies touching biblical and also secular interpretation: notably, Locke's own practical criticism of the Bible, the extension of Locke's principles in the work of his deistic follower Anthony Collins, and a rebuttal of Collins by the great textual scholar Richard Bentley, whose implicitly destructive textual criticism is then also challenged. What is perhaps most important in the comparison of these three eminent figures is their similarity of assumption despite the sometimes sharp differences of opinion. All accept the view that biblical interpretation must proceed according to the standards for any other text, and that the Bible has the historical and verbal impedimenta of all ancient texts. Furthermore, the truths of Christianity, all concede, are dependent on some kind of textually based historical veracity, a textuality inevitably problematic. The demand for referentiality is then often displaced by prior concerns about textuality. In fact the question of the materiality of the text is raised so often that it seems to have eclipsed concerns for context.

In "An Essay for the Understanding of St. Paul's Epistles By Consulting St. Paul Himself," Locke regards the interpretive difficulties to be those of language and context, as in any other old texts: "Expressions now out of use, Opinions of those times, not heard of in our days, Allusions to Customs lost to us, and various Circumstances and Particularities of the Parties, which we cannot come at."[49] In addition, he sees the Pauline text as representing individualized aspects of its human author despite its presumed inspiration by a divine author:

> He was, as 'tis visible, a Man of quick Thought, warm Temper, mighty well vers'd in the Writings of the Old Testament, and full of the Doctrine of the

[49] John Locke, "Preface" to *A Paraphrase and Notes on the Epistles of St. Paul*, 2 vols., ed. Arthur W. Wainwright (Oxford: Clarendon Press, 1987), 1:112.

New: All this put together, suggested Matter to him in abundance on those Subjects which came in his way: So that one may consider him when he was writing, as beset with a Crowd of Thoughts, all Striving for Utterance. (1:104)

Locke, nevertheless, takes the view that a reading of the kind he proposes, one that attempts to grasp St. Paul's larger purposes and meaning, will "carry us a great length in the right understanding" of the epistles (1:113).

Locke's deist disciple Anthony Collins's interpretive perspective has much in common with Locke's, but Collins finds the condition of the biblical text itself a problem. In A Discourse of Free-Thinking, he attacks the textual integrity of the Bible as well as the confusions that have been occasioned by the biased and multiple interpretations of what is in any case obscure.[50] For Collins the massive contextual demands for understanding the Bible create interpretive problems rather than resolutions: "The Compass of such a History shews that no Art or Science can be untouch'd in it" (p. 9). Rather than finding a book from which meaning emanates, Collins finds one that demands all the independent resources of human scholarship for a construal that will even then be thwarted by textual difficulties.

The great classical scholar Richard Bentley responded by impugning Collins's learning, claiming that Collins "understands not the mere Grammatical sense, much less the application and import of any old Passage he cites" and also lacks knowledge of the customs of biblical times (pp. 48–49).[51] Bentley particularly focuses on the charges of the textual corruption of the Bible, endeavoring not so much to refute Collins as to deny the significance that he finds. Using classical scholarship as the standard, Bentley argues that the biblical text is more than adequate. And accepting the view that the Bible is subject to the same vicissitudes of text and interpretation as any other book, Bentley concludes that disagreements in these areas are inevitable. According to Bentley, the real question Collins asks is, then, whether revelation can "be communicated and convey'd to us in Books" (p. 56). In a sense Bentley stakes the veracity of the Bible on his own position as the representative of the continuing technical advances of humanist textual scholarship: it is his kind of historical scholarship that keeps alive both the classics and scripture. Collins's view would either return history to conjecture or demand a constant miracle on behalf of the Bible: "Either a posteriori all Antient Books, as well as the Sacred, must now be laid aside as uncertain and precarious; or else to say a priori, That all the Transcripts of Sacred Books should have been privileg'd

---

[50] Anthony Collins, A Discourse of Free-Thinking, Occasion'd by The Rise and Growth of a Sect call'd Free-Thinkers (London, 1713).

[51] Richard Bentley, Remarks Upon a late Discourse of Free-Thinking in a Letter to N. N. By Phileleutherus Lipsiensis, 6th ed. (Cambridge: Cornelius Crownfield, 1725), pp. 32, 48–49.

against the common Fate, and exempted from all Slips and Errors whatever" (p. 75). In contrast to Collins, Bentley asserts that a kind of truth is reached through the textual scholarship that achieves resolution by means of the comparison of a multiplicity of copies and variants: "Since Time and Casualties must consume and devour All; the subsidiary Help is from the various Transcripts convey'd down to us, when compar'd and examin'd together" (p. 66). In Bentley's view Collins's problems with the Bible arise not from excessive historicism but from insufficient historicism.

Bentley and Collins disagree violently about orthodox Christianity, but they do not contest the grounds from which they reach disagreement. Belief in Christianity is text based, and the text must be interpreted according to the methodology appropriate for other texts. The hermeneutical methods of Bentley and Collins are consistent with those of Locke, although Bentley's textual criticism is beyond anything that either Locke or Collins were capable of. Bentley's methods, which look forward to the higher criticism of the nineteenth century, produce a less dependent relationship with a text, making it reveal much that it won't tell directly. But Bentley's methods are implicitly destructive too (just as Collins's are), having a demonstrated potentiality for the subversion of seemingly authoritative texts as well as mending them to enhance their authority. The destructive possibilities of Bentley's criticism and analysis are evidenced in the very "Remarks" in which Bentley confutes Collins's attack on the authority of the biblical text, where Bentley does to Homer what Collins wanted to do to the Bible: Homer, Bentley states (as had others), "wrote a sequel of Songs and Rhapsodies, to be sung by himself for small earnings and good cheer, at Festivals and other days of Merriment; the *Ilias* he made for the Men, and the *Odysseis* for the other Sex. These loose Songs were not collected together in the form of an Epic Poem, till Pisistratus's time about 500 years after" (p. 18).

Bentley's enemies repeatedly charged that if his methods of criticizing classical texts were accepted, the Bible too would be destroyed, not just Phalaris and Aesop. In response to Bentley's *Dissertation*, Boyle charges that St. Paul's epistles must be found spurious on the same principles: "The Writings that carry his Name must be Four hundred Years Younger than We Christians suppose 'em: and the Epistle to the *Romans* could not be the Genuine Work of that *Apostle*. . . . Shall we allow Dr. Bentley to be a Scurvy Critic, or shall we in Tenderness to his Honour, give up our Bibles?"[52] Bentley eventually proposed an edition of the New Testament, "So that the Reader has under one View what the first Ages of the Church knew of the

[52] *Dr. Bentley's Dissertation on the Epistles of Phalaris and the Fables of Aesop* (London: Thomas Bennet, 1698), p. 62.

Text . . . what has crept into any Copies since, is of no Value or Authority"; this proposed work may "last when all the Antient MSS here quoted may be lost and extinguish'd."[53] Conyers Middleton, himself thought by some to be no good friend to Christianity, went on the attack: "Our Author, we see with all his Zeal for *Common Christianity*, makes no Scruple to destroy here at once the Authority of all our *published Scriptures*, and by a kind of *Papal Edict* cries down all our *current Editions* as corrupt and adulterate, 'till coined and stamped anew by his Authority" (p. 5). Included in Middleton's attack is the charge that the true motivation for Bentley is the printing industry, Grub Street, not permanence, or, presumably, Providence: "For having invented a *rare Secret* to make *Paper* more durable than *Parchment*, and a printed Book, however used and tumbled about, to *outlast any manuscript* preserved with the utmost Care, he presently *takes in a Partner, opens Books for Subscriptions*, and does not in the least question but that *Bentley's* Bubble will be as famous and profitable as the best of them" (p. 18).

These interpreters often have difficulty getting beyond the status of the text itself. But to find the truth in the text, the appropriate interpretation must be historical and referential. The interpreter must reconstruct the putative events to which the texts refer, or if there are no such events, "give [in Frei's words again] credible historical explanations for the accounts having been written in their specific way" (p. 134). An interpretation is thus called upon to define a historical situation that accounts for, and is in turn illuminated by, the narrative. But as we have seen, the text is itself the first obstacle that history raises before explication can even begin. A text and language itself are known to have a history and must be part of the arsenal of historicist interpretation.

In the claims to historical status found in some of the major narratives of eighteenth-century fiction, we can see a number of parallels to the situation Frei describes. Narrative meaning without some referential claim, however attenuated, apparently condemns the fictional work to an inferior status. The approved kind of referential narration is implicitly and sometimes explicitly characterized as *lacking* the effects that would put it in the category of romance—or poetry—and *having* the appearance of an account by someone whose qualifications resemble those of a witness. This quality of the writing, like the realism of the biblical accounts, is regarded as making the claim to

[53] *Dr. Bentley's proposals For Printing a New Edition of the Greek Testament and St. Hierom's Latin Version With a Full Answer to all the Remarks of a late Pamphleteer* (London: J. Knapton, 1721), p. A2. This edition contains the response by Conyers Middleton, as well as Bentley's answer to Middleton's *Remarks, Paragraph by Paragraph, upon the Proposals Lately published By Richard Bentley. etc.*

history plausible if not certain. Such realism is valued in itself even when external verification is absent or shaky. When Hugh Blair praises Defoe (*Lectures on Rhetoric and Poetry*, 1762), his terms suggest that his implicit standard is historicality: "No fiction, in any language, was ever better supported than the *Adventures of Robinson Crusoe*. While it is carried on with that appearance of truth and simplicity, which takes a strong hold on the imagination of all readers, it suggests at the same time, very useful instruction" (Williams, *Novel and Romance*, p. 251). His specific praise of this use of verisimilitude to *support* the fiction is at least as prominent as his praise of the instruction. Furthermore, the "instruction" Blair specifically praises includes the practical matters of surviving without assistance, a kind of everyday instruction that has little relationship to the kind of instruction required by apologies for poetry like Sidney's. His explicit extension of the instruction to matters not immediately connected to the category of the moral tends to merge the instructional capacities of the fiction he approves with those of history.

IV

The crucial relationship of the eighteenth-century novel to history is, however, both more complex and even more pervasive than those relationships to which attention is directed in these critical statements, prefaces, and manifestos. Eighteenth-century fiction is not commonly *historical* fiction, but very often it is *historicized* fiction. Its claims to history are most prominently and meaningfully found in its enactment of the historicist terms for the interpretation of narrative in the eighteenth century.[54] The preface to *The Castle of Otranto* (1765) exemplifies this tendency of eighteenth-century fiction to put itself within the parameters of historical interpretation

[54] John F. Tinkler argues in an important article, "Humanist History and the English Novel in the Eighteenth Century," *Studies in Philology* 85 (1988): 510–37, that the novel took the side of rhetorical history in response to the division of humanist history into antiquarianism and rhetorical history. Although I agree with this view in some respects, particularly because the novel responds opportunistically to fill in the inevitable hiatuses caused by history's increasingly sophisticated criteria of evidence, it appears to me to be incomplete. The eighteenth-century novel also, I argue, parodies, critiques, and simulates evidentiary concerns raised by the increasingly influential, although not dominant, antiquarianism. Tinkler sees humanist forms other than history also as affecting the novel, such as, for example, the collection of letters as pioneered by Petrarch being replicated in Richardson's fiction (p. 511 n. 6). I suggest that by making the collecting, editing, and interpreting of the letters a major focus of attention within the book, Richardson redirects our attention to historiographical implications of the fiction.

even when it conceives of its reporting of events as violating probability. This first Gothic novel is conceded to be fiction in its preface, even though not all its truth claims are abandoned. But the frame presents the text as derived from an ancient document in which the narration of marvelous events must be excused as according with prejudices of a former time, thus giving these episodes the historical status of time-bound narration. Walpole concedes that many of the events of the story "are exploded now even from romances," an acknowledgment that is a plea for historical sympathy with the author, who "would not be faithful to the *manners* of those times" if he omitted "all mention of [prodigies]. He is not bound to believe them himself, but he must represent his actors as believing them" (Williams, *Novel and Romance*, p. 264). The story is given plausibility and made accessible to historicist analysis by being narratively rooted in the mistaken assumptions of a definable past.

The specification of narrative perspective—for example, the narrator, the circumstances of narration, the authenticity of the narrator's relationship to the story, narrative intentionality—is a feature that eighteenth-century fiction shares with historicist inquiry into past documentary evidence. But questions of narrative perspective and authority are examined in this fiction (or tortured, depending on the novel and one's attitude) beyond any casual pursuit of verisimilitude. Richardson's *Clarissa* has no authoritative narrator, narration being given to a multiplicity of voices, none of them always authoritative, each requiring and frequently thwarting evaluation. Sterne's parodic novel *Tristram Shandy*, for an extreme example, exposes narrative strategies and dilemmas to the point at which it implicitly questions narrative choices and the grounds for authority in any representation of a purported reality. For the reader of *Tristram Shandy*, evaluating a narrative perspective frequently leads to irresolution, not conclusion. Rather than fulfilling the expected function of such evaluation in historicist inquiry—that is, estimating the meaning and authority of a report—the narrative perspective itself often remains a perplexing object of attention.

Eighteenth-century fiction takes the process of simulating a documentary foundation well beyond mere gestures toward potential external verification.[55] There are of course analogues in prior works of fiction—in many romances, for example, and in extended fashion in *Don Quixote*, where the

---

[55] Commentaries on sources are of course not unique to eighteenth-century history or fiction. The critical questioning of sources had long been a practice of historiography (in Thucydides for a notable example) and was central to the efforts of the humanist scholars. For discussion of pseudo-documents in relation to fictional developments, see Nelson, *Fact or Fiction*, chap. 1, "From Fraud to Fiction," and Percy G. Adams, *Travel Literature and the Evolution of the Novel* (Lexington: University Press of Kentucky, 1983), pp. 97–100.

account of the Arab historian Cid Hamete Benengeli is cited as source (see especially part 1, chapter 9) and is compared with other sources.[56] But eighteenth-century British fiction sometimes extends its representation of its own documentation to the point at which it appears to be representing not so much the history of the past as the traces of the past, in a sense taking verisimilitude to a disintegrating point at which it is not an account but an artifact, striving to be the past, not only to tell it. A book like *Robinson Crusoe*, for example, incorporates into its narrative extended portions of Crusoe's purported journal, a re-embedded artifact surviving from the island sojourn, a recovered trace rather than a subsequent narrative. Richardson makes a version of this technique the basis of his entire narrative. Epistolary fiction creates the entire story from what are purported to be a series of documents written in immediate proximity to the events and sometimes bearing material traces of the events, such as tears and a shaking hand.

The editorial fiction common in the eighteenth century—the fiction that a novel is put together by an editor who orders the documentary evidence in such a way that it narrates its own story—is a gesture toward giving writing the status of event, a gesture that unleashes a dizzying series of dissolves. Making writing the event results in an equation of event and narration that often apparently leads from narration to narration rather than from narration to even a putative foundational event. The narrator of *Robinson Crusoe* is also an editor who presents us with a single document, formerly written—the "Journal"—that is the basis for his later narration. Yet that leaves the single document as a foundation still in writing, vouched for only by the narrator

---

[56] The deep connection of *Don Quixote* to the later novel and to the novel's relationship to history has long been noted. Walter L. Reed, *An Exemplary History of the Novel: The Quixotic versus the Picaresque* (Chicago: University of Chicago Press, 1981), finds that "novels are pseudohistorical, in the sense that they raise the question of documentation," a respect in which *Quixote* is markedly influential (p. 268). Studies of *Don Quixote* that are relevant to the themes pursued here include the following four: Bruce W. Wardropper, "*Don Quixote*: Story or History?" *Modern Philology* 63 (1965): 1–11, who analyzes Cervantes' exploitation of the ambiguities of *historia* as story and history; Oscar Kenshur, *Open Form and the Shape of Ideas* (Lewisburg: Bucknell University Press, 1986), who argues that "although Cid Hamete is concerned with grasping reality, Cervantes' subject matter is not reality itself, but the human efforts to comprehend it" (p. 67); McKeon, who begins his sustained readings of fiction with *Don Quixote*: "The text of *Don Quixote* encloses a development from the self-criticism of romance, to the naive empiricism of 'true history' to a final orientation of extreme scepticism; and in a correlative movement, from an early and progressive ideology to a late and conservative one" (*Origins*, p. 273); and Elizabeth Wanning Harries, *The Unfinished Manner: Essays on the Fragment in the Later Eighteenth Century* (Charlottesville: University Press of Virginia, 1994), pp. 24–27, who connects the found-manuscript of *Don Quixote* with the implications of the fragment, making "visible the uncertainties that mark all narrative" (p. 27).

who is also the author as well as editor of this evidentiary foundation. A more complex use of the editor is entailed in Richardson's presention of his story as reconstructed fragments, the editor making the story appear out of its pieces. Each piece is in a sense a new document, even if it is a continuation, as its writer is in a new position or circumstance.

Perspectives correct each other but they also confuse each other. The editorial fiction is not even a unitary one in *Clarissa*, as Clarissa's editorship is succeeded by Belford's, and Belford is himself finally enclosed in a more encompassing editorial perspective. Tristram Shandy operates as an author seeking his lost foundations but also as editor introducing a variety of others' documents. Rather than establishing foundations outside the book, Sterne's use of the editorial motif so complicates our sense of provenience that it implies a precariousness in the authority of narrative itself, which can only with difficulty be reconciled to anything purportedly lying outside it. Perhaps the most sustained novelistic version of the eighteenth-century editorial fiction is to be found in Henry Mackenzie's *Man of Feeling* in which the text is presented as having been reconstituted by its editor from torn strips of paper that were destined to be used as gun wadding. The authenticity of the text is vouched for by the obtrusion of its hiatuses.

The textualization of meaning is thus, like the trace, sometimes represented as a reduction to mere material or to latent meaning waiting for construal. Lurking behind the representation of the search for verification in eighteenth-century fiction is the image of the book as paper, its undeniable reality.[57] This reduction of the book to its material is implicit in the tattered remains of *The Man of Feeling* and in those black and mottled pages of *Tristram Shandy* that mystify us, rather than elucidate the opacities of

[57] Relevant to this sense of the material text is Richard W. F. Kroll's examination of neo-Epicureanism in *The Material Word: Literate Culture in the Restoration and Early Eighteenth-Century* (Baltimore: Johns Hopkins University Press, 1991), which links English neo-Epicureanism of the seventeenth century to the understanding of the materiality of sign systems: "Neoclassical linguists were fascinated by the phenomenon by which words occur as the physiognomic maneuverings of the mouth, tongue, palate, and lips. The Restoration frequently resorted to the metaphor of printing to emphasize this plastic quality in language: the age seems to have delighted in the concreteness of the page impressed by visible marks, ascending atomically from letters to words, to sentences, to entire discourses" (p. 14). This connection of the material with language was also used in anti-Epicurean satire of the eighteenth century, providing the argument that the world could no more have been created by the fortuitous concourse of atoms than a book by the fortuitous concourse of the alphabet (see, for example, Irvin Ehrenpreis, "Four of Swift's Sources," *Modern Language Notes* 70 [1955]: 98–100). I think it possible that mid- and late-eighteenth-century novelistic playing on the materiality of books and language as mediated by printing are linked to the uneasiness caused by neo-Epicurean conceptions of the material.

writing.[58] The editorial fiction with its promise of persuading the traces themselves to speak also threatens that the narrative may never quite be constituted from these fragments, thus leaving the traces as no more than the detritus that reminds us of the loss of meaning. The novel embodies the ambiguity in the textual scholarship espoused by Bentley and his followers; they rescue texts from their material enemies—worms, dust, decay, and even transcriber's errors—yet they also destroy texts, restoring fragmentation instead of creating wholeness.

Through these often skeptical explorations and evocations of historicist procedures, eighteenth-century fiction makes history vulnerable. History will have to notice and eventually justify its similarity to fiction. Yet as I argued earlier, the eighteenth-century novel is not pyrrhonist any more than eighteenth-century historiography is. Its demonstration of the capacities of fictional construction is also an imputation of potency to historical narration. History is challenged to differentiate the traces it accepts as foundational from those teased into meaning by novelistic narration, yet both historical and novelistic narrrative retain their potential for meaningfulness.

---

[58] Terry Castle, *Masquerade and Civilization: The Carnivalesque in Eighteenth-Century English Culture and Fiction* (Stanford: Stanford University Press, 1986), comments in similar fashion on the implications of the domino costume of the masquerade: "With its shifting, undulating materiality, the domino represented on the one hand a kind of Ur-costume, a paradigmatic swatch of cloth from which any sartorial fancy might be formed: an emblem of potentiality. By its sheer incommunicativeness, it was on the other hand a sign of negativity, of the erasure or voiding of all form" (p. 77).

CHAPTER 2

From Figura to Trace:
Bunyan and Defoe

I

For Hume, the master narrative that orders all other historical narratives is the secular story of the development of civilization. His idea of history includes prominently the economic and cultural aspects of civilization as well as the more narrowly political aspects.[1] He rejects the very different master narrative that had long been assumed by his culture—the Bible. Regarding historical narrative as properly placed within the biblical story entails a providential conception of events; ultimately, every event must fit into God's unfolding plan for the world, and any apparently secular narrative remains incomplete until it finds its conclusion in this master narrative. Jacques-Bénigne Bossuet's *Discours sur l'historie universelle* (1681) is a notable expression of this conception of biblical history.[2] Early in his history Bossuet lists a number of "epochs" of ancient history that to our eyes confuse biblical and classical myth with secular history: the entire list begins with "Adam, or the Creation" and ends with "Charlemagne, or the Establishment of the New Empire" (p. 5); within this list, "The Fall of Troy" is placed between "Moses, or the Written Law" and "Solomon, or the Foundation of the Temple." Bossuet conceives of biblical events both as part of the same temporal continuum as secular history and also

[1] Nicholas Phillipson, *Hume* (New York: St. Martin's Press, 1989), chap. 2, "Politics, Politeness and Men of Letters," defines the deep interconnections of political ideas and broader cultural and economic concerns in Hume's thought.

[2] Jacques-Bénigne Bossuet, *Discourse on Universal History*, trans. Elborg Forster, ed. Orest Ranum (Chicago: University of Chicago Press, 1976).

as providing an interpretive pattern that gives seemingly secular history its meaning.

In *Augustan Historical Writing*, Laird Okie finds that the changes in eighteenth-century rewritings of English history tend toward the elimination of providential interpretations: "Theocentric, providential history, written primarily by clerics, gave way to the mundane, naturalistic approach favored by political writers and professional journalists."[3] Hume's narration of the Battle of Dunbar illustrates the less than respectful treatment of providential interpretation that Okie finds developing earlier in the century. Describing how Cromwell and his parliamentary army were placed in jeopardy by the king's Scottish forces under Lesley but gained the victory through the military ineptitude of Lesley's Presbyterian advisers, Hume creates an ironic juxtaposition of the language of religious superstition with that of historical causation. He first narrates the episode from the perspective of the Scottish enthusiasts, a narrative strategy that gives their antagonist Cromwell's later cry of victory—"The Lord has delivered them into our hands"—an ironic resonance suggesting the impotence of a providence unsupported by military tactics. Hume's irony is not only directed at the Scots but also at providential interpretation itself:

> Night and day the ministers had been wrestling with the Lord in prayer, *as they termed it* [my emphasis]; and they fancied, that they had at last obtained the victory. Revelations, *they said* [my emphasis], were made them, that the sectarian and heretical army, together with Agag, *meaning Cromwel* [my emphasis], was delivered into their hands. Upon the faith of these visions, they forced their general, in spite of his remonstrances, to descend into the plain, with a view of attacking the English in their retreat. Cromwel, looking through a glass, saw the enemy's camp in motion; and foretold, without the help of revelations, that the Lord had delivered them into *his* [Hume's emphasis] hands.[4]

In Hume's rendition, Cromwell uses the terminology of providence without assuming any need for inspiration, a view that places providence within the boundaries of discernible power relations, whereas the Scottish enthusiasts are shown to have an internal persuasion of their inspiration that is disastrously contradicted. Hume's integration of the two perspectives within one skeptical narrative voice demonstrates the need for a discourse

[3] Laird Okie, *Augustan Historical Writing: Histories of England in the English Enlightenment* (New York: University Presses of America, 1991), p. 209.

[4] David Hume, *The History of England*, vol. 6 (1778; reprint, Indianapolis: Liberty *Classics*, 1983), p. 30.

other than the providential to account for outcomes determined in this world.

The process being discussed is the alteration of an entire cultural perspective and demands more than just eliminating some suspect causes; it requires the constructing of a new discourse.[5] Timothy Reiss has indicated essential components and assumptions of this emergent discourse of the seventeenth century in his term "analytico-referential"—a discourse that asserts "the adequacy of concepts to represent objects in the world and . . . of words to represent those concepts. . . . [T]he properly organized sentence . . . provides in its very syntax a correct *analysis* of both the rational and material orders."[6] Reiss's definition is related to Michel Foucault's designation of two ruptures in Western culture, each with a definable *episteme*. The first rupture—the Classical age—occurs in the mid-seventeenth century and

[5] Robert Markley, *Fallen Languages: Crises of Representation in Newtonian England, 1660–1740* (Ithaca: Cornell University Press, 1993), shows the interconnectedness of religious and scientific ideologies in this period and rejects accounts that find a triumphant scientific ideology to be the overwhelming cause of a new discourse. He quite persuasively argues that some histories of the period create a progressivist narrative, one emphasizing the modernity they are already committed to when positing a break between the early modern and the modern (see, for example, pp. 21–22).

[6] Timothy Reiss, *The Discourse of Modernism* (Ithaca: Cornell University Press, 1982), p. 31. Richard Kroll, *The Material Word: Literate Culture in the Restoration and Early Eighteenth Century* (Baltimore: Johns Hopkins University Press, 1991), protests against the view that the assumption of the period he discusses was that language used properly is transparent and unproblematical. Rather, he suggests, there was assumed to be the need for the interpreter to judge on "limited, probable grounds": "The talk about the 'plain' places of Scripture does not amount to a belief in linguistic transparency; rather it describes those points at which textual evidences are 'sufficient' to provide minimal agreement about the sense of a passage" (p. 241). It does not appear to be necessarily inconsistent with Kroll's views to accept Reiss's formulation of "analytico-referential discourse" as a discourse of the late seventeenth and eighteenth centuries. This discourse posits a potentially adequate concept and a potentially adequate language for it, a formulation that does not necessarily imply a transparency of language to the object of which one holds a concept. Foucault's formulations do sometimes appear to imply that Enlightenment writers assumed a transparent language, yet these formulations may be taken as Enlightenment programmatic goals for an ideal language rather than as evaluations of contemporary fact: "The profound vocation of Classical language has always been to create a table—a 'picture': whether it be in the form of natural discourse, the accumulation of truth, descriptions of things, a body of exact knowledge, or an encyclopaedic dictionary. It exists, therefore, only in order to be transparent" (*The Order of Things: An Archeology of the Human Sciences* [New York: Random House, 1970], p. 311). Of importance to any estimation of the close connections of language to experience in empiricism is the study of Jules David Law, *The Rhetoric of Empiricism: Language and Perception from Locke to I. A. Richards* (Ithaca: Cornell University Press, 1993), who suggests that "empiricist characterization of perceptual knowledge is articulated explicitly in terms of linguistic distinctions: between signifier and signified, proper and improper, true and false analogy, literal and metaphorical, voice and print, character and word, and so on. . . . [T]he empiricist account of *what we see* is inseparable from an account of *what we say*" (p. 3).

corresponds roughly to what is usually called the "Enlightenment" in world history; the second rupture, which Foucault characterizes as the modern age, succeeds the Classical age in the nineteenth century.[7] The Classical episteme is characterized by criticism and classification, as distinguished from the commentary and relations of resemblance characteristic of the previous episteme. Foucault describes these shifts in relation to the historian's task: before the mid-seventeenth century "the historian's task was to establish the great compilation of documents and signs . . . to restore to language all the words that had been buried" (pp. 130–31); for the Classical age, however, the task became "that of undertaking a meticulous examination of things themselves for the first time, and then of transcribing what [has been] gathered in smooth, neutralized, and faithful words" (p. 131).

Because the fiction being discussed in this study extends from the early eighteenth century to its end, a brief consideration of Foucault's second rupture may also be useful. That rupture is characterized as the invention of "man". Foucault is aware of the seeming counterfactuality of his view, noting the possible objection that no other period than the Classical "has accorded more attention to human nature, has given it a more stable, more definitive status, or one more directly presented to discourse" (p. 309). Yet he states categorically that in the Classical episteme "there was no epistemological consciousness of man as such," a view that may appear merely provocative within the contours of an intellectual history that has long recognized the Baconian and Royal Society suspicion of, yet inevitable dependence upon, a subject who must remain the creator and interpretor of those very tools that are meant to supplement human limitation and also of those methodologies that are invoked to elude bias. But Foucault responds (albeit with a Cartesian example) by urging that the very limitation of seeing man only in the context of the linkage between his being and his thinking is an occlusion: "The transition from the 'I think' to the 'I am' was accomplished . . . within a discourse whose whole domain and functioning consisted in articulating one upon the other what one represents to oneself and what is" (pp. 311–12). The result is that within Classical discourse "no interrogation as to the mode of being implied by the *cogito* could be articulated." In Foucault's view then, only from outside Classical discourse can man appear "in his ambiguous position as an object of knowledge and as a subject that knows" (p. 312).

Despite Foucault's heuristic commitment to a methodology of discontinuity, of rupture, he acknowledges that man could not have burst upon the scene quite so precipitously: "It must not be supposed that he suddenly

[7] Foucault, *Order of Things*, pp. xxii, xxiii.

appeared upon our horizon, imposing the brutal fact of his body, his labour, and his language in a manner so irruptive as to be absolutely baffling to our reflection" (p. 317). Seeing aspects of the Foucaultian "episteme," then, not as revolution but as an emergent discourse that eventually achieves dominance, we may find those epistemic changes that bracket the period of the consolidation of the novel to be relevant to our understanding of some of the epistemological functions of eighteenth-century fiction. If we look at the fiction of Defoe, Richardson, Fielding, and Sterne, we see writing that encounters the emergent and soon dominant empirical or Classical discourse, mediating its conflicts with the figural. The novel after its midcentury consolidation may then also be amenable to an analysis that finds it an adumbration of the onset of "man" in Foucault's sense—one who must be understood in his own right, a producer of knowledge about man and also simultaneously an object of that knowledge.

Some complexities of this version of man are evoked by Hubert L. Dreyfus and Paul Rabinow in their characterization of man as an "organizer of the spectacle in which he appears."[8] This statement is a reference to Foucault's articulation of his argument through a complex analysis of Valesquez's *Las Meninas*. In the words of Dreyfus and Rabinow, "The central paradox of the painting turns on *the impossibility of representing the act of representing*. If the essential undertaking of the Classical Age was to put ordered representations onto a table, the one thing this age could not achieve was to put its own activity on the table so constructed" (p. 25). In Foucault's description the painting presents the "entire cycle of representation" (p. 11), but all who are represented in it are oriented toward a space at the front of the painting where the viewer and also the objects of the painting, King Philip IV and his wife Mariana, stand. The presence of these objects of the painter's gaze are confirmed by a dim reflection in a mirror at the rear of the room, a reflection of which all inside the painting are unaware. But not only does Foucault's analysis reveal the absence of "man" in the Classical episteme, it also adumbrates his obscure presence at the advent of the modern episteme. While all are represented as gazing on that figure who is represented only dimly in the mirror away from their gaze, the painter looks not only at that object but presumably also at himself as object on his canvas, *this* canvas that represents him representing (p. 308). Eighteenth-century fiction's intense flurry of experiments with narrational perspectives may be seen as an attempt to consider the paradox that Foucault assigns to *Las Meninas*. An effect of this fiction's sometimes

[8] Hubert L. Dreyfus and Paul Rabinow, *Michel Foucault: Beyond Structuralism and Hermeneutics*, 2d ed. (Chicago: University of Chicago Press, 1983), p. 29.

corrosive scrutiny of a predecessor's techniques of representation may be the perhaps erratic and intermittent but nevertheless persistent uncovering or creation of the "man" who must from then on be suspected as the organizer of his own spectacle.

Returning then to the earlier "rupture"—the shift from a providential discourse to an "analytico-referential" one—we see a process that entails not a sudden revolution but a gradual alteration of a nexus of relationships; the change proceeds haltingly through contestation and negotiation, not through decisive victories. One of the most familiar statements in support of this alteration of discourse is that of Thomas Sprat in his *History of the Royal Society* (1667), a book perhaps more accurately described as a polemic in favor of the Society's program than a history of so relatively new a group. Sprat's own language is imbricated in a mythology and epistemology not conceptually unified with the program he seemingly espouses:

> To return back to the primitive purity, and shortness, when men deliver'd so many *things*, almost in an equal number of *words*. They have exacted from all their members, a close, naked, natural way of speaking; positive expressions; clear senses; a native easiness: bringing all things as near the Mathematical plainness as they can: and preferring the language of Artizans, Countrymen, and Merchants, before that, of Wits, or Scholars.[9]

This imagined representational language is founded on notions of an originary pastoral condition ("primitive purity") that is transferred to a later georgic in which artisans and merchants are connected to countrymen. The original language—"naked" and "natural"—is approximated by the "Mathematical plainness" that distinguishes the valorized language from that of sophisticates like scholars and wits. A myth of progress is here assimilated to one of the Fall, with the new science cast as a redeemer from Adam's sin; the language here being sought is rendered as putatively pristine as that formerly in Eden. Yet at the same time no mode of expression is found by Sprat that even approximates naked innocence, his traverse through history being revealed through a language of complex allusion to multiple versions of the pastoral and in relation to the social realities of late-seventeenth-century England in which merchants of the City are antagonized by wits of Westminster. Sprat's evocation of "Mathematical plainness" is an insinuation of a series of narratives that mediate between new and old epistemologies,

[9] Thomas Sprat, *History of the Royal Society*, ed. Jackson I. Cope and Harold Whitmore Jones (St. Louis: Washington University Studies, 1958), p. 113.

juxtaposing or assimilating the contested yet still powerful myths of the past to the new social and religious world.

It seems plausible, then, that we should include among the many cultural functions already attributed to the novel, the mediation of a discursive conflict similar to the one Sprat evokes, one between the narrative construction of the past as conceived through empirically authorized documentation and the narrative uncovering of a preexistent meaning by reference to the biblical master narrative that governs history.[10] When the biblical master narrative is assimilated or juxtaposed to analytico-referential discourse, the conflict of perspectives requires the narrator/author of eighteenth-century fiction to rationalize a discourse that threatens to fragment. Plausible connections to a biblical master narrative tend to deteriorate in the presence of the particularities of accumulated foundational documentation; presumed meaningful details then turn into decontextualized traces of the past that yield only a limited authority for a sustained narrative. The narrator (sometimes putative editor) of eighteenth-century fiction displays the process of adjudicating among these discourses and structuring a narration that will enable a provisional meaning resistant to the incipient fragmentation. Fiction's scrutiny of such narrative adjudications is of significance to history, which faces similar problems but is expected to maintain a decorum that suppresses metanarrative intrusions.

II

As a way of analyzing the contribution of the novel to the adjudication of these interpenetrating and competing discourses, I use the concept of "figura" to represent and question the older providential discourse and "trace" to represent and question the newer attempt at empirically justifiable discourse. Neither of these concepts is precisely *within* the discourse that it represents and for that reason each provides salutary resistance to the assumptions of that discourse. "Figura" derives from traditions outside the Judeo-Christian and thus takes no sides in the Reformation controversies

[10] Melvyn New, " 'The Grease of God': The Form of Eighteenth-Century English Fiction," in *Telling New Lies: Seven Essays in Fiction, Past and Present* (Gainesville: University Presses of Florida, 1992), argues that eighteenth-century fiction occupies a position between two worldviews: "The major novelists of the age imaged forth in their writings neither the Christian world view, which was slowly giving way, nor the secular world view, which we now recognize as having replaced it; rather . . . their fictions reflect with surprising consistency and complexity—if not full consciousness—that historical moment when the imaginative resources of their culture were transferred from one system of ordering experience to another" (pp. 30–31).

about allegory, and "trace" questions the efficacy of the empirical construal of its meaning. "Figura" as developed here is conceptually indebted to the discussion by Erich Auerbach in his classic essay "Figura," and "trace" to the already referenced discussion by Paul Ricoeur in his magisterial *Time and Narrative*, although the uses made of these conceptions are not always consistent with either writer's philosophical outlook.[11]

A "trace" is a material remnant of a past that counts as evidence, authorizing our attempts to provide a more complete version of that past for our imaginative consideration. A trace bears witness to the past, thus pointing toward a context that is absent or incomplete even while the trace continues to exist within a present context. Interpreting a trace is to a large extent the restoration of the vanished context by means of the resources found in its present one. Such resources include other traces as well as the intellectual and imaginative powers relevant to construal. Traces can be both the written works of the past—often ones *intended* to be "documents"—and other artifacts lacking the "voice" that documents possess as an integral part of their ostensible functions. Yet the seeming transparency of those traces that appear themselves to be interpretations or descriptions may be deceptive; as Ricoeur notes, following Levinas, the trace indicates a "passage . . . not some possible presence" (p. 125). The trace may thus tease us with its present palpability while seeming to allude to something more evanescent and perhaps beyond recovery. Applying this hint to those writings we call "documents," we see that surrounding the seeming interpretive precision of a past report is perhaps an absence of context as crippling to the understanding as in the case of isolated artifacts. Such written traces acquire their status as documents by appearing to be detached from their objects of scrutiny, commenting on them from outside. Yet writings are finally only one trace among others, artifacts requiring the exercise of our ingenuities before they speak to our concerns. Connoting absence, the trace resists assimilation to a preexisting master narrative, a significant difference from the figura.

The figural connects several events in a diachronic pattern of significance with the later of two events regarded as the "fulfillment" of some implicit aspect of the former, as when Christ is regarded as the fulfillment of essential features of Moses's life and mission. But as Auerbach makes clear, Christian uses of the figural insisted on the full historicity of all connected events.

---

[11] Erich Auerbach, "Figura," in *Scenes from the Drama of European Literature* (New York: Meridian, 1959), pp. 11–76; the segment of Ricoeur most important to this discussion is "Archives, Documents, Traces," pp. 116–26, in *Time and Narrative*, vol. 3, trans. Kathleen Blamey and David Pellauer (Chicago: University of Chicago Press, 1988), chap. 4, "Between Lived Time and Universal Time."

Moses did not exist *only* as an adumbration of Christ but *also* as an adumbration of Christ, having his own reality within history just as Christ did. The figural thus exists as a web of connections within a master narrative, designating elements of the historical as transcending their own particularity and achieving a connection to other, ultimately all, times and places.

The figural requires that the many possible historical narratives be subordinated to, and find their places within, a master narrative. The question of provenience is then both submerged and obtruded: the divine author may control the world and thus validate certain representations of it, but narratives nevertheless come into being through particular narrators in particularizable circumstances. The presumption of divine authorship gives the Christian master narrative its authority but obscures its historicity. "In the beginning God created the heavens and the earth" asserts divine authority over the earth and implies divine authorization of the writing, yet by making God's activity the content of a narrative, a problem is raised about the absent standpoint for the narrator. God's purposeful activity in creating "lights" for "signs and seasons" is construable only in a human context absent at the putative time of the narrative, consequently introducing into the narration a later particularizable history by means of which this narrative came into being. The master narrative appears then to be subject to the same historical contingencies as other narratives. Such leveling of narratives endangers the authority of any figural conception, implying that what is called the figural is a subjective creation of its narrator(s).

In his philological analysis of the figural, Auerbach finds hints of the deceptive in the pre-Christian background that are later also present, if even further subdued, in the Christian foreground. In Ovid, for example, "*figura* is mobile, changeable, multiform, and deceptive" (p. 23), and in Augustine too it sometimes appears "as idol, as dream figure or vision" (pp. 37–38). The figural, like some of Christ's parables, keeps the uninitiated unenlightened, protecting the divine mysteries from contamination by outsiders. On the one hand, figural interpretation is then validated by the small but fit community of believers; on the other hand, if it is relegated only to coterie use, the figural vacates any broad historical claims to being the pattern to which all other narratives can be meaningfully subordinated. If the figural is relegated to the status of esoteric narrative interpretation, its status as the revelation of the meaning of all histories is vitiated.

The conceptions of trace and figura as used in this analysis can be mapped on Foucault's previously mentioned description of the rupture between the Classical episteme, characterized by criticism and classification, and the preceeding episteme, characterized by commentary and relations of resemblance. Defining this shift in terms of *figura* and *trace* entails placing figura in the earlier episteme and trace in the succeeding Classical one. Figurae are connected by webs of resemblances that include the self-justifying commentary by which the figural is constituted. Loosened from the commentary in which they are embedded, the elements of the figural become traces, which can then be reorganized by another classificatory scheme. The development of archives and inventories, as described by Foucault, was a "way of introducing into the language already imprinted on things, and into the traces it has left, an order of the same type as that which was being established between living creatures" (p. 132). Although elements that were formerly commentary may be included as traces, they find their present meanings through deployment in a classificatory scheme that allows criticism or analysis. The figural, in contrast, fosters a reliance on the self-justification of commentary that leads to an ever enlarging synthesis.

Regarded as coterie interpretation, or even as fossilized tradition, the figural may appear to be authorized only by the subjective choices of its narrator. The trace, on the other hand, appears to be an element of the past itself—rudimentary perhaps but not laden with false significance. Deploying the traces in a classificatory grid then appears to create a past that is responsive to the questions we ask of it. For example, the burgeoning archaeology and geology of the eighteenth century used "cabinets of curiosities" to provide not only a comparative display but also to further the understanding of artifacts or natural objects through systematic comparison—notably the coins and medals of antiquity and the accumulating specimens of fossils. Such reorganization of traces, each placed in its compartment according to a defined classificatory system, gave increasing insight into both the geological history of the earth and the Roman presence in Britain.[12] The meagerness of the traces in comparison to the richness of the past in which they participated is compensated by the analytical context that replaces the literal vanished one.

Yet this new classificatory analysis raises questions about its presumed objectivity also. Put simply, are the results not somehow as much represen-

[12] See Joseph M. Levine, *Dr. Woodward's Shield: History, Science, and Satire in Augustan England* (Berkeley: University of California Press, 1977), esp. chap. 6, "The Collector," and chap. 8, "Roman London," for useful descriptions of actual problems in classification within cabinets of curiosities. Eilean Hooper-Greenhill, *Museums and the Shaping of Knowledge* (New York: Routledge, 1992), traces the development of the cabinet from the "cabinet of the world" of the sixteenth century, designed to bring together a variety of artifacts that "represent or recall either an entire or partial world picture" (p. 78), to the very different classificatory schemes developed during the age of the Royal Society: "The documents of this new history were not other works, or texts, but unencumbered spaces in which things were juxtaposed.... [T]he classical age stripped away much of the contextualizing material that had accrued to things and ideas during the Renaissance" (pp. 137–38).

tative of the analytical scheme as of the seeming objects of analysis? The ancients and moderns controversy in some of its manifestations appears to be concerned with this issue. When through the techniques of modern philology Richard Bentley and his cohorts and followers redate ancient manuscripts and destroy long-accepted proveniences, the suspicion is aroused that history is not being determined by testimony about what happened but being created by the techniques of analysis themselves. Temple, Swift, Pope, and others ask, at least by implication, whether the seeming gains in precision are sufficient compensation for the eroding of a long-existing tradition of classical history that appears to have as much testimony on its side as the new history does. As Levine has shown, the victory of the moderns was not definitive: "Modern scholarship continued to threaten to undermine the whole neoclassical edifice that it had been invented to serve, but each time it faltered before the pressure of an unreconstructed *ancienneté*."[13]

The constitution of the category of "novel" in the eighteenth century is an enlistment of it on the side of modernity, a definition of the novel as a new form however long its features had existed. The novel then has the implicit task of addressing new shapes of society and emerging epistemologies. It performs that task, however, not by taking the analytico-referential as the dominant, but as an emergent, discourse, and by taking the figural as a residual but still functional discourse. The newly constituted, or about to be constituted, form's comprehensiveness is then able to articulate its society's contradictions. *Robinson Crusoe*, written before the consolidating achievements of Richardson and Fielding, yet still often regarded as one of the central originary works of the English novelistic tradition, exhibits pointedly some of the distinctions between figura and trace on which this present discussion rests, as well as some of the strains resulting from the attempted adjudication of competing discourses.[14]

Crusoe's "Journal" is the putative foundational trace on which the larger narrative depends, whereas the single footprint in the sand is uncanny—mysterious, evocative, and evanescent but never foundational. The sprouting

---

[13] Joseph M. Levine, *The Battle of the Books: History and Literature in the Augustan Age* (Ithaca: Cornell University Press, 1991), p. 415.

[14] Maximillian E. Novak, *Realism, Myth, and History in Defoe's Fiction* (Lincoln: University of Nebraska Press, 1983), aptly describes Defoe's as "a fiction rooted in reality and history but with the generality of myth and fairy tale," having characters "both highly individualized and mythic, firmly based in history, and capable of floating free from time" (pp. 16, 17). J. Paul Hunter, *The Reluctant Pilgrim: Defoe's Emblematic Method and Quest for Form in Robinson Crusoe* (Baltimore: Johns Hopkins University Press, 1966), and George A. Starr, *Defoe and Spiritual Autobiography* (Princeton: Princeton University Press, 1965), are the fullest analyses of Defoe in relationship to figural thought and providential patterning.

corn, which Crusoe first thinks is miraculous but then attributes to natural causes, is figural, a reality like other realities, yet eventually linked by Crusoe to biblical providential events that reveal the patterns governing God's management of the natural world. Traces make evident the past existence of a context but also need to have that past context construed; the figural purports only to uncover a preexistent meaning that is already an articulated and comprehensive story into which the figura can be fitted. The footprint, then, is a trace that resists connection to a larger narrative; the sprouting corn is a figura that claims participation in a preexisting providential narrative standing above the particularities of Crusoe's narration; and the "Journal" rests uneasily between the seeming limits of particular events and the construal that attempts to link them to the larger providential narrative. The "Journal" records those events that Crusoe attempts to connect to the larger biblical story, yet it also persistently points to the shaping elements of the human subject and medium, speaking of distance from the source of meaning, of construal rather than presence.

About noon one day, Crusoe comes upon the "Print of a Man's naked Foot on the Shore."[15] This episode is only perfunctorily connected to the remainder of the plot; presumably intended to be related to the later visits of the cannibals, it is in fact tied to those episodes only in inferential terms. This trace is apparently irrefutable evidence of a former presence—but of what? Only one foot and in sand: it is in jeopardy even in so marginal a form as the trace of a mystery. Unable to find any other impression elsewhere in the sand, Crusoe thinks his "Fancy" responsible, yet finds on his return "the very Print of a Foot, Toes, Heel, and every Part of a Foot" (p. 154), an allegory of the verisimilitudinous romance, improbable yet precisely delineated.[16] Crusoe, however, has difficulty in placing this trace within a surrounding explanatory narrative, even thinking for a time that it might be the Devil's work, but concluding that this master of deceit would have acted in accord with probability and not have left a "Mark in a Place where 'twas Ten

[15] Daniel Defoe, *Robinson Crusoe*, ed. J. Donald Crowley (Oxford: Oxford University Press, 1981), p. 153.

[16] David Blewett, *Defoe's Art of Fiction: "Robinson Crusoe," "Moll Flanders," "Colonel Jack," and "Roxana"* (Toronto: University of Toronto Press, 1979), finds the footprint to be a turning point in Crusoe's island sojourn: "It shatters Crusoe's tranquil existence and opens the movement of the second half of the novel, the story of Crusoe's return to the world" (p. 39). Michael Seidel, *Exile and the Narrative Imagination* (New Haven: Yale University Press, 1986), brings the footprint into proximity to issues of narrative and politics: the print evokes the political situation of one who having had no rivals now has to recognize potential opposition; it may be applied to the "status of narrative as sovereign on the one hand, sufficient unto its made-up self, and representational on the other, reflecting the contingencies and necessities of the supposed real world it imitates" (pp. 36, 37).

Thousand to one whether I should ever see it or not, and in the Sand too, which the first Surge of the Sea upon a high Wind would have defac'd entirely" (p. 155). This juxtaposition by Crusoe of a spirit world and a world of probability leads him to reflect on the possibility of a divine ordering process being refracted through the appearance of this footprint. The best elucidation he can achieve is the evasive, "How strange a Chequer Work of Providence is the Life of Man," a formulation that accepts the defeat of human notions of providential ordering even as it evokes them. The print is neither explained nor explained away.

The later appearance of cannibals apparently verifies that uncanny single footprint, yet they shed no light on its singleness. They imply mystery and moral complexity rather than resolution, having occupied a notably ambiguous position in Western mythologies, as in Montaigne where their status as the ultimate perversion of nature is shown to be amenable also to the interpretation that their nature rises above our culture.[17] Crusoe's cannibals are given a palpable reality in the narrative, yet they remain to some degree Crusoe's imaginary creation, never achieving a narrative reality unconnected to his obsessive fantasies of eating and being eaten (with the exceptions of Friday and his father). They are appropriately associated with that earlier print of one foot in the sand, which is only interpreted through narratives reflective of the self and is never plausibly explicated in its one-footed individuality, a trace too marginal even to be attributed to the devil—or, inferentially then, a divine pattern. The elusive cannibals of Coetzee's *Foe*, sought by the writer Foe's imagination yet never seen by the island's inhabitants, reflect an implication of Defoe's book.

The treatment of the sprouting corn [barley] underscores the process of reconciling trace to figura. As the green shoots of barley are to him at first inexplicable, Crusoe turns to "miracle" as a category of explanation, which belief he finds from his later more religious perspective to be a decisive turning away from his earlier erroneous propensity to attribute events to chance rather than to providence. When, however, Crusoe remembers that he had shaken out a bag of chicken feed where the grain now grows, he rejects the providential explanation, a rejection that the narrator characterizes as error: "For it was really the Work of Providence as to me, that should order or appoint, that 10 or 12 Grains of Corn should remain unspoiled . . . as if it had dropped from Heaven" (p. 79). The increases in grain that he records over the years, his planting and careful husbanding,

---

[17] Claude Rawson, "Cannibalism and Fiction," part 1, "Reflections on Narrative Form and 'Extreme' Situations," *Genre* 10 (1977): 667–711; and part 2, "Love and Eating in Fielding, Mailer, Genet, and Witting," *Genre* 11 (1978): 227–313, discusses the cultural meanings and literary uses of cannibalism.

suggest the parable of the sower, thus connecting this rather mundane earthly event to the biblical narratives that have authority over human life. Yet even as the case for a figural meaning is narratively compiled, Crusoe and Defoe introduce a contradictory biblical allusion that puts the apparent meaning in question: "And now indeed my Stock of Corn increasing, I really wanted to build my Barns bigger" (p. 123), an allusion not to the increases praised in the parable of the sower, which are equated with spiritual fruitfulness, but to the foolishness of the rich man whose plentiful harvest led to his decision to "pull down my barns, and build greater," thus allowing his "soul" to take its "ease" and "eat, drink, and be merry." Rather than consistently leading toward an explanation of Crusoe's success, the figura of the grain now appears to have turned against Crusoe, indicating a foolish reliance on the material: "So is he that layeth up treasure for himself, and is not rich toward God" (Mark 12:16–21).

Ambiguities invade Crusoe's (or Defoe's) attempts to bring material event and spiritual meaning together; the trace becomes figura only at the cost of raising suspicions of duplicity. The "Journal" that underwrites so much of the island narrative is an example of the resistance of the trace to being placed in relation to the Christian master narrative. This "Journal" (pp. 70ff.) purports to be Crusoe's account at the time of his sojourn on the island, an activity of the sojourn as well as a documentation of it: "I began to keep my Journal, of which I shall here give you the Copy (tho' in it will be told all these Particulars over again) as long as it lasted, for having no more Ink I was forced to leave it off" (p. 69). This introduction to the "Journal" insists on its artifactuality, its dependence on the resources available on the island and its independence from the usual constraints of purposeful after-the-fact narration. The "Journal" is a source that is incorporated without being entirely absorbed by the book, thus implying a claim to be historical verification of the narrator's later account and having the epistemological advantage over the retrospective account of being closer in time to the described events as well as the ontological advantage of being one of those events.

The "Journal" beginns as repetition of events described earlier, which permits the seeming objectivity of a very spare account; that style, however, is not maintained and the "Journal" soon expands to include increasing amounts of commentary from the narrator's later and presumably more spiritually illuminated perspective. Thus the "Journal" signifies the weaknesses in the attempt to bridge the gap between trace and figura: meaning does not inhere in the events denominated in the summary account of the "Journal" but is produced by the narration within which the "Journal" is placed. Even the "Journal's" putative identity as trace is easily vitiated. Its writing and ink do not, of course, survive the printing press, which erodes the material basis of its status as artifact. And from the early pages, the entries betray interventions that signal distance and mediation, traces of traces, not an originary document. For example, this following entry appears to be retrospective summary that may be based on a journal, but does not have the immediacy of a direct transcription: "*Nov.* 4. This morning I began to order my times of Work, of going out with my Gun, time of Sleep, and time of Diversion, *viz.* Every Morning I walk'd out with my Gun for two or three Hours if it did not rain, then employ'd my self to work till about Eleven a-Clock, then eat what I had to live on, and from Twelve to Two I lay down to sleep, the Weather being excessive hot, and then in the Evening to work again" (p. 72). The specificity of "this morning" turns into the retrospection of "Every morning," implying that actuality is here at most the object of a gesture. The "Journal" appears to have been produced as much by the narrator *now* as left by the character *then*. The seeming palpability of the trace metamorphoses into the fantasy that is produced by authors and shared by readers.

III

Here then may be the place to pause (before proceeding to longer analyses) to consider how the larger issues of this discussion can be placed in relation to several current theories of the definition, rise, and function of the English novel. Clearly there are affinities with the circumstantial realism defined in Ian Watt's influential study, although much more play is here given to the figural. Two other comprehensive studies that inevitably intersect with concerns here are those by John Bender and Michael McKeon—books focusing respectively on the consequences and the origins of the novel.[18] Neither addresses precisely the same object as I do, each constituting the field of the novel in somewhat different terms. The following discussion is an attempt to highlight some of these differences in constituting an object of study.

Recent theories of the British novel have often foregrounded questions of origin while at the same time blurring those lines of demarcation that have conventionally organized the study of this genre. Watt's influential *Rise of the*

[18] Ian Watt, *The Rise of the Novel: Studies in Defoe, Richardson, and Fielding* (Berkeley: University of California Press); John Bender, *Imagining the Penitentiary: Fiction and the Architecture of Mind in Eighteenth-Century England* (Chicago: University of Chicago Press, 1987); Michael McKeon, *The Origins of the English Novel, 1600–1740* (Baltimore: Johns Hopkins University Press, 1987).

Novel (1957) posited Defoe, Richardson, and Fielding as the major originary figures, even while recognizing that many features of their writings had been adumbrated in earlier fiction. Subsequent criticism has complicated this history by including fiction marginalized by Watt, for example that of Aphra Behn, Delarivier Manley, and Eliza Haywood.[19] Such inclusions place the romance less sharply in opposition to the novel, in contrast to Watt's demarcation, which was based on a wide-ranging, although not absolute, opposition between the main line of eighteenth-century novelistic fiction and the romance. Watt identifies "formal realism" as the salient novelistic characteristic, that is, the text's claim to be in compliance with appropriate evidentiary tests that distinguish it from the merely imaginative. This version of the novel emphasizes a simulated evidentiary basis that conforms to the criteria for plausibility established through the activities of civil society. Among Watt's memorable formulations is the dictum that juries don't take evidence from someone called Mr. Badman (p. 31). Yet romances too are sometimes liberally sprinkled with devices apparently designed to validate their evidentiary basis—establishing the putative authenticity of the story by describing the finding of a foundational manuscript, for example. Furthermore, what is plausible in the context of the activities of civil society, even in presentations to a jury, has varied significantly. One might then argue that the novel is not simply in opposition to the romance but is rather the romance as it appears in an empiricist moment.

McKeon's recent analysis, *The Origins of the English Novel, 1600–1740*, incorporates Watt's powerful argument, which had been under attack for years yet remained significantly more plausible than alternative theories. McKeon regards the novel as having been established as a category in response to the needs of early to mid-eighteenth-century British society, but he also finds that the actual epistemological and social problems addressed in the texts of Richardson and Fielding from the early 1740s "had a long prehistory of intense and diversified public debate" (p. 410). This early modern fiction is defined by its dialectical, not absolute, character: McKeon's history of fiction moves from narratives designated as romance

[19] John Richetti, *Popular Fiction before Richardson: Narrative Patterns, 1700–1739* (Oxford: Clarendon Press, 1969), argues that Watt's teleological bias imposes a restrictive view of what counts as the novel and thus omits from serious consideration fiction such as that of Haywood and Manley. Jane Spencer, *The Rise of the Woman Novelist: From Aphra Behn to Jane Austen* (Oxford: Basil Blackwell, 1986), apparently alludes to Watt in her title, making the points that (1) the early novel was first associated with women as part of the bias against both women and novels, and (2) that when the novel gained prestige women's connection with it was suppressed (p. viii). She finds Richardson to be writing in a tradition already established by women, a tradition that, after Richardson, tended to define the expectations held for writings by women, expectations contrasting to those for the Fieldingesque novel (pp. 88–90).

if regarded from an empirical perspective, through narratives that incorporate empirical criteria of evidence, to narratives that reject the empirical perspective itself, which is designated as naive from a succeeding skeptical perspective.

Romance is not, then, in McKeon's view simply superseded but is instead recovered by this skeptical disenchantment with the "naive" empiricism that had itself brought the seeming fallacies of the romance into view: what he labels as "extreme skepticism" manifests itself in a turn toward the romance that had been rejected by empiricism. Thus McKeon's analysis incorporates much of Watt's description of the novel but makes the features there emphasized part of a longer history in which the prominence of the novel in eighteenth-century England is brought about by the social needs it serves rather more than by the uniqueness of its features. The seemingly new rejection of the romance is in fact part of a long-operative dialectical pattern in which the romance is continuously rejected but also reincorporated. The history McKeon writes engages fiction in an often repeated developmental pattern, although the eighteenth century remains the period in which the novel was constituted as a category of literature. This constitution of the novel resulted, however, from a synchronic conceptualization of what was in fact a limited phase of a persisting dialectical pattern.

Crucial to McKeon's argument is the confluence of both social and epistemological conflicts in what became known as the novel—namely, the conjunction of "questions of virtue" with "questions of truth." In order to bring the development of both kinds of questions together within a dialectic of fictional forms, McKeon links, or even assimilates, empiricism to a progressive view of the social order. In dialectical opposition to empiricism is skepticism, which is then linked to a conservative view of the social order. Both views of the social order—conservative and progressive—are responses to the incommensurabilities of status with worth; the conservative skeptical view, however, derives additionally from its recognition of the propensities of progressive ideology to create anomalies in the social order analogous to the ones it rectifies. These connections of social to epistemological conflicts are, however, somewhat tenuous; McKeon's arguments tend to proceed by analogies between the two realms, and he explicitly acknowledges that questions of truth and of virtue are in the early modern period "propounded by contemporaries as distinct questions" (p. 265). Yet the novel in his view finally brings the two ranges of questioning together, or, more precisely, calls attention to the untenable division between them: "The origins of the novel's mediatory project mark the discovery not of the relation between these realms but of an increasing division between them that is too great to ignore" (p. 420).

McKeon is of course writing about the constitution of the category of the novel in and through the oppositions of Richardson and Fielding, not about the later development of the novel. He remarks that *both* Richardson and Fielding in the course of their careers exemplified "naive empiricism and extreme skepticism, progressive and conservative ideologies," a comprehension that "attests not only to their supreme virtuosity but also to the fact that these oppositions are losing their intellectual and social significance" (p. 418). And he suggests that by the end of the century, "the questions of truth that have thus far organized the origins of the English novel are not so much solved . . . as drastically reformulated" (p. 419). I take up these questions of truth as they appear mainly after *Pamela* and *Joseph Andrews*, and thus continue and build on the epistemological inquiry that is a large part of McKeon's enterprise. Yet the epistemological has an apparent priority in this book that alters the emphasis of McKeon's, which treats epistemology and social ideology as convertible into each other: "In the context of early modern narrative, epistemological choices have ideological significance, and a given explanation of the meaning of social mobility is likely to imply a certain epistemological procedure and commitment" (p. 266).

It would be foolish to challenge the view that epistemologies have ideological implications, a view I accept as a truism. Yet I am not fully persuaded that epistemologies correlate or necessarily connect with social views in a consistent manner, although McKeon has convincingly argued several specific cases. In using the epithet "naive" in connection with nearly all empiricism and "extreme" with nearly all skepticism, McKeon motivates and elucidates the dialectical interchanges and mutual supplantations of these epistemological perspectives; he is thus also able to connect the complementary fallacies of progressive and conservative social ideology to these already marginalized epistemological perspectives. While McKeon acknowledges the existence of a variety of empiricisms that encompass both naive and more skeptical versions, the heaviest work of empiricism in his text is to display naïveté. Substantial debate during the century, nevertheless, attempts to extend the empiricist view, despite the acknowledged liabilities of the senses, experience, and testimony. Especially in historiography, when events already past are at issue, an empirical ideology invites skepticism; the eighteenth century, however, frequently and even characteristically attempted to confine skepticism to limits that would save an empirical outlook. When McKeon attempts to connect "extreme" skepticism with the "conservative plot," he sometimes appears not to be defining either skepticism or any version of empiricism, but a mystification: conservative plots "generate a desire for the return of an earlier order whose vulnerability has now by one means or another become more resistant to skeptical reduction" (p. 231).

And what he calls "naive" empiricism sometimes appears to be fraud rather than an epistemology: he suggests that in Fielding the criminal biography with its "characteristic devices of authentication" is regarded as the "'new romance' of naive empiricism," which uses "modernized methods of imposing on the credulity of the reader" (p. 383). Here a reader's naïveté may be at issue but empirical epistemology is not: perhaps a "romance" simulation of empiricism is represented but not the naïveté of empiricism.

The differences between the views on epistemology represented by me and by McKeon are easily exaggerated (and have perhaps already been); as suggested previously, the differences derive primarily from our differing assumptions about the possibility of consistently mapping epistemological perspectives on social ideologies. Yet the center of gravity of this book is the already constituted novel of midcentury, not as in McKeon the process of that constitution. There is in fact evidence in McKeon's book that empiricism occupies a broader and more flexible position in his thinking than the repeated epithet "naive" suggests. He states that Fielding seeks "to distinguish between a naively empiricist and a more 'imaginative' species of belief," yet Fielding "is also at pains to emphasize the crucial degree to which he is in accord with the empiricist perspective, and to distinguish his preferred sort of belief also from the sheer creativity of romance" (p. 404). Perhaps what he describes here as "more 'imaginative'" is empiricism without the epithet. McKeon also allows for a skeptical empiricism, although within this text he limits it to his own authorial role: "Anyone who would seek to disclose the dialectical process of historical experience must be in some committed (if skeptical) way an empiricist, responsible to the evidence at hand lest it appear that by 'history' one means finally that realm where everything can be found to equal everything else" (p. 421).

In *Imagining the Penitentiary: Fiction and the Architecture of Mind in Eighteenth-Century England*, John Bender explores the relationship of the eighteenth-century novel to the social consequences of the epistemological rupture defined by Foucault and called the Classical episteme. Within this episteme, conceptualization is often and characteristically a form of classification: "Stripped of all commentary, of all enveloping language, creatures present themselves one beside another, their surfaces visible, grouped according to their common features, and thus already virtually analyzed, and bearers of nothing but their own individual names" (*Order of Things*, p. 131). Such understanding through classification is in *Discipline and Punish: The Birth of the Prison* related to the ordering that constitutes the modern social world. Foucault presents the instructions given to a town during a time of plague at the end of the seventeenth century as a paradigmatic instance of the power that is disclosed within classificatory ordering.

The town is to be closed, partitioned, and inspected, and complete records identifying every habitation and inhabitant are to be produced: "It lays down for each individual his place, his body, his disease and his death, his well-being, by means of an omnipresent and omniscient power that subdivides itself in a regular, uninterrupted way even to the ultimate determination of the individual, of what characterizes him, of what belongs to him, of what happens to him."[20]

The implications of this classificatory system of surveillance are expressed in Jeremy Bentham's image of a "Panopticon," in which every inmate of a prison or worker in a factory is separated from every other and observable at any moment, although the observed is not able to see the observer and thus not able to discern whether he or she is under observation or not at any particular time. The effect is to create a sense of constant visibility, a persisting internalized version of the less persistent external perspective. The "penitentiary idea" described in Bender's book is the outcome of this potentially precise placement or classification and, thus, seeming knowledge of people: the aberrant individual can presumably be reformed, reconstituted, through subjection to the surveillance of the invisible authoritarian figure. From Bender's perspective certain features of the eighteenth-century novel participated in the formation of this coercive world, most notably the novel's fostering of the illusion of the transparency of authority, which appears less and less to be embodied in identifiable people but in "passive, disinterested, objective, and transparent" rules (*Imagining the Penitentiary*, p. 176). The very conventions of realist fiction, its presentation of itself as the kind of discourse validated by civil society, confirm and are confirmed by the power exercised through a classificatory epistemology: "Formal realism, transparency, judicial objectivity, bureaucratic neutrality and consistency—the very instruments that allow the separation of relevant from irrelevant fact, of perjury from honest testimony, of the evidential from the incidental, of distortion from reality—are all representational systems of assent that at once constitute and validate authority as densely particularized, closely reasoned differentiation" (p. 177).

Such description of the eighteenth-century novel appears to be counterfactual. Rather than making authority invisible, this fiction foregrounds issues of authority, openly showing narrative to be a formulation arising from a definable perspective rather than from some supposed objective source. The questions aroused by this fiction appeal to the reader's judgment just as strongly as its assertions inculcate the omniscience of the

---

[20] Michel Foucault, *Discipline and Punish: The Birth of the Prison*, trans. Alan Sheridan (New York: Random House, 1979), p. 197.

narrator. Richardson's *Clarissa*, for example, appears to be exposing the narrational strategies of the principals as attempts to accrete power of various kinds. Although Clarissa's claims are valorized, her perspective is not assumed to be unbiased but is subjected to the critical scrutiny of her friend Anna Howe as well as of Lovelace, and she herself must question her own understanding and the adequacy of its embodiment in her narration. When Richardson discovers that his multivoiced narrative has produced multivalent commentary, he introduces more of his own evaluations into the notes to the text, hoping to define the parameters within which readers must interpret. His attempt to recover the authority that he had ceded to the reader reveals both the author's tyrannies and their ineffectuality. Sterne's *Tristram Shandy*, for another example, can be read as an exposure of the arbitrariness of narration, the reality it claims to represent reducible to an intelligible order only by the choices of its narrator and the conventions of narrative. Not the illusion of transparency but the delusiveness of claiming transparency is what Sterne conveys through Tristram's meditations on the intractability of his medium. Neither of these novels is dealt with by Bender, whose concern is with the "novelistic" as distinguished from the more restrictive "novel."

It is with the notions of the "novelistic" and "novelization" that Bender counters the interpretation that eighteenth-century fiction is an apparent exposure of, and resistance to, the authority imposed by narrative convention. Following Bakhtin, Bender regards the novel not as a genre but as a compilation of competing genres that establish a dialogue both internally and externally, the internal dialogue among the genres becoming an external dialogue with connected social institutions. Rather than regarding these competing voices as a deterrent to hegemony, however, Bender argues that the dialogic within the eighteenth-century realistic novel participates in a discourse that creates a more inclusive hegemony: "The realistically illustrated minutiae of present life become subject to the discourse of debate—a discourse in which evidence based on observation is central and in which narrative coherence forged from multiple voices delineates authority, government, and reality itself" (pp. 135–36).

What the novel insinuates, then, as Bender sees it, is not the resistance to totalization that the dialogic implies, but the monolithic terms within which the dialogue is conducted and through which any resolution can be imagined. Some of the characteristics of eighteenth-century fiction, again, evade this conclusion. Eighteenth-century fiction notably focuses on narrators and characters, their conflicting and contradictory subjectivities being at least as emphatically presented as other dialogic possibilities. The subjectivity so fully rendered in, for example, Richardson, and sometimes even celebrated in Sterne, is ill-suited to the function of aiding in the creation of an internalized oppression that is supposedly the result of the acceptance of analytico-referential discourse. Arguably, eighteenth-century fiction is a turn toward the individualistic, a locating of interest and value in the person and a weighing of even the acknowledged power of the community in the balances provided by individual judgment and well-being. Yet even such a view of eighteenth-century fiction does not entirely evade Bender's argument. For Bender, the resistances of these individualistic novelistic characters to the world in which they are embedded (a world of analytico-referential discourse) are an essential element in the formation of the penitentiary idea. Only through such resistance can the illusion of a self persisting through changed and changing circumstances be maintained: "The nature and function of novelistic realism lie in its ability to produce meaning by containing its own contradictions and thus to leave the impression that consciousness and subjectivity are stable across time" (p. 48). Such illusions of the stability of subjectivity are essential to the penitentiary idea, for "the exact aim of the penitentiary as an institution" is the manipulation of "identity by recomposing the fictions on which it is founded" (p. 38).

For McKeon the conventions of realism are constantly receding into the ineffectuality of the naive and being subverted by a recrudescence of romance, whereas for Bender these conventions, however different from one another, are all versions of a dominant epistemological frame for late-seventeenth- and eighteenth-century discourse. The self that is constructed and the social order that is constituted within this period are for Bender a decisive change requiring a redescription that emphasizes rupture more than continuity. Bender finds a uniformity within the instantiations of novelistic realism even while also recognizing differences similar to those that McKeon's dialectical model incorporates. Among the broadest variations that Bender describes are the movements in the novel "between points of view that imply surveillance and enclosure," the more limited point of view requiring the reader to "enter the mental world of a single character and thereby fictionally view reality as a network of contingencies dependent upon observation" and the broader narrative perspective allying readers "with the controlling power of an omniscient narrator" (p. 61). At this point Bender and McKeon converge in the perception that "epistemological choices have ideological significance, and a given explanation of the meaning of social mobility is likely to imply a certain epistemological procedure and commitment" (McKeon, *Origins*, p. 266). Just as Bender implicitly reduced the opposition between Richardson and Fielding (an opposition signaled by their contrasting limited and omniscient narrative procedures) by finding both to be in the service of a more comprehensive ideology that embraces enclosure *and* surveillance, McKeon also links these two authors (in his dialectical system they are foundational *because* oppositional) as expressions of the "conflict between naive empiricism and extreme skepticism, between progressive and conservative ideologies" (p. 266). Conservative ideology reincorporates the romance features that have been excluded by the empiricist progressive ideology, and the dialectical oppositions between the two ideologies/epistemologies present a persistent and comprehensive critique of both aristocratic and progressive values.

At this point I wish to define a space for a different kind of analysis, one that is, nevertheless, in some ways closely related to the methods and materials of both McKeon and Bender. History, considered as the *construal* of patterns of humanly significant change through time, is central to McKeon's dialectical method, and he frequently comments on the interactions of historical with fictional narrative in the eighteenth century and before. Renaissance historicism is in fact at the root of his version of the novel's dialectic of naive empiricism and extreme skepticism (p. 48). In McKeon's view, the periodizing perspective of the Renaissance led in two very different directions, both characterizable as scientific (p. 41). One of these views, which corresponds to naive empiricism, "encourages an optimistic ambition to construct the positive laws of universal history," whereas the other view, which corresponds to extreme skepticism, "promotes the more chastened belief that every historical period is singular and perhaps unknowable from without" (p. 41). My pursuit of the topic of eighteenth-century fiction and historiography in this study focuses not primarily on the role of history in the origin of the novel but on the role that the scuffles between history and fiction play in eighteenth-century novelistic developments. Specific attention is devoted to the epistemological implications of the novel's attempts to usurp historical space, as well as to the changes in the formal structures of novels that this conflict entailed. My emphasis is less on the novel in formation and more on its midcentury consolidation in texts such as *Clarissa*, *Tom Jones*, and, somewhat later, *Tristram Shandy*.

In focusing on this slightly later era, I include in my approach a view of changes in eighteenth-century historiography similar to Foucault's construal of the Classical episteme, an episteme that emphasizes a classificatory logic intended to allow the historian to evade the bondage to written sources characteristic of previous history. Although the historian always, of course, needs sources, in the Classical episteme written documents are dispersed in a classificatory grid like the exhibits of natural history, allowing linguistic phenomena themselves to become objects of analysis: "The establishment of archives, then of filing systems for them, the reorganization of libraries, the drawing up of catalogs, indexes, and inventories" are all a response to the need to reorder past discourse analytically and critically (*Order of Things*, p. 132).

This dispersal of sources according to a classificatory scheme is, I think, manifested in the eighteenth-century novel, which among other things is a representation of a variety of schemes for managing information, its characteristic effort the preservation or recovery of the bits of information that can be brought to an unforeseen meaning through their embedding in a narrative network: one thinks of the complex clues of *Tom Jones* that remain individually without significance until brought into contiguity by the narrator; of the archive that is collected and contested in *Clarissa*; of the interpolated documents and the search for an appropriate narrative disposition of the details that will construct the sought-for past in *Tristram Shandy*. Catalogs, indexes, and inventories, the detritus of learning in Swift, often become essential if sometimes comic tools in the construction of this later form of writing. In their broadest manifestations such classificatory schema exemplify the discourse to which Bender attaches the conventions of realism that distinguish the eighteenth-century novel and participate in the formation of the "penitentiary idea."

Both Bender and McKeon see the novel as a particularizable cultural artifact of the eighteenth century, yet the object of investigation for both is the cultural matrix or continuum in which the novel participates. McKeon defines changing elements of a historical continuum that make possible the consolidation of the "category" of the novel in the eighteenth century, and Bender defines the novel's participation in a matrix that produces a society in which conformity is enforced through the internalization of authority. Neither argument can be easily controverted (except possibly piecemeal) if one agrees on the end to which the argument appeals. If indeed the novel was formed as a category in the eighteenth century despite all its evident diversity, then the argument that it was formed through the dialectical development of preexisting contradictions is patently plausible. And if the eighteenth century eventuated in a world in which power was dispensed through the internalization of authoritative surveillance, then the novel surely played some part in that outcome; even if the novel resisted, it must still in some way have been implicated in the matrix from which that world ensued.

As the *connection* of past and present, history must inevitably include a version of the past that can only be retrospectively understood—or even noticed. Nevertheless, it is also true that the refocusing of a past event exclusively either in relation to its causes or consequences constricts the possibilities for description. Both Bender's and McKeon's books are admirable refocusings of eighteenth-century fiction in relation to its origins and consequences, yet their insights inevitably come at the expense of certain related exclusions. McKeon's dialectical method constrains him to construct a narrowed version of the empiricism engaged by fiction, thus providing little incentive for a sustained assessment of the role of the novel in the attempted marriage of narrative with one or another of the empiricisms central to eighteenth-century historical and religious discourse. The eighteenth-century novel has marked significance as a critique (admittedly somewhat rough and ready) of history during an era dominated by an empirical ideology. And in rereading eighteenth-century fiction from the perspective of its iteration or pre-iteration of aspects of an evolving penitentiary idea, Bender sometimes disregards the more resistant role that fiction itself claims. Fiction's configuration of the problems of a subject in accounting for the diversity of meaning in a world is for Bender only an insinuation of the emerging notion of a stable subject.

For Bender the world confronted by the confused subject in eighteenth-century fiction is visible only within the limits of analytico-referential discourse. He discounts any claims of eighteenth-century fiction to be revealing conflicts between the subject and this discourse, sustaining this analysis by considering subject and discourse as separable components of the penitentiary idea—the one validating the idea of the subject and the other the idea of the analytico-referential, even though they sometimes appear to be in opposition. My point is not that this division of features of the novel and their connection to diverse sources of later oppression is erroneous from the perspective of a matrix of ideas later triumphant, but that as a description of novels it is inadequate. The novel, like eighteenth-century philosophy, makes the *self* into a problem, and it makes the discourse within which the self and the novel construct themselves a problem. Bender's view that such problematizing is merely the process of the insinuation of both—self and discourse—into a position of ideological dominance may be a plausible view of the "novelization" of eighteenth-century culture, but it does not account for eighteenth-century fiction's actual positioning of itself.

Eighteenth-century fiction, like Bender's book about it, is concerned to scrutinize the relationship of the subject to the discourse within which subjectivity is formulated. The major novels of the midcentury reveal a relationship to that discourse somewhat different from the one Bender finds dominant in the "novelized" culture of the time. Bender's premise is that "from the eighteenth-century onward, the realist novel has attempted the appearance of having removed all distance between itself and the processes of daily life: it pretends to be a transparent, unmediated form of knowledge about that life" (p. 8). This formulation may hold true for many *nineteenth*-century novels, but it is an implausible description of *Clarissa, Tom Jones,* and *Tristram Shandy*. These novels persistently expose the discrepancies between various discourses and "the processes of daily life." I find Lionel Gossman's description of eighteenth-century fiction more persuasive: "The characteristic feature of eighteenth-century fiction is the ironic distance most eighteenth-century novels establish between the narrator and the narrative, and the complicity they set up between the reader and the narrator over against the narrative—that is to say, the clear distinction they make between *discours* and *histoire*."[21]

My argument is not that I can recover this fiction in its own terms—in my analysis I obviously use a conceptual apparatus that was not available to eighteenth-century writers—but that I include in that analysis the explicit or implicit responses of eighteenth-century fiction both to the history that it claimed as a relative and to those larger aspects of epistemological change that it recognized. The later eighteenth century was very conscious of the need to rewrite much history and also of the possibilities for doing so that arose out of the new learning. While "naive empiricism" is obviously a useful term for placing this interest in a dialectical continuum, it does not adequately describe or motivate the reconceptualization of historiography within an eighteenth-century intellectual world that accepts an empirical ideology. And our sense that these alterations in historiography may be part of a matrix of changes in epistemology and discourse that facilitates the internalization of relations of power leaves still to be discussed the question of the implied disposition of the novel toward those subsequent developments.

IV

As a way of clarifying my approach to the novel and the larger discourse in which it participates, I propose here to analyze two familiar texts that border the novel and precede its full consolidation, Bunyan's *Pilgrim's Progress* and Defoe's *Journal of the Plague Year*, guiding the discussion with the concepts of figura and trace. These works by Bunyan and Defoe are

[21] Lionel Gossman, "History and Literature: Reproduction or Signification," in *The Writing of History: Literary Form and Historical Understanding*, ed. Robert H. Canary and Henry Kozicki (Madison: University of Wisconsin Press, 1961), p. 22. See Elizabeth Deeds Ermarth, *Realism and Consensus in the English Novel* (Princeton: Princeton University Press, 1983), for a perspective on the "realism" of eighteenth-century fiction that is relevant to mine. Realism is in Ermarth's view a matter of consensus among viewpoints within the fiction as mediated by the narrator. She finds that Defoe and Richardson engage with realistic premises in her sense but ultimately subvert them.

implicitly connected by similarities of structure and of the interpretive questions they entertain, yet they represent remarkable diversities of discourse. *The Pilgrim's Progress* (1678) appears to be a recuperation of an earlier discourse, having more in common with Augustine than with Bacon. Yet Bunyan's book also shows the strains resulting from its rejection of its own location within a modern political world that endorses an empirical epistemology. Defoe's *Journal* foregrounds those strains, showing the City of Destruction as London after the Stuart restoration and exemplifying the movement toward narrative subjectivity that is occasioned by an attempt to extract figural meaning from an empirically conceived world. When *The Pilgrim's Progress* is reconstructed within history, it must found itself on the authorizing traces from an actual past; before those traces can be reconceived as figurae, however, they must be construed in relationship to a multiplicity of historical events constituting a pattern of significance. Such construal implies a narrator's effort to evade the constrictions of any specified time, a strategy that conflicts with the somewhat different enterprise of attempting to reconstruct a single historical event in its individuality, which requires the narrator both to be aware of the limitations of a present and to seek the particularities of a past.

Defoe's emphasis on the dual roles of his narrator in *Robinson Crusoe*—as actor in the events and as producer of text about them—foregrounds questions of narrative authority. In contrast, *The Pilgrim's Progress* presents its narration as authoritative by emphasizing its narrator's role as observer rather than as producer of text: the recounted story is a monitory dream that is given an authority to which the narrator must submit. His story opens with his account of the coming of the dream to him, and it is punctuated by repeated versions of the phrase "Now I saw in my dream," thus implying a claim that the story both exceeds the narrator's personal authority and the canons of the empirical: the dream represents the factual basis of the Christian journey as if it were a definitive meaning without any necessary dependence on the observer. The narrator-observer does become an increasingly active presence in the narration, but this activity indicates an enlarged understanding of, and response to, the meaning of the narrative, not primarily a larger role in shaping it. The narrator can perceive Christian's experience more precisely than Christian can during the trials of the "Valley of the Shadow of Death," having of course the benefits of the visual presentation.[22] He later introduces his tentative, rather flat, moralizing into the text: "Then I thought that it is easier going out of the way when we are in, than going in

<hr>

[22] John Bunyan, *The Pilgrim's Progress*, ed. Roger Sharrock (New York: Penguin, 1965), p. 98.

when we are out" (p. 151). And he subsequently contributes his own admonitory note/song, in emulation of the songs through which Christian and his companions distill their experiences: "When saints do sleepy grow, let them come hither, / And hear how these two pilgrims talk together" (p. 176). His role develops in the direction of participation in the events of the story—starting as bare observer, becoming an interpreter, and then actually entering the narrative when a gardener in Beulah inquires directly of him, "Wherefore musest thou at the matter?" (p. 197). On the arrival of Christian and Hopeful into the heavenly city, he wishes himself "among them," a hint of an intent to replicate their journey, which he has proleptically begun.

But *The Pilgrim's Progress* is a far more conflicted text than is suggested by this account of the basis for its claims of narrative authority. In presenting the dream motif as an evasion of human subjectivity, the narrative merely defers the question of the source of authority. The figural method of the narrative connects it to its master text—the Bible—and raises questions about the need for, and the authority of, intermediary texts. Such questions about the text as a totality are reinforced by the conflicts within the narrative itself, which is largely an account of Christian's perplexities about authoritative interpretation, his journey having as an early necessary component a course of instruction in the house of Interpreter and as one of its last episodes the encounter with Ignorance, whose persistence in, and punishment for, error remain not easily framable (even by Christian and Hopeful) within the boundaries of ordinary ethical judgments.

Bunyan's book begins with an "Author's Apology," which displays the underlying premise that the book repeats the truths of its master narrative, the Bible, and is thus as justifiable by the same reasoning as the hortatory function of the preacher. Yet a persisting irritation for Bunyan and his interlocutors in the "Apology" is the book's *darkness*, the obscurity of its allegory. What can justify an *obscure* repetition of truths already sufficiently presented in the Bible? The "Apology" finally rests on the analogy between biblical obscurity and Bunyanesque obscurity: the "sober man" will attempt to understand "what by pins and loops, / By calves, and sheep, by heifers, and by rams, / By birds and herbs, and by the blood of lambs / God speaketh to him" (p. 34). While it is true that the figural view of reality proposed by *The Pilgrim's Progress* demands an allegorical presentation, Bunyan's "Apology" is notably defensive about his allegory, responsive perhaps to Protestant and especially Puritan valorizations of plainness and clarity in religious forms and formulations.

The narrative itself makes problematic interpretation a prominent subject matter. The "Way" of Bunyan's allegory is the outward configuration of the

Christian life: all true Christians travel on it, but not all who travel on it are true Christians. The most basic metaphor of the book is thus a problem in interpretation rather than an answer; "Formalist" and "Hypocrisy" are on the Way just as Christian is (p. 72). "Ignorance" is perhaps the most serious challenge to the attempts of Christian and Hopeful to rationalize their understanding of the Way in comprehensive moral terms. His excuse for not sharing their particular self-critical religion and for not entering the Way at the beginning where he might have received the requisite certificate is that he is following the religion of his country, just as he urges them to "be content to follow the religion" of theirs (p. 162). Ignorance insists on the centrality of behavior to salvation and opposes his true Christian fellow travelers openly only when they proclaim the importance of a direct revelation of Christ: "I believe that what both you, and all the rest of you say about that matter, is but the fruit of distracted brains" (p. 189). Attempting to rationalize this apparent imperviousness to their own anguished form of religion, Christian later remarks to Hopeful that he believes such pretended Christians have stifled former convictions of their sinfulness, a formulation that makes ignorance a variant of willfulness (p. 190) and allows the true pilgrims to persist in maintaining the universality of the truths of their religion.

The Pilgrim's Progress grounds religion in a history that elides diachronic as well as synchronic difference. Being Christian is a process of connecting chronologically disparate events to the constantly changing present in a manner that reveals (or creates) a stasis, an underlying meaning that is constant however much the superficies appear to change. An active interpretive effort is required, as the merging of a completed past with an evanescent present can achieve significance and unity only through constant adjustment. The "Way" of The Pilgrim's Progress sometimes resembles an interactive museum in which the emphasis is on the connectedness of past to present rather than on the pastness of the past. The focus is on the present of the journey, with the past appearing not precisely as it was but as a constant refocusing that establishes a relevance to changing present occurrences. Some of the past is animated, revealing persisting meaning through the continuous variations of typological actions; whereas other aspects are monumental, fixed, and thus requiring construal to establish meaning and relevance. Demas, for example, entices the pilgrims to leave the path to observe a silver mine, a rather fuller and more active narrativization of the figure than that given in the New Testament, where Paul merely remarks somewhat enigmatically, "Demas hath forsaken me, having loved this present world" (2 Timothy 4:10). This Demas is, however, sometimes associated with Demetrius, a silversmith of Ephesus who led a rebellion against Paul, whose gospel was hurting the trade in "silver shrines" (Acts 19:24ff.). Christian's identification of Demas from his typological actions allows him to extend the story and his explication of it even further, for Demas's actions place him within the lineage of prior biblical figures: "Gehazi was your great grandfather, and Judas your father, and you have trod their steps" (p. 145). Shortly thereafter they see "an old monument," which they cannot identify until Christian construes some "writing in an unusual hand": *"Remember Lot's wife"* (p. 146). This combination of a monument to Lot's wife with Demas's repetitive but not identical actions allegorizes the twin demands of the book's implied hermeneutic: adherence to a fixed text and the connections of meaning to ever evolving circumstances.

Rather than being content to take these two incidents—the actions of Demas and the monument to Lot's wife—as independent, the pilgrims proceed to turn them into a monitory whole, Lot's wife representing the kind of spectacle they themselves might have become had they left the "Way" to inspect Demas's silver mine. Demas's failure to heed the warning implied by this monument so near to him is then interpreted as an intensification of his sin, an interpretation glossed by the biblical account of Sodom, whose inhabitants were judged to be unusually wicked "because they were sinners before the Lord, that is, in his eyesight" (pp. 147–48). Meaning is created by connecting the artifacts and events of the biblical-historical world to one another through an ever expanding web of narrative resemblances, thus achieving a transhistorical significance that can be integrated into a present.

A systematically artifactual approach to the Christian journey is presented at the palace named "Beautiful," Christian's first place of sustained rest and instruction after his visit to the house of "Interpreter."[23] In the house of Interpreter, he finds pictures and tableaus that are already composed into a pattern suited to the conveyance of moral meaning to one with the appropriate interpretive skills. After attaining the necessary competence to be fully responsive to the instruction found in these images, Christian is sent on his way. His later experience at the palace Beautiful has a somewhat different educational goal, seeming to aim at confirmation more than elucidation, and thus focusing on the past. Included is a visit to the "study," where he is shown "records of the greatest antiquity," including "the pedigree of the Lord of the Hill . . . some of the worthy acts that some of his servants had done . . . [and]

---

[23] David J. Alpaugh, "Emblem and Interpretation in *The Pilgrim's Progress*," *ELH* 33 (1966): 299–314, discusses Christian's learning of the art of interpreting emblems, an art leading to turning "immediate experience" into emblematic interpretation and "reexamining . . . past experiences from a vantage point of increased understanding" (p. 302).

several other histories of many famous things" (pp. 86–87). After being shown this written documentation, Christian is taken to the "armoury," where he sees the "furniture, which their Lord had provided for pilgrims" and also a large collection of "engines" referred to in biblical accounts, including "Moses' rod, the hammer and nail with which Jael slew Sisera, the pitchers, trumpets, and lamps too, with which Gideon put to flight the armies of Midian" (pp. 87, 88).

This description of a collection of proto-Christian antiquities appears to verge, perhaps parodically, on the discourse of empiricism.[24] The composed pictures of the house of the Interpreter may be construed as forming an initiation into figural interpretation, while the artifacts of the house Beautiful may be seen as the traces confirming the biblical history that is the foundation for the figural. Bunyan, however, means his "armour" to be of the spirit and his antiquities to attest to a transhistorical meaning even while his faith in their historicity remains. This collection is perhaps closer to the reliquary than to the museum, which does not yet exist in its modern public form. Yet we should not fail to notice Bunyan's sensitivity to the analytico-referential discourse that he is repulsing. The character "Shame," described as "bold-faced," is his representation of the coerciveness of the modern world in which religious pilgrims are contemptible because of their "ignorance of the times in which they lived, and want of understanding in all natural science" (p. 107). Bunyan's resistance to modernism betrays his awareness of its threats.

The Bible is the pretext for *The Pilgrim's Progress*, yet it appears inadequate, apparently needing supplementation, interpretation, and confirmation. The opening portrayal of Christian is of him reading a book that causes him to fear but does not succeed in giving him a course of action. Evangelist supplements this book with a "parchment roll," directing Christian to "fly from the wrath to come" (p. 41). And when Christian loses his evil burden, he is given a "roll" (p. 70), which is both "to comfort me by reading" (p. 73)

[24] Alpaugh remarks that "Bunyan conceives of the mind almost in a Lockean sense. . . . [O]ne must reason from sense impressions," although the object is spiritual understanding (ibid., p. 302). McKeon addresses possibilities for literalizing interpretation within the allegory: Christian's freedom from his burden has affinities with the "liberated vagabondage of the masterless men," and those who attempt to fill in the Slough of Despond appear to be engaging in a "national system of highway maintenance" rather similar to efforts in Bunyan's time (*Origins*, p. 303). Christopher Hill, *A Turbulent, Seditious, and Factious People: John Bunyan and His Church, 1628–1668* (Oxford: Clarendon Press, 1988), examines *The Pilgrim's Progress* in the context of the Restoration and the memories of the Civil War: for example, he notes that the pilgrim is given a sword, which is "the sword of the spirit" but neverthless recalls the arming of the New Model Army, enabling it to resist the gentry just as Christian can now resist Apollyon (p. 199).

and to be the certificate needed for entrance into the celestial city. Whatever the allegorical meanings in relation to Protestant theology, the suggestion seems inescapable that the printed book needs supplementation by the personalization of the manuscript. Ernst Robert Curtius states that "it was through Christianity that the book received its highest consecration"; he also notes that the invention of printing degraded the status of the book: "The written book had a value which we can no longer feel. Every book produced by copying represented diligence and skilled craftsmanship, long hours of intellectual concentration, loving and sedulous work. Every such book was a personal achievement."[25] The various manuscripts referred to within *The Pilgrim's Progress* are of inestimable importance in relation to its ideology, and their meaning is not or cannot be fully replicated by print.

The verbal in *The Pilgrim's Progress* attains authenticity only as connected to the person, yet personal authority must in turn be found in the book—the biblical master narrative. Talkative is rejected as one whose religion "hath no place in his heart," despite his familiarity with scripture (p. 113), while Ignorance's confidence in the goodness of his heart despite his not possessing a certificate is derided by Christian: "Except the Word of God beareth witness in this matter, other testimony is of no value" (p. 185).[26] When Bunyan attempts to justify his own book's efficacy, he concludes his "Apology" with the admonition to "lay my book, thy head and heart together" (p. 37). Several versions of this formulation occur repeatedly within the narrative itself, where the book referred to is the Bible, not *The Pilgrim's Progress*.

Even the master text is not, however, justified as admonition and historical narrative alone, but as the divine person. Attempting to persuade Pliable of the reliability of scripture, Christian urges that the "truth of what is expressed therein . . . is confirmed by the blood of him that made it" (p. 43). Christ as the Word is thus a guarantor of textual meanings, yet as a living presence he introduces meanings that are not only those of a past history. Bunyan's activity in making this living biblical text not a monument but a part of his own new text is an acceptance of the continued evolution of its

[25] Ernst Robert Curtius, *European Literature and the Latin Middle Ages*, trans. Willard R. Trask (Princeton: Princeton University Press, 1973), pp. 310, 328. Curtius's view of the text in a religious context needs to be balanced by the statements of many others who argue that only through the printing press could the proliferation of variants be somewhat staunched.

[26] James F. Forrest, "Bunyan's Ignorance and the Flatterer: A Study in the Literary Art of Damnation," *Studies in Philology* 60 (1963), examines the contextual reasons for Bunyan's treatment of Ignorance, ascribing them to the Calvinist thought that construes Ignorance's unbelief as willful, although the modern reader may find the incident "an outrageous flaw in the work" (p. 12).

meanings. Room for flexibility of interpretation is implied in Christian's response to Faithful's ingenious reading of the Mosaic law in relation to Talkative: "He cheweth the cud, he seeketh knowledge . . . but he divideth not the hoof, he parteth not with the way of sinners" (p. 116). Christian responds: "You have spoken, for aught I know, the true Gospel sense of those texts."

Such flexibilities of text in concert with its crucial and determinate position as the standard for judging all human activity and motivation produce an anxiety that leads to textual materialization and fetishizing. The text itself becomes body and is combined and recombined without necessary reference to standards of interpretation. The extension of the figural to the contemporary sometimes involves the reconfiguration of numerous segments of text to recompose them in a manner responsive to a current issue, as illustrated in Christian's encounter with Demas and the monument of Lot's wife. And Bunyan's book goes even one step further toward a materialized text by using the biblical language knowingly and explicitly but yet sometimes without any determinate allusive relevance: the Bible is reconfigured and reconstituted at the level of the words themselves. Perhaps relevant here is the remark by St. Francis of Assisi when explaining his saving of all written scraps of parchment, even if from pagan books: his scrupulosity stems from the recognition that even pagan writings are made up of the same letters as form God's name (account by Thomas of Celano cited by Curtius, *European Literature*, p. 319).

Bunyan's reconstitution of scripture in *The Pilgrim's Progress* is accomplished only through its fragmentation. His belief or hope that these fragments may be revivified is possibly implied by Christian's validation of his book in response to Pliable's questions: not only is the book guaranteed by the blood of its maker but also it leads us to a place where those who were "cut in pieces, burnt in flames, eaten of beasts, drownded in the seas . . . [are] all well, and clothed with immortality" (p. 44). The resurrection of the body is analogous to the wholeness of truth that may be derived from what appear to be dispersed fragments.

The Pilgrim's Progress maintains its figural view of history by looking forward to a time of completion when the apparent fragments will find their place within a finally stablized pattern of meaning. The urgencies of the present do of course intrude into *The Pilgrim's Progress*, as, for example, the very first of Bunyan's marginal notes indicates when it identifies the "den" as "The gaol" (p. 39), the place where Bunyan is confined and writes, thus bringing to direct attention the then current religio-political context. A *present* makes continuous interpretive demands on any conception of the figural, obtruding discontinuities that need to be reconciled within the constraints of a past history and a future faith. Yet the very program of *The Pilgrim's Progress* is designed to elucidate everything in terms of a future but also completed process whose meaning is already understood. The meaning of the moment is to be found only in its subšumption, not in its isolation. Defoe's *Journal of the Plague Year* may be understood as a contrasting attempt to write an account of an overwhelming event in terms of an incompleted meaning, thus allowing a recent present to exert its full force, which is to say its full perplexity. The figural master narrative is available to the narrator of the *Journal*, yet his experience often retains the enigmatic quality of the trace, resisting subsumption in the master narrative. Christian and his companions Faithful and Hopeful narrate their experiences repeatedly, distilling them until they are reduced to the morally assimilable, their reconstructed narrative often losing its particularity in the generalized form of one of their songs. The *Journal*, however, maintains a perspective that insists on its continued proximity to the particularity of the described events and ends with a cessation of the plague rather than a conclusive meaning. The *Journal* is put together from putative memoranda written at the time of the plague, and it represents the bafflement of the plague for both participant and historian; while the narrative acknowledges its after-the-fact compilation and includes later reflection, the truth of the plague is sought as if from within the experience itself. The experiences of Bunyan's hero in civil society are divided between the City of Destruction and Vanity Fair: Christian is fleeing from the former and is consequently merely passing through the latter. Defoe's H.F., in contrast, describes the paroxysms of the City of Destruction itself without being able to identify himself as a citizen of another country with a vantage point outside the destruction. Defoe creates a sustained narrative out of the scraps of evidence, yet the narrative does not combine perspectives internal and external to the event in a comprehensive view.

The *Journal* does not separate itself from the future by ignoring it. When published in 1722 it insinuated itself into the web of history, connecting itself to a continuous time within which its meaning must be sought. As Manuel Schonhorn has shown, the street configurations prior to the great fire are carefully reproduced in Defoe's book.[27] When combined with the ruminations in the narrative about the changes London has undergone, this authenticity of detail creates a sense not merely of *then* but of a reconstructed then—a then that has been brought into a present. As John Bender puts it: "H.F. lives simultaneously in modern, metropolitan London and in an old

[27] Manuel Schonhorn, "Defoe's *Journal of the Plague Year*: Topography and Intention," *RES*, 2d ser., 19 (1968): 387–402.

city that, following presentiments of future growth after the Civil War, died away at the height of the plague into a kind of archeological site" (*Imagining the Penitentiary*, p. 75). Yet the plague year remains unincorporated into its future because it is as rationally unassimilable now as then. The return of the plague via Marseilles is a motivation for Defoe's writing, yet the moral meaning of the plague is no more fully understood through this present account than it was formerly understood. Louis Landa has shown that Defoe does indeed suggest certain preparations for the plague that would mitigate disruption and suffering; however, the plague and the subsequent fire are also regarded within the *Journal* as inescapably linked to divine agency and purpose.[28] No reformation of the populace of London is, nevertheless, perceived, although the prevailing assumption is that divine castigation is motivated by a desire for human improvement. The cessation of the plague is even more mysterious than its beginning, without empirical or rational explanation for its end: "Those Physicians, who had the least Share of Religion in them, were oblig'd to acknowledge that it was all supernatural, that it was extraordinary, and that no Account could be given of it" (p. 247). The significant point is not only that the cessation is a miracle but also that no account can be given of it. It is rupture not development, fitting securely into no intelligible pattern of meaning then or now.

Interpreting the *Journal* as if it recounts the experience of the plague year in isolation from a completed future meaning suggests several potential emphases for the narrative. It might focus on an immediate and private response that exists as supplementation to the public record of the plague; or it might focus on how the plague was publically understood then rather than now. Defoe's narrative interacts with both of these concerns. The plague as public disaster becomes an increasingly individual affair: "Death now began not . . . to hover over every ones Head only, but to look into their Houses, and Chambers, and stare in their Faces" (p. 34). But H.F. wishes to write of the public impact of this private fear and misery, exfoliating the private world according to standards of verifiability and bringing it within history. To achieve this intersection of private and public, he uses the figural language that places his account within the biblical master narrative, reflecting the received interpretations of the plague that identify its meaning within the contexts of both individual and national punishment and salvation. But in the interests of verifiability, he also describes the plague as fully as possible according to the canons of empirical discourse. As he transcends the private, he also implies questions about the figural, which is

---

[28] Daniel Defoe, *A Journal of the Plague Year*, ed. Louis Landa (London: Oxford University Press, 1969), "Introduction." References are to this edition.

no more verifiable than much that is reputed to occur within the closed houses.

A significant portion of Defoe's book is explicitly metanarrative, reflections of its narrator on the procedures for, and the occasion of, putting together his story of the plague.[29] The narrative is structured around his personal experiences, bringing together his direct observations and his collection of documentary evidence. His evidentiary concerns are explicit, his narration including critiques of public documents and also of presumably less authoritative private reports and even casual stories. His recurrences to his own decision to remain in London place his integrity as observer in the foreground, calling it in question through his various suspect justifications of an action that appears in many respects to be willful and rash; at the same time his unsparing exposure of his own muddy motivations validates his integrity as narrator.

H.F.'s account of the formation of the foundational document for his narrative locates it within his private memoranda, which were produced in the context of the emotional turmoil generated by the plague:

> Terrified by those frightful Objects, I would retire Home sometimes, and resolve to go out no more, and perhaps, I would keep those Resolutions for three or four Days, which Time I spent in the most serious Thankfulness for my Preservation, and the Preservation of my Family, and the constant Confession of my Sins. . . . Such intervals as I had, I employed in reading Books, and in writing down my Memorandums of what occurred to me every Day, and out of which, afterwards, I [took] most of this Work as it relates to my Observations without Doors: What I wrote of my private Meditations I reserve for private Use. (pp. 76–77)

H.F.'s desire to purge his account of the purely private reflects his chosen obligation to historical discourse, which he understands as transcending the private and restraining the hortatory, although both are necessarily embedded in the narrative.

The private is at the root of the experience of the plague and of its narration, and the didactic, hortatory functions of inculcating a recognition of its divine ordering and of fostering human mitigations of the suffering caused by the plague are the justifications for the narration; these are,

---

[29] John J. Burke Jr., "Observing the Observer in Historical Fictions by Defoe," *Philological Quarterly* 61 (1982), finds that *Memoirs of a Cavalier* and *A Journal of the Plague Year* "are not simply about their narrators. They are not simply about the history they report. They are about how they report history, about the narrators' responses to history, and these responses are the center of interest" (p. 13).

nevertheless, components regarded as subsumable in the main purpose of historical construction. H.F. suggests that the religious divisions between the conflicted protestants of England were, and could continue to be, resolved by "a near View of Death," but then retreats from this obviously hortatory view to define a purpose that is more purely historical: "I mention this but historically, I have no mind to enter into Arguments to move either, or both Sides to a more charitable Compliance one with another" (p. 176). At the inexplicable cessation of the plague, H.F. cuts short his remarks on the obligations of thankfulness to God by saying: "Perhaps it may be thought by some . . . preaching a Sermon instead of writing a History, making my self a Teacher instead of giving my Observations of things; and this restrains me very much from going on here" (p. 247). His purpose in foregrounding the historical appears to be not so much to suppress his sense of obvious moral conclusions as to create a decorum that will enable the book to be read primarily as a description of what happened according to direct evidence and only very cautiously admitted hearsay.[30] He regards both the hortatory and private aspects of his topic not as erroneous but as detractions from his "Observations of things," the empirically structured discourse that can become foundational for other reflections.

The empirically described plague year, however, is a year in which conventional sources of empirical evidence are suspect. Not only the figural but also the evidence of public documents and official numbers is inconclusive and unproductive of definitive description. H.F.'s account of the plague year appears sometimes to be an analysis of the failures of public information, and ultimately of history, in a time of plague. H.F. does, of course, record much that he regards as factual and admits even more to his account that he finds

---

[30] Robert Mayer, in his important article "The Reception of *A Journal of the Plague Year* and the Nexus of Fiction and History in the Novel," *ELH* 57 (1990), suggests that "Defoe and his publishers can reasonably be thought of as having presented this narrative to their readers as a genuine work of history" (p. 534). Our belief that "fictional elements within the text disqualify its being reasonably construed as history" is, in his view, anachronistic. Questions about the genre of the *Journal* remain insistent because "Fiction and history exist in dialogue"; because "The nexus of history and fiction is a constitutive feature of the form"; and because the *Journal* asks the question: "What is the relationship between history and fiction in novelistic discourse?" (p. 546). Lennard J. Davis, *Factual Fictions: The Origins of the English Novel* (New York: Columbia University Press, 1983), discusses a relevant issue in his chapter 3, "News/Novels: The Undifferentiated Matrix," in which he argues that the news ballads were the "first intersection of print and narrative that was a genuine product of the technology of moveable type" (p. 45). Noting an etymological relationship between "news" and "novels," Davis finds that a characteristic of news/novels discourse is a "disinclination to distinguish between fact and fiction as a signifier of genre" (p. 51). Perhaps then the *Journal*'s obtrusion of questions of genre is part of its creation of a discourse that succeeds the news/novels matrix without supplanting all of its features.

at least plausible, yet a significant part of his story may also be described as
an account of what is lost to history in this time. For example, he believes
it certain that many survived because of the charity of "well-minded
Christians" but he cannot find specific information: "But as such Multitudes
of those very Officers died, thro' whose Hands it was distributed; and also
that, as I have been told, most of the Accounts of those Things were lost in
the great Fire which happened in the very next Year, and which burnt even
the Chamberlain's Office, and many of their Papers; so I could never
come at the particular Account, which I used great Endeavours to have seen"
(p. 93).

H.F. is concerned to elucidate the components that make a meaningful
event of the plague, an event in which a baffling natural history is brought
into juxtaposition with a human history that includes values and pur-
posefulness. His view of the authority of natural philosophy and of the
human propensities to disregard it is summed up in his analysis of his own
persuasion that the comets preceeding the plague and fire had predictive
value:

> I saw both the Stars; and I must confess . . . that I was apt to look upon
> them, as the Forerunners and Warnings of Gods Judgments. . . . But I
> cou'd not at the same Time carry these Things to the heighth that others
> did, knowing too, that natural Causes are assign'd by the Astronomers for
> such Things; and that their Motions, and even their Revolutions are calcu-
> lated, or pretended to be calculated; so that they cannot be so perfectly
> call'd the Fore-runners, or Fore-tellers, much less the procurers of such
> Events, as Pestilence, War, Fire, and the like. (p. 20)

He attempts to mediate between these seemingly conflicting discourses of
religion and natural philosophy, rejecting the claims of religious "enthusiasts" that all is supernaturally contrived and also those of a naturalism that
will not speak of first causes. A perhaps overweening conclusiveness in the
claims of natural philosophy is hinted at in the phrase "calculated, or pretended to be calculated." In attempting to balance the claims of both discourses, H.F. interprets the plague figurally but attempts also to include its
natural origins and progress in his history.[31]

Crucially limiting to the possibilities for the historical in the *Journal* is the
loss of human identity in the plague. H.F. tells a story in which the baffling
but inexorable natural history of the plague gradually absorbs human history,

[31] Ilse Vickers, "The Influence of the New Sciences on Defoe," *Literature and History*
13 (1987), shows that "Defoe was familiar with the tenets of the Baconian experimental
philosophy" (p. 200).

which is dependent on a context of social organization and expectation. Human history is a constituent of the society that is its object or its audience, and is thus inconceivable without a social framework for its analysis. (As we know, what is called "natural history" is not fully distinct from "human history" but in the *Journal* H.F. attempts to keep the emphases separate.) From within the time of the plague, H.F. narrates the apparent disintegration of the structures that organize and individuate human life, leaving finally only one story to be told—that of the irrestibility of a plague whose effects are approaching the indescribable and whose causes are uncontrollable.

Economic and social conditions deprive Londoners of their categories of self-definition. Families, whether fleeing or staying, reduced or eliminated their servants, and "all Trades being stopt, Employment ceased" (p. 95). Burials are relatively early performed "promiscuously," the pressures for the disposal of bodies not allowing differentiation or memorializing (pp. 62–63). As was noted before, official documentation is suspect, and eventually people simply vanish, remaining unburied and not even included as a number in the plague toll: "It was known to us all, that abundance of poor despairing Creatures, who had the Distemper upon them . . . wandred away into the Fields, and Woods, and into secret uncouth Places, almost any where to creep into a Bush, or Hedge, and DIE" (p. 100). Returning after the plague, inquirers find that "some whole Families were so entirely swept away, that there was no Remembrance of them left" (p. 230). Moral structures too are in the process of vanishing. Despite many mitigations, exceptions, and disclaimers, H.F. acknowledges that the continuation of the plague "took away all Compassion; self Preservation indeed appear'd here to be the first Law"; this return to a Hobbesian state of nature is legitimized by a condition in which "every one had Death, as it were, at his Door" (p. 115). The final inexplicable relief from the plague comes at a time when "a few Weeks more would have clear'd the Town of all, and every thing that had a Soul: Men every where began to despair, every Heart fail'd them for Fear, People were made desperate thro' the Anguish of their Souls, and the Terrors of Death sat in the very Faces and Countenances of the People" (p. 245).

H.F. believes that "such a time as this of 1665, is not to be parallel'd in History" (p. 236), thus making it analogous only to the imagined apocalyptic. H. F.'s remark is a rationalization of his refusal to judge conduct during the plague according to moral standards that would apply in less terrifying circumstances. For him the plague year is unique and ultimately incomprehensible; yet the very judgment that it is without parallel also places it partially within the historical imagination of the narrator, who on some level finds measures of relationship possible. Events taken singly often have historical analogies; for example, H.F. uses the comparison of London to Jerusalem at the time of its destruction by Titus. What H.F. must mean is that even if specific aspects of the plague year have analogies, in its totality the plague year exceeds all seemingly analogous past events, and can thus not be represented by those historical formulations that conventionally are used to make events meaningful.[32]

The difficult position of H.F. as historian of that which exceeds the dimensions of history links him to other narrators of extreme events—the "Terror" of the French Revolution, for example, and more notably the Holocaust. The role taken is that of "witness," one who keeps in remembrance that which affronts history by not being subsumable in its conventional patterns, and defends against history's presumed tendency to normalize or to suppress.[33] H.F. thus insists on the plague year as unparalleled and not fully explicable even as he renders as fully as possible its ineluctable horrors and separates the demonstrable from mere hearsay, maintaining the reality of the experience by empirical criteria while revealing the inadequacy of history to assimilate the plague narrative to existing canons of human experience. The "witness" resists any reduction of the experience to fit the conventions of historical construal, yet insists that history must acknowledge the experience as a challenge to the limits of its understanding of existence.

Survival, then, of the witness and of the depending account is a goal that succeeds, even supersedes, the goal of understanding. H. F.'s references in his narrative to events subsequent to the plague and fire are tokens of hope in the bleakest of times, green leaves brought by a dove, harbingers of a survival that connects the world before and after the cataclysm. The sense of triumph is directly acknowledged in the final doggerel—"an Hundred Thousand Souls / Away; yet I alive!"—and is earlier more subtly underlined by an apparently interpolated note: "N.B. The Author of this Journal, lyes buried in that very Ground, being at his own Desire, his sister having been buried there a few Years before" (p. 233). This note reveals H.F.'s exemption from

---

[32] Paul K. Alkon, *Defoe and Fictional Time* (Athens: University of Georgia Press, 1979), argues that Defoe in the *Journal* "departs from previously available forms without taking a new shape which obviously 'contains' experience in an orderly way." He finds this departure "appropriate as the reflection of a time that was unlike other times by virtue of being so highly disordered" (p. 184).

[33] Paula Backscheider, *Daniel Defoe: His Life* (Baltimore: Johns Hopkins University Press, 1989), identifies H. F. as a version of the "witness," who often "bear[s] the responsibility for an alternate history": "His scornful remarks about the king and court and his criticism of some of the quarantine regulations stand in contrast to the 'history' of the time as it was offered immediately after the plague" (p. 505).

the oblivion that he describes. It interrupts his account of the expansions of the burial grounds of London during the plague and the uses to which some of these grounds were subsequently adapted, many of them now unidentifiable as burial grounds, the bodies then buried promiscuously and the very places now unremembered. H.F. states with precision where in his current London these graves are covered over, specifying also that Sir Robert Clayton was responsible for building upon one of the burial grounds:

> After which the Bones and Bodies, as fast as they came at them, were carried to another part of the same Ground, and thrown all together into a deep Pit, dug on purpose, which now is to be known, in that it is not built on, but is a Passage to another House, at the upper end of *Rose Alley*, just against the Door of a Meeting-house, which has been built there many Years since; and the Ground is palisadoed off from the rest of the Passage, in a little square, there lye the Bones and Remains of near Two thousand Bodies, carried by the Dead-Carts to their Grave in that one Year. (pp. 232–33)

H.F.'s account resists the disappearance of the major remaining evidence of the ferocity of the plague—the mass graves of the victims—while the note identifying the location of his own grave marks his evasion of the obliteration of individuality suffered by the victims promiscuously buried in sites that are subsequently disturbed but not memorialized. His survival of the plague year is personal and his exemption from the common obliteration of memory is monumental—a reiteration of his chosen function as witness.

This analysis of H.F. as witness supports Bender's contention that Defoe's "innovation" is to construct "fictions whose contents are not consistent with reference to any moral but only with reference to a central consciousness" (*Imagining the Penitentiary*, p. 49). Bender goes on to argue that the construction by this central consciousness of a moral world despite the depiction of "materially realistic conditions that erode or even contradict it" purveys the ideology "that such representational constructions [of the moral world] are real and material in themselves" (pp. 49–50). Thus Bender implies that Defoe's *Journal* participates in the development of a society in which authority acquires the reputation of omniscience because unconstrained by a clear demarcation of its limits. However compelling this view of the "novelization" of eighteenth-century society appears, Defoe's *Journal* resists it. As witness, H.F. exposes the incommensurability of human moral structures with the plague, rather than concealing their factitiousness, and his frequent accounts of the activities of the authorities often pay tribute to their well-meaningness but usually also emphasize their ineffectuality. His attempts to link private to public in a complete history reveal the limitations of this enterprise in the face of the great plague, rather than recommend or even insinuate the efficacy of analytico-referential ordering. While empirical observation is assumed without debate to be an appropriate form of discourse, its limits, rather more than its triumphs, are shown.

Bender's analysis rests on the assumption that whatever H.F. states, his *Journal* recommends the values of isolated self-scrutiny, with the object of bringing self and authority into congruence:

> In H.F. we witness the private self being constituted narratively through isolated reflection on its relation to circumstance; individual personality appears as the internal restatement of external authority, as a principle of order in face of chaos, comprehension in face of the arbitrary, representation in face of endless disordered perception, a principle of life as opposed to death, reformation as opposed to execution. (p. 77)

The two strands of this analysis should perhaps be separated: first, the constitution of the self, and, second, the relation of self to authority. The construction of the private self described here applies to H.F. and also to Christian (as well as to other selves from spiritual autobiography), whose isolation begets a changed identity and results in a program to conform to authority. Christian does not, however, fully fit the strand of Bender's analysis that relates to authority because he conforms to an authority outside civil authority and to a great extent opposed to it; it would thus be tendentious to deny that H.F. is far more implicated in civil authority than Christian is (despite the notable impingements of the contemporary historical scene on Bunyan's book). But H.F.'s isolated meditations do not imply either a validation of isolation or of civil authority. Isolation is recognized as an impediment to his understanding of the plague. Although it does produce apparently beneficial reflection (as Bender suggests), it nevertheless leads to little sense of comprehension: "I cannot speak positively of these Things; because these were only the dismal Objects which represented themselves to me as I look'd thro' my Chamber Windows" (p. 103). The adjudication of the figural and empirical discourses requires that he both reflect on the plague and also enter the public spaces in order to observe it; he cannot accede to the kind of incarceration that Bender finds is the book's recommendation, but is torn between his desires to isolate himself from the dangers of the plague and his compulsion to observe it by becoming a participant in the public experience of it.

H.F.'s recommendation is that of *The Pilgrim's Progress*—flee: "tho' Providence seem'd to direct my Conduct to be otherwise; yet it is my opinion, and I must leave it as a Prescription, *(viz.) that the best Physick against the Plague is to run away from it"* (pp. 197–98). He here regards his own decision to remain as possibly providentially motivated, yet he has already repented of it. Encountering a waterman who remained to preserve his wife and child, H.F. decides that his own decision to remain to preserve his business was "meer Presumption, his a true Dependance, and a Courage resting on God" (p. 108). The inserted story of the three men from Stepney is a miniature version of the wanderings of the Israelites and illustrates H.F.'s recommendation to flee the plague.[34] This recommendation is not one of subservience to civil authority, any more than Bunyan's is, but of evasion and resistance, as necessary, to the civil authorities both of London and the surrounding towns. H.F.'s own conflicted decision to remain illustrates the clash of discourses that is stabilized in his assumption of his role as witness.

The plague, like the City of Destruction, must be fled if Salvation is to be achieved, yet understanding can only be based on empiricist description. Such description, however, records an experience of bafflement and horror, thus reinforcing the admonition to flee. Defoe's *Journal*, then, illustrates powerfully one of the functions of eighteenth-century fiction—describing in analytico-referential discourse those human experiences that yield themselves easily but no longer entirely satisfactorily to figural interpretation. But rather than unquestioningly representing the triumph of empiricism, the new fiction also exposes its limits, contesting the adequacy of this emergent and finally dominant ideology to analyze exhaustively the kind of experience represented in the novel. The novel shares with history, then, the problem of representing human experience in a manner that uses the resources of the new epistemology, yet avoids reducing that experience to the limits of the empirical.

[34] See Everett Zimmerman, *Defoe and the Novel* (Berkeley: University of California Press, 1975), chap. 5, for a fuller analysis of figural aspects of Defoe's *Journal*.

CHAPTER 3

A Battle of Books: Swift's *Tale* and Richardson's *Clarissa*

A Tale of a Tub and *Clarissa* are unlikely yokemates, yet as Swift perceived, opposites are prone to meet. The clashes of these two books exemplify conflicting elements of the arguments of Sir William Temple and William Wotton, the principal antagonists in the ancients and moderns controversy of late-seventeenth-century England. While less directly engaged in these issues on behalf of the moderns than Swift, Temple's protégé, had been on behalf of the ancients, Richardson explicitly acknowledges his hostility to his predecessor. Nearly a half century after the publication of the *Tale*, Richardson expresses his antagonism to Swift in *Clarissa*, once directly in a footnote and elsewhere by allusions associating Swift's *Tale* with Lovelace. And Richardson encouraged the writing of, and then published, one of the final salvos of the ancients and moderns controversy, Young's *Conjectures on Original Composition*, which repeatedly cites Swift denigratingly, while extolling the moderns' potential for greatness and including Richardson among examples of modern excellence.

The late-seventeenth-century battle of the "ancients and moderns" in England may be baldly summarized as one between two views of history—that of the humanists, who valued knowledge of the past only insofar as it was intrinsically valuable for the present, and that of the antiquaries, who valued whatever understanding of the past became available no matter how estranged from present concerns. Richard Bentley, the great classical scholar and a principal combatant in the controversy, exemplifies much that was associated with antiquarianism. In his *Dissertation* attached to the second edition of William Wotton's *Reflections upon Ancient and Modern Learning*, he exposed the spuriousness of the epistles of Phalaris with a thoroughness that many thought inappropriate to the seeming inconsequentiality of the task. Bentley's analysis pointed to the implausible hiatuses in the history of the transmission of the text and to historical anachronisms, including references to inappropriate coins and the use of an inappropriate dialect. Among Bentley's achievements, C. O. Brink remarks, are his demonstrations that "not only literary genres . . . have a 'history', but also stylistic forms of language such as the Attic and neo-Attic. . . . Even words come to be seen historically."[1]

An Essay Concerning Curious and Critical Learning, written by someone identified only as T.R., presumably not one of the principals in the ancients and moderns controversy, gives some sense of what the views of the more traditional among the educated observers may have been. This writer values history for "conveying down such Notices and Observations from Antiquity, as may be of Service in the Conduct of all future Occurrences in Humane Life"; however he cannot understand why anyone cares "whether *Homer* or *Hesiod* did really live first."[2] From his perspective, those who have traced "the rise and progress of *Words*; and have written Volumes concerning particular *Letters*" have "miserably lost their time" (p. 8). The knowledge of the antiquaries is in his view "at best but Uncertain and Conjectural, being drawn out of defaced *Monuments*, *Coins*, *Inscriptions*, *Calendars*, *Traditions*, *Archives*, *Fragments*, and scattered passages of lost Books" (p. 16).

This particular commentator emphasizes the stodginess as well as the hypothetical nature of antiquarian scholarship. But Bentley was capable of unintentional self-parody, which was easily taken advantage of by his enemies. His edition of Milton still strikes many as scholarship gone mad, a proto–*Pale Fire*. Bentley argues for four sets of errors—those committed by the amenuensis, by the bookseller/printer, by a "friend," and by Milton himself. The "friend" is metamorphosed into an "editor," even without any more substantial evidence of his existence than that changes for the worse are introduced in the second edition: "If anyone fancy this *Persona* of an Editor to be a mere Fantom, a fiction, an Artifice to skreen *Milton* himself; let him consider these four and sole Changes made in the second Edition."[3] This "editor" is in Bentley's view easily isolated, for the "Editor's Interpola-

---

[1] C. O. Brink, *English Classical Scholarship: Historical Reflections on Bentley, Porson, and Housman* (New York: Oxford University Press, 1985), p. 59.

[2] *An Essay Concerning Critical and Curious Learning* (London: R. Cumberland, 1698), pp. 15, 16. The author, identified as T.R., Esq., also dislikes Bentley's antagonist Boyle, finding that the controversy was "prosecuted with as much Heat and Contention on both sides, as if some article of Eternal Life was immediately concerned in it" (p. 54).

[3] Richard Bentley, *Milton's Paradise Lost: A New Edition* (London: Tonson, 1732), "Preface." William Empson, *Some Versions of Pastoral* (New York: New Directions, 1960), pp. 141–

tions are detected by their own Silliness and Unfitness" and can be "cured by printing them in the Italic letter, and inclosing them between two Hooks." Milton, however, creates more formidable problems, and his "Slips and Inadvertancies cannot be redress'd without a Change both of the Words and Sense." Here was ample material for the satirists, and they helped themselves to it.

The satire of the earlier eighteenth century allied itself with the older view of history, in contrast to the novel's tendency to make an alliance with the newer historicism. Satire parodied the fragmentation created by the Bentleyan scholars, whereas the novel often created a narrative web out of apparent fragments.[4] Swift's *Tale of a Tub* mocks the claim that a tattered, fragmented text can be raised to significance by annotation and interpretation, and it scorns Richard Bentley as well as other historicists who appear to value authenticity and exactitude above coherence. Perhaps the salient eighteenth-century attack on historicist scholarship is Pope's *Dunciad*. Modern scribblers appear in a text that is annotated in distracting detail, parodically resembling a text edited according to Bentley's or Theobald's principles and thus ridiculing the self-display of the scholar who produces fragmentation rather than a more complete version of what is already known.[5]

Eighteenth-century novelistic fiction, on the other hand, frequently aligns itself with the historicist scholarship by simulating a concern for documentary authenticity. Richardson and Sterne, for example, attempt to define the proveniences of their fictional texts, locating them in precise relationship to their narrators. Apparently fragmented texts—letters, interpolated documents, and truncated tales—then find their place in a coherent scheme that may be called an editorial performance as well as an authorial one. Sterne's

---

83, takes Bentley's criticisms of Milton seriously: "English critics adopt a curious air of social superiority to Bentley; he is the Man who said the Tactless Thing. There seems no doubt that he raised several important questions about Milton's use of language" (p. 149).

[4] The novel's alliance with the newer historicism is not programmatic or consistent. As John F. Tinkler has shown in "Humanist History and the English Novel in the Eighteenth Century," *Studies in Philology* 85 (1988): 510–37, eighteenth-century fiction often defines itself as if it were humanist rhetorical history that focuses on character in contrast to antiquarianism. I would, however, add that the novel also is responsive to, even imitative of, evidentiary issues of historiography that derive from the antiquarian tradition travestied by Swift and Pope. J. Paul Hunter, *Before Novels: The Cultural Contexts of Eighteenth-Century English Fiction* (New York: W. W. Norton, 1990), studies the cultural contexts for the modernism represented in the novel, defining an "Augustan moment in English culture" that puts the question of ancients against moderns in a way that "modernity had to answer if in fact a modern literature was to develop" (p. 26).

[5] See Joseph M. Levine, *The Battle of the Books: History and Literature in the Augustan Age* (Ithaca: Cornell University Press, 1991), chap. 7, "Pope and the Quarrel between the Ancients and the Moderns," for discussion of Pope and Theobald.

mockery allies him with Swift in some respects, yet his narrator's construction of his story in relation to historicist procedures is not represented as merely aberrant even if it is made the matter of comedy. While there is a strong element of parody in Sterne, the entire editorial performance is never fully assimilable to parody. Authenticity, in addition to (sometimes instead of) the more abstract, universal truths of the satirists, is this fiction's apparent claim. Fielding is the exception, for he self-consciously adopts a stance opposing the kind of novelistic fiction here described; he presents an architectonic structure that subsumes the fragmentation that appears in the near view. Nevertheless, his fiction is also a demonstration that coherence depends on a narrator who brings the fragments of existence to meaning through a process of selection and evaluation.

The contrast between Swift and Richardson exemplifies many of these differences that arise from the conflicting versions of history underlying the ancients and moderns controversy. An apparent point of entry into the complex system of differences that divides and unites these two writers is through their responses to the modern literary establishment, which is increasingly molded by the social and economic consequences of the technology of printing.[6] Printing was, of course, a significant part of Richardson's identity. He managed his professional responsibilities, which included aspects of what we would now call publishing as well as printing, with consummate skill, and as author benefited from his own ministrations.[7] The proliferation of prefaces, dedications, notes, and other addenda that Swift replicates scornfully as evidence of the corruptions brought by the the press (although in justice one must note that Swift found similar corruptions resulting from patronage too) are skillfully manipulated by Richardson for the advantage of his own reputation and what he thought of as the proper reception of his works. A *Pamela* and, especially, a *Clarissa* with all their accretions resemble in this respect *A Tale of a Tub*, but what Richardson

---

[6] Alvin Kernan, *Printing Technology, Letters and Samuel Johnson* (Princeton: Princeton University Press, 1987), argues that the full social impact of the invention of printing was not felt until the late seventeenth and early eighteenth centuries when "the more advanced countries of Europe [were transformed] from oral into print societies, reordering the entire social world, and restructuring rather than merely modifying letters" (p. 9). Mark Rose, *Authors and Owners: The Invention of Copyright* (Cambridge: Harvard University Press, 1993), analyzes the changing roles of the author as patronage declined and authors increasingly supported themselves by writing for the enlarged reading public: "The literary-property question was a legal and commercial struggle, but it was also a contest between representations of authorship at a time when writings were becoming commodities" (p. 104).

[7] William M. Sale Jr., *Samuel Richardson: Master Printer* (Ithaca: Cornell University Press, 1950), surveys major aspects of Richardson's printing career and lists books known to have been printed by his press.

regards as support of his text is from a perspective like Swift's a symptom of textual spuriousness, a failing effort to nudge inconsequential writing into significance. And running through Swift's writings are the irritable whines of authors or putative authors directed at booksellers and printers, who lose manuscripts, print the names wrong, make promises they can't or won't keep, and see the purpose of making books as selling them.[8]

Attitudes toward the significance and consequences of the printing press mark important points of divergence between Sir William Temple and William Wotton in the controversy that fueled the *Tale*. In *An Essay upon the Ancient and Modern Learning* (1690), Temple represents the printing press as irrelevant to the propagation of true knowledge. He believed that the ancients were likely to have had just as many books as the moderns; seeming differences in numbers are accounted for by the many ancient writings that have been destroyed. The printing press merely proliferates *copies*, not books. Furthermore, many existing books are themselves repetitious: "Few . . . can pretend to be authors rather than transcribers or commentators of the ancient learning."[9] And Temple rejects the view that books are essential to learning; not only could much have been transmitted through oral tradition, but also books are "dead instructors" (p. 41). Wotton in contrast emphasizes the crucial importance of modern technology for the advancement and mediation of learning—the telescope, microscope, engraving, and, most important of all, printing: "The Use of *Printing* has been so vast, that every thing else wherein the Moderns have pretended to excel the Ancients, is almost entirely owing to it."[10] Included in his rehearsal of the conventional advantages of books over manuscripts are their cheapness, readability, and textual accuracy. Among the less conventionally prominent conveniences of books that Wotton cites are that notices of their publication are dispersed, thus bringing them to the attention of those seeking learning, and that they often include indexes and "other necessary Divisions" too cumbersome for manuscripts, which enable desired information to be found expeditiously (pp. 171–72). These latter economically motivated and techno-

---

[8] Pat Rogers, *Grub Street: Studies in a Subculture* (London: Methuen, 1972), studies the satirists' responses to the writing and publishing culture of the early eighteenth century known as "Grub Street." He deals specifically with Swift's responses to hack writers in *A Tale of a Tub* in chap. 4, "Swift and the Scribbler" (pp. 220–35). Angus Ross, "The Books in the *Tale*: Swift and Reading in *A Tale of a Tub*," in *Proceedings of the First Münster Symposium on Jonathan Swift*, ed. Hermann J. Real and Hans J. Vienken (München: Wilhelm Fink, 1985), pp. 209–16, examines the "sense of a world of books" in the *Tale*.

[9] *Five Miscellaneous Essays by Sir William Temple*, ed. Samuel Holt Monk (Ann Arbor: University of Michigan Press, 1963), p. 41.

[10] William Wotton, *Reflections upon Ancient and Modern Learning* (London, 1694; facsimile edition, Hildesheim: Georg Olms, 1968), pp. 170–71.

logical conveniences of books are notable objects of Swift's later satiric attack.

Wotton's lengthy refutation of Temple encompasses many of their conflicting views of history, yet a significant number of the disputed issues can be connected to, or exfoliated from, their divergent views concerning the seemingly narrower subject of printing. Wotton rejects Temple's belief that human learning can be preserved over a long period of time without some form of inscribed communication (p. 82), finding implausible Temple's theory that great civilizations and masses of learning were orally based and have now entirely disappeared. Wotton's implied view is that any civilization leaves behind interpretable traces: "The History of Learning is not so lamely conveyed to us, but so much would, in all probability, have escaped the general Ship-wrack, as that, by what was saved, we might have been able to guess at what was lost" (p. 139). The intricacy of such guessing requires the full apparatus of philology, which Wotton finds to be one of the glories of the moderns. This means for understanding a past from which the printing press is missing is dependent for its development, however, on the invention of printing. With printing, books that were available previously only in a relatively few manuscripts can be compared and examined with ease, and they are no longer in danger of being lost or "hurt by Copiers" (p. 312). Thus Scaliger, Casaubon, and others "may have had a very comprehensive View of Antiquity . . . a much greater than, taken together, any one of the Ancients themselves ever had" (p. 312).

Perhaps Swift's fullest exploitation of a potential absurdity in Wotton's argument with Temple is related to Wotton's praise of the moderns' philological knowledge. Swift finds the moderns' self-congratulation on philological knowledge—a knowledge with the end of recovering what the past was already fully in possession of—to be absurdly paradoxical. But Wotton finds no absurdity whatsoever in the notion that knowing the ancients means that we know more than the ancients did: "For the Ancients did not live all in one Age . . . upon a nearer View, they will be found very remote each from the other; and so as liable to Mistakes when they talk of Matters not transacted in their own Times" (pp. 311–12). The issue then is whether moderns understand their past better than the ancients understood theirs, a question that Wotton decides in favor of the moderns, noting that the moderns have detected and corrected mistakes about chronology and geography in apparently authentic ancient writers (p. 315). Wotten is arguing for a history that does not merely reprise evidence from the writings of others, but attempts to achieve an understanding of the past not possible even to those then alive; in short, he argues for a criticism that is based on the wide readings and comparisons that were possible only "when Copies of Books, by Printing, were pretty well multiplied" (p. 319).

The multiplication of books is not, however, without its own problems. The responses of Temple and Wotten to ancient and modern learning can be regarded as attempts to subdue the anxieties produced by a proliferation of books. Temple's wish to accept a canon that reduces modern books to relative unimportance and calmly acquiesces in the irrecoverability of large portions of antiquity is a way of keeping learning within boundaries that are masterable. Not only need he not deal with large numbers of modern books that from his perspective are inevitably repetitious, but he may also safely ignore modern realignments of the boundaries of the canon: questioning of the existing canon is in Temple's view highly conjectural and merely pedantic. But if modern critical philology in Wotton's sense is taken seriously, antiquity is rendered an unsteady concept requiring constant adjustment, the fragmentary not safely confined to the irrecoverable nor the seemingly whole sequestered from potential fragmentation. Temple's very acquiescence in loss stabilizes a canon by placing limits on what may be learned about it. For Wotton, on the other hand, critical philology can potentially incorporate a newly understood ancient world into the remarkably expanded modern one. But just as Temple wishes to reduce the modern intellectual world to manageable dimensions by setting up against it an overshadowing but largely lost, and thus unchangeable, ancient world, Wotton too must find ways to comprehend the overwhelming modern world that he is constituting. Yet incipient in both Temple and Wotton is this question, Who can possibly truly assimilate the vast knowledge that is claimed in potentiality?

Wotton's sense of a rapidly expanding knowledge—books begetting books—focuses attention on what our more recent moderns call information retrieval and management. Wotton, like the philologists he praises, is alert to the retrieval of summary accounts that make possible the assimilation of the learning even of writers whose books have been lost. Within a single book he can find layerings of history that suggest at least the outlines of not fully known, yet not entirely lost, intellectual worlds. For example, Pliny included abstracts of others' writings on natural history; Galen listed the views of others on medicine; and Ptolemy gave an account of the old astronomy (p. 85). On the other hand, Temple's view that the modern world is unlikely to produce as many *lasting* original books as those in the Ptolemaean library is criticized by Wotton on a number of grounds, including Temple's possibly anachronistic view of what constitutes a volume in the catalog of an ancient library (pp. 82–83). Wotton's ambitious endeavor is to encompass ancient learning without diminishing either ancient or modern learning; modern learning, after all, is the precondition for the retrieval of the ancient.

Wotton makes central to modern achievement the ordering of information, which is not just needed for the retrieval but also for the constitution of knowledge: "The Moderns have made clearer and shorter Institutions of all Manner of Arts and Sciences than any which the Ancients have left us" (p. 337). Ancient observations in natural history, for example, have been made useful by modern organization and classification. Pliny uses systems of classification that "signifie nothing to the Understanding of the Characteristical Differences of the several Plants" (p. 254); in contrast, John Ray develops a system for ordering descriptions of plants that enables an observer to "consider those Things Philosophically, and comprehend the whole Vegetable Kingdom . . . under one View" (p. 256). The advantages of a methodical classification include the acquiring of knowledge about the unknown through the classification system itself: an unfamiliar plant will be better understood by means of the system that orders information about it. But adaptation to human capabilities is also at issue, as an inadequate system of classification makes knowledge depend too much "upon an uncommon Strength of Memory and Imagination" (p. 254). Elsewhere, Wotton remarks too that "Abridgements" in mathematics "save Abundance of Labour, and make Knowledge pleasant" (p. 338).

Wotton's own book is a compendium of others' achievements, designed to give a survey of all the kingdoms of knowledge, ancient and modern. His remarkably confident Baconian purpose is to facilitate the identification of those areas of investigation that may be most profitably pursued, "By which Means, Knowledge, in all its Parts, might at last be compleated" (Preface). In surveying the achievements of the Royal Society, he recommends a selection of books that will suffice "if it shall be thought too tedious a Work to examine all their Writings"; then realizing that even his pared list may be too long, he recommends a single book "to comprehend all under one," *Philosophia Vetus et Nova ad Usum Scholae accommodata* (written by Jean-Baptiste DuHamel), which will adequately substantiate his views (p. 307). Even as he praises the achievements of modernity, he betrays an anxiety about their possibly unassimilable quantity that is not fully allayed by modern skills in abridgment and indexing. As, for example, he describes the achievements of philology, Wotton expresses not only a sense of plenitude but also of loss of control: his description of "The *Bodleyan* and *Leyden-* Libraries," which "can witness what vast Heaps of *Eastern MSS.* have been brought . . . into *Europe*," hints at chaos in the cataloguing department of the library's manuscript division. Wotton's recognition of the difficulties in providing orderly access to these materials is followed by his reflections on the problems of summarizing the multitudinous productions of modern philology that result from these heaped manuscripts: "One would think I were drawing up a

Catalogue . . . if I should enumerate the Books which have been printed about the *Oriental* Learning, within these last Seventy Years" (p. 314). His own survey, even if at times summary of summary, is hard pressed to comprehend the volume of modern learning.

As we moderns know too well, inaccessible or unassimilable information is only another form of ignorance. However complete in a theoretical way knowledge may be, it counts only to the extent that it is appropriated. As Wotton praises the increase of knowledge, he is also intuiting its approaching fragmentation. The possibility of the completion of knowledge that he, like Bacon and others, asserts is a way of imagining a static state that coheres without disintegrating. Thus Wotton *and* Temple are seeking a form of "sufficiency," the vice Temple finds particularly characteristic of moderns and regards as their motive for attempting to detach themselves from the ancients.

The conceptual apparatus for managing information entails systematic devices not only for maintaining information but also for gathering it into wholes and for reducing it to fragments, which are then recombinable into previously unanticipated wholes.[11] The indexed book, for example, enables its user either to accept the book's apparent purposive arrangement or to use the words and topics of an index to rearrange its structure and modify its purported function. Such rearrangement may be used in the interest of a simplification of detail, thus allowing a reduction in the time alloted to the book, or it may be used in the interest of applying the book to a purpose that does not correspond precisely to its ostensible one. In either case the whole is fragmented in a way that evades the full authorial conception as embodied in the written book, although indexical devices may also entail authorial collusion. The index permitting such simplification and reorganization ordinarily places words from the book, and words for other concepts that are designated to represent the book, in alphabetical order, using this arbitrary alphabetical scheme to make the book's contents accessible to the widest variety of counterorganization. A concordance is a kind of index allowing access to a book by means of a rearrangement of all the words in it, thus facilitating a questioning of the book on grounds not exclusively topical: what subject areas are its vocabulary drawn from; what do the proper names suggest about geographical and ethnic variety, for some examples. Such indexing is, however, ordinarily selective rather than complete, and is

---

[11] For an extension of some of the concepts discussed here into the realm of recent technology, see George P. Landow and Paul Delaney, "Hypertext, Hypermedia and Literary Studies: The State of the Art," in *Hypermedia and Literary Studies* (Cambridge: MIT Press, 1991), pp. 3–50.

supplemented by topical listings that direct attention to what the writer conceives of as the book's conceptual and substantive content. A topical listing represents an interpretation of the book, a selection designed to be at the appropriate level of abstraction to make portions of the book available to those deemed to be using it properly. The listing must, of course, be at a lower level of abstraction than chapter or sub-chapter headings in order not to be redundant. On the other hand, it needs to be high enough in generality to be usable by those who have only a subject area in mind and do not know the precise level of information they are seeking. As the level of generality diminishes, individual units signify less of their context. The lower the level of abstraction, that is, the smaller the unit of information that is indexed, the more easily the book will yield itself to purposes far from those embodied in its organization. The reduction to absurdity of such specificity is represented by the movement through an alphabetically organized concordance to, finally, the letters of the words themselves. At this stage the arbitrary organizing device of the index and the signifying devices of the book have melted into each other with all context lost. Meaning is then fragmented below indexical recovery.

For the purposes of his satire, Swift represents both Wotton's quantitative estimate of the proliferation of modern books and Temple's qualitative views of the repetitiousness of modern learning. He expresses these views by figuring modern books as bales of paper, which metonymically constitute two alimentary metaphors: books are a bare livelihood or, ultimately, mere refuse, depending on whether the paper is used as bread wrapping or ends in a jakes.[12] Grub Street is the world of the garret, of fasting, and of an overwhelming need that hints at the urgencies of defecation: "*Considering my urgent necessities*, what . . . might be acceptable this month" (p. 207). The modern learning garnered from books and needed to produce them is acquired by reading titles or, preferably, getting "a thorough Insight into the *Index*, by which the whole Book is governed" (p. 145). Indexes are characterized as "*Back-Door*" learning, the usually shameful but nevertheless urgent end of the human trunk, which end is shared with the source of the sole modern contribution to writing, "deducing Similitudes, Allusions, and Applications . . . from the *Pudenda* of either Sex" (p. 147). As the "Digression in Praise of Digressions" illustrates in form and content, the applauded modern production of books is enabled by indexes, compendiums, quotations, lexicons, systems, and abstracts—all seemingly

[12] Jonathan Swift, *A Tale of a Tub*, 2d ed., ed. A. C. Guthkelch and D. Nichol Smith (Oxford: Clarendon Press, 1958), pp. 35–36.

second-order forms of information ordering and retrieval that Wotton regarded as facilitators of progress, but which Swift represents as forms of degenerative repetition.

Yet for quantitative reasons, these books are not, despite their seeming evanescence, benignly biodegradable. The regularizing of the new forms of learning has increased the number of writers, thus allowing their existence as quantity to withstand their self-canceling repetitiveness. However vacuous, airy, or elusive modern books are in the *Tale*, they are also an oppressive presence, from their representation as "Bales of Paper" in the "Epistle Dedicatory" (p. 35) through the proliferation of titles in the course of the narration. Although books have many ways of leaving the world, they are also a swarming if useless presence within it. For example, the *Tale*'s opening includes a list of eleven treatises written by its author and waiting to be published, which titles the narrator reiterates as extensions or preemptions of topics discussed throughout the succeeding text; and in the "Introduction," a competing modern, John Dunton, is announced to be preparing the publication of twelve folio volumes of the speeches of condemned criminals (p. 59). Combined with the constant references to multitudinous other productions of Grub Street and the acknowledgment of the vast numbers of books that are ransacked to produce even one more book, such persistent reference to the burgeoning of books evokes a claustrophobic sense of a paper world closing in on nature, truly creating a need for a tale of a tub to amuse those dangerous wits "appointed . . . with Pen, Ink, and Paper" (p. 39).

The "modern's" anxiety in response to the constant production of printed materials is premised on Swift's reduction to absurdity of the notion that the most recent is most authoritative. The narrator of the *Tale* claims that "as the *freshest Modern*" he has "a Despotick Power over all Authors before" (p. 130), a view that permits him to retain his authority only as long as he continues to write. Temple, in contrast, allows only a very modest sphere for modern authority: the occasional genius, Pico della Mirandola, for example, may rival the ancients, but most modern writing has only that authority which it has derived from the ancients. (Temple, *Essays*, p. 67). While not necessarily definitive on all matters, ancient writers provide a standard for the evaluation of modern achievements; consequently, modern writings that connect themselves to ancient authority are enhanced by it, and writings that exceed its parameters have an unusual burden of proof placed upon them. Moderns who attack the ancients are to Temple analogous to the Goths or Vandals who defaced the "admirable statues of those ancient heroes of Greece or Rome, which had so long preserved their memories honoured."[13] Temple makes a monument of the classics, using them to stabilize a post-Renaissance cultural construct that validates his views and supports the social structure from which his eminence (now somewhat diminished) had derived. Thus any new understanding of the classics is potentially threatening.

Swift's satiric conflation of modern repetitiveness and productiveness leads to a version of the human mind and endeavor that is both energetic and circular: "The mind of Man . . . sallies out into both extreams of High and Low" but eventually the extremes meet "like one who travels the *East* into the *West*; or like a strait Line drawn by its own Length into a Circle" (pp. 157–58). The circular image is one of imprisonment within a restrictive pattern that permits no escape from the limitations of Temple's world, Wotton's version of supersession being from Temple's perspective merely fruitless emulation. As W. B. Carnochan remarks, "This parody of the happy prison comes close to being the real thing."[14] "The Digression concerning . . . Madness" presents innovation as the effort of an overturned reason, whereas "the Brain, in its natural Position . . . disposeth its Owner to pass his Life in the common Forms" (p. 171), presumably without any serious desire to escape from this confinement. Yet happiness is dependent on delusion, "*the Possession of being well deceived*" (p. 174). The treadmill of language that results from Swift's conflation of Temple's static world and Wotton's world of unceasing endeavor is unbearable.

The culminating subject of the *Tale* is exhaustion—of narrator and of the narrated, but perhaps not of narration itself: "I am now trying an Experiment very frequent among Modern Authors; which is, *to write upon Nothing*; When the Subject is utterly exhausted, to let the Pen still move on" (p. 208). The writing meanders until it concludes in the decision to "here pause awhile, till I find, by feeling the World's Pulse, and my own, that it will be of absolute Necessity for us both, to resume my Pen" (p. 210). Exhaustiveness generates exhaustion, but in a world of repetitiveness not necessarily completion. Exhaustiveness may be attempted either by the multiplication of summaries or the extension of commentary. Within this tubbian interpretive framework, a book can recapitulate the many texts of the larger world or the commentator may exfoliate complexities from within a seemingly inert single text. The aim of the *Tale* as announced in the "Epistle Dedicatory" is to give to posterity a "faithful Abstract drawn from the Universal Body of all

---

[13] This quotation is from *Some Thoughts upon Reviewing the Essay of Ancient and Modern Learning*, a posthumously published work of Temple's that was prepared for the press by Swift. It is here cited from Monk's edition, p. 72.

[14] W. B. Carnochan, *Confinement and Flight: An Essay on English Literature of the Eighteenth Century* (Berkeley: University of California Press, 1977), p. 91.

Arts and Sciences" (p. 38); abstracts, however, are linked to past texts and can be made to encompass posterity only through the constant interpretive efforts of the commentator.

When Homer, like many epic poets thought to be a master of the learning of his time, is dealt with as if a summarizer, the narrator finds many omissions (p. 127). He demands that his *Tale* be accorded a different, more personalized, treatment: he has opened his vein for the universal benefit of mankind, and he invites his readers to find in his book whatever meanings they need: "The Reader truly *Learned* . . . will here find sufficient Matter to employ his Speculations for the rest of his Life. . . . [S]even ample Commentaries on this comprehensive Discourse . . . will be all, without the least Distortion, manifestly deduceable from the Text" (pp. 184, 185). His embodied text is to be treated like a sacred text in which, through commentary, all essential meanings are to be found. Thus the *Tale* will contain a summary of all past knowledge and will also exfoliate all future knowledge through the efforts of the skilled reader. Although digressions and tale are not systematically discriminated by theme, the digressions, especially those "in the Modern Kind" and "in Praise of Digressions" tend to explore the possibilities and liabilities of repetitiveness, of summary, whereas the allegorical tale of the three brothers explores the possibilities and liabilities of commentary.

In the allegory, the Will is presented as a document from which the brothers are expected to infer subsequent appropriate conduct. The interpretive value apparently enjoined is simplicity, and the valorized method of interpretation is literality. The brothers, however, find various ways to accommodate the Will's literality to a larger range of meanings. Behind many of their expedients is the historicist perception that meaning must be adjusted in relation to language and culture if intention is to be preserved beyond its origin: for example, "These Figures were not at all the *same* with those that were formerly worn, and were meant in the Will" (p. 89). Their interpretive choices are not entirely untrammeled, however, for we learn that the Will already exists in a context of prior commentary about coats: the brothers need a positive precept to change the lining, "the Lining being held by Orthodox Writers to be of the Essence of the Coat" (p. 87). Among the various methods that they use to find positive precepts in the Will are ones referred to earlier in this chapter as implicit in an index—a reduction to components with the aim of adapting information to purposes not necessarily included in authorial intention. As the father's apparent intention becomes increasingly difficult to evade, they reduce the Will to words—a concordance—then to syllables and finally to an alphabet in order to make their meanings out of its presumably still authoritative language. As even these techniques are too restrictive for the intensity of their desires, they eventually lock the Will away (pp. 83–84, 89–90).

The reader's relationship to the Will is to allegory, whereas the brothers' relationship is to a literal Will. When the brothers subject the Will to allegoresis, we see, according to the allegory, that they are misinterpreting, placing their multiple wills before their father's singular one. A literal perspective is privileged within the allegory, whereas the reader is asked to interpret an allegory.[15] The allegory as a whole has a defined focus on the development of Christianity, but, nevertheless, the literal narrative of the three brothers and their hermeneutical adventures within an allegory suggest a less focused interpretation than that imposed by the historical pretext of a Church of England version of church history. The clothes philosophy, introduced as part of the explanation for the brothers' complex and willful deformations of literal interpretation, implies ambiguities in the status of the Will itself. The Will, dealing as it does with coats, has the answers to all exigencies of human life only if the clothes philosophy, which figures a hypocritical emphasis on appearance, is in some sense authoritative and comprehensive. Otherwise presumably the brothers' following of their father's Will might remain a piety, but it could not be the decisive issue in their existence. But in a world in which the clothes philosophy prevails and in response to a Will in which the wearing of coats is the central concern, the brothers must find in that Will a complete institute of clothes, and clothes themselves must be allegorized to include much else.[16] The Will must be interpreted in a way that authorizes a literal capable of enabling an allegory that encompasses existence itself.[17]

Elizabeth L. Eisenstein remarks that the multiplication of books made possible by printing allowed scholars to be less "engrossed by a single text. . . . The era of the glossator and commentator came to an end" and was succeeded by comparison and compilation as more characteristic scholarly activities.[18] In the *Tale* Swift finds both kinds of activity to be similarly

---

[15] Richard Nash, "Entrapment and Ironic Modes in *A Tale of a Tub*," *Eighteenth-Century Studies* 24 (1991), concludes that "a reader hoping to work out the meaning of the text must be willing alternately to accept and reject the literal meanings of the text without falling into the easy codes of a strictly allegorical or a strictly ironic interpretation" (p. 431).

[16] Deborah Baker Wyrick, *Jonathan Swift and the Vested Word* (Chapel Hill: University of North Carolina Press, 1988), describes the clothes as "intertextual signs, reaching beyond their host textile to link with other orders of meaning. They act, in other words, like words" (p. 132).

[17] For additional comment on these topics, see Everett Zimmerman, *Swift's Narrative Satires: Author and Authority* (Ithaca: Cornell University Press, 1983), chap. 2, "The Hermeneutics of Self."

[18] Elizabeth L. Eisenstein, *The Printing Revolution in Early Modern Europe* (Cambridge: Cambridge University Press, 1983), p. 42.

perverted by the desire for totalization, a version of "sufficiency." The brothers use what we take to be an allegory as if it were an encyclopedia. The aim of the encyclopedia is to be all-encompassing and discursive, to arrange all available knowledge according to a scheme that will make portions of it accessible for any purpose. Allegoresis, on the other hand, allows a single text to imply increasing complexity, but it does not permit totality unless founded upon a radically allegorical conception of reality in which any element of the world is connected to every element—the kind of allegory Augustine implies when he finds that words point to things and that things, including words, each have their own meanings, all connected to the totality of conception that is God's.[19] In such a schema even the alphabet has a meaning, but not in Swift's *Tale*: here the dissolution of words leads to an alphabet that is incomplete, and from which the only meaning derivable is that constructed by the desire of the moment. Swift has created a text in which summary and commentary are in conflict. The summarizing characteristic of an encyclopedia enjoins a literalistic interpretation, but a single narrative, as opposed to multiple entries each arranged under their proper topic, demands expansion by commentary in order to engage the manifold exigencies of life through allegoresis. Martin and Jack reject the irresponsible allegorizing that characterizes Peter's assertion of self above the literal meaning of the will. Yet Jack's subsequent behavior shows the limits of the Will in a literal interpretation. Not finding an authentic phrase from the Will for inquiring the way to a jakes, he dirties himself, but will not clean himself because of the scriptural phrase "he which is filthy, let him be filthy still," a dubious phrase that may have been "foisted in by the Transcriber" (p. 191). Here even the details of the text, the Will that is the basis for interpretation, literal or allegorical, is of limited authority.

Foucault's definition of the shift from resemblance to representation is relevant to these conflicts of interpretation. The preclassical episteme assumes no sharp division between reality and the language used to present it, as resemblances can be discovered between words and the things they designate: indeed understanding is dependent on discovering the resemblances that connect all. In the "Classical episteme," however, language facilitates an analytical understanding that assumes a separation of the representation from the thing represented, the analytical tool from what is analyzed. This separation is the basis of "analytico-referential" language, as previously discussed. In Foucault's sense, the preceeding episteme is based on repetition, the connection of all into a great web of similarities in which

---

[19] See Augustine, *On Christian Doctrine*, trans. D. W. Robertson, Jr. (Indianapolis: Bobbs-Merrill, 1958), bk. 1, sec. 2; bk. 2, secs. 1 and 28.

adjacency is not adventitious.[20] In the sense implied by Swift's *Tale*, however, the subsequent Classical episteme is also based on repetition because the modern learning is a disguised repetition of that achieved by the ancients. The summary that is characteristic of a book like Wotton's is for Swift a tendency of all knowledge; the aim at completeness of knowledge turns into an encyclopedic repetition of one fragmented piece of knowledge after another. But a return to interpretation by resemblance is also rejected in the *Tale*. Allegoresis, which is the expansion of meaning by resemblance, avoids the discursiveness of fragmented summary, but for Swift it is in practice governed by desire and is thus a private aberration that evades the common forms. Systems, totalizing schemes, are also governed by resemblance, no matter how "modern" they appear. The placement of disparate fragments within a context that clarifies their meaning (as in the "cabinet of curiosities" of an eighteenth-century antiquarian or natural philosopher) if seen in Swiftian terms is the creation of arbitrary meaning by the imposition of contiguity and the discovery of elements of resemblance; in contrast, the "modern" sees it as an attempt to generate meaning through a system of classification that is distinct from the fragments. While attacking the Classical episteme, Swift grants no alternative validity to the preclassical episteme: when language is reduced to an alphabet, or to things, meaning vanishes because the analytical device for ordering and representing meaning has been dissolved. It is not in itself meaningful.[21] The brothers thus have a Will that may be admirable but much of the interpretation that extends it to new times and circumstances reflects either the ludicrous literalization of regressive summary as sometimes exemplified by Jack or the uncontrolled resemblance sometimes exemplified by Peter; each of these interpretive moves is a willful distortion motivated by private desire.

Martin, of course, represents the preferable alternative to Peter and Jack, yet his behavior does not validate the demand for literality implied by the interpretive excesses mocked in the satire. His response is related to a modified uniformitarian conception of history that accepts neither a radical difference of past from present nor the past's identity with the present. He stops short of attending precisely to the Will's instructions and thus avoids destroying the "substance" of the coat, a violation of the Will justified as

[20] See Michel Foucault, *The Order of Things: An Archeology of the Human Sciences* (New York: Random House, 1970), pp. 46–77.

[21] Frank Palmeri, "The Satiric Footnotes of Swift and Gibbon," *The Eighteenth-Century: Theory and Interpretation* 31 (1990), finds that "Swift satirizes the paradigm of criticism and representation in the footnotes to *A Tale of a Tub* (5th ed., 1710)" (p. 249). In some of the notes, Palmeri concludes, "Swift seems to undermine his own text by extending its uncertainties rather than resolving them" (p. 256).

according with its "True intent and Meaning" (p. 136). Jack's ripping and tearing in opposition to Peter is an attempt to recover some pristine originary state, a denial of his history, whereas Martin's less fervent response acknowledges his experience, which has brought about an irreparable distanciation from the Will. Although his coat continues to harbor the signs of his alienating history, it also creates some connection to an essential meaning that has power even when no longer literally applicable. Jack's tearing is analogous to Swift's version of a modern like Bentley whose meticulous analysis of the ancients reduces them to shreds, whereas Peter's desertion of the Will for his own advancement is analogous to Wotton's rejection of dependency on the ancients. Martin's response to the Will thus represents an acknowledgment of history—a connection to the past, but a rejection of a historicism that would make the difference of the past centrally important. The "phlegmatic" Martin shapes his conduct as much by a concern for the continuity of "common forms" as by a stringent view of the Will's meaning.

The institutions of book, encyclopedia, and archive are related to the form of the *Tale*, or perhaps more properly to the strains on its apparent formal organization. The notion of creating the "bulk" of a book by summarizing others and digressing from oneself suggests that the work is a book only in terms of material form, yet the taleteller's metaphoric expansion of the text to his own authorial body creates a putative organic unity. The topical multiplicity, the unrestrained inclusiveness, however, leads to the analogy of book to world, an expansion that imposes an impossible demand in a "modern" world with unassimilable amounts of information. Allegoresis is used to supplement the text, but it fragments the book by its introduction of conflicting and unrationalized interpretive norms. The demands of inclusiveness subvert order and result in the reader being empowered to remove a digression "into any other Corner he pleases" (p. 149), a move toward the arbitrary order necessitated by an encyclopedic goal.[22] But eventually the book moves toward an archival self-conception as the narrator tries to create significance for his commonplace book by emptying it into the *Tale*, and as Swift in subsequent editions adds footnotes, including material from Wotton's attack. The *Tale* simulates a modern text and a modern version of an ancient text

---

[22] Richard Yeo, "Reading Encyclopedias: Science and the Organization of Knowledge in British Dictionaries of Arts and Sciences, 1730–1850," *Isis* 82 (1991): 24–49, points out the "apparent absurdity" confronting those who attempt encyclopedic organization, that is, "the combination of universal knowledge and alphabetical order" (p. 24). The eighteenth century, Yeo states, has been identified as both an age of encyclopedias and of classification, both characteristics reflected in, for example, Chambers's *Cyclopaedia* and the *Encyclopédie* (pp. 26–27): "Chambers warned that 'a reduction of the body of learning' in the form of an encyclopedia was 'growing every day more necessary'"(p. 27).

simultaneously. It is ragged with missing passages, defaced pages, and editorial explanations, as well as with multiplications of prefatory materials and excerpts from others' commentary that change from one edition to another. It becomes a lopsided, stuffed collection of papers and implies a conception of its potentiality that requires the reordering, indexing, and storage that are not possible within the covers that are the conventional demarcations of books. Swift's parodic version of a book responds to the moderns' conception of an uncontrolled increase in knowledge that finds its salient manifestation in the burgeoning of the printing industry; this parodic book's exemplary contrast is the concise book that expresses conclusions rather than explores the conditions for its own hegemony, a book that has a limited coherent scheme with a controlled and controlling narration. Such values imply a canon and a library as their larger models. The canon negotiates a compromise that reduces mere repetition and avoids conflicts of values, thus keeping the library small and free of battles, not the library of Babel or the Prince Regent's library but Temple's library.

A summary of some conventional differences between archive and library may be useful for identifying issues in the historical outlook of ancients and moderns that are relevant to understanding the contrasts between Swift and Richardson. Although the terms "archive" and "library" overlap and are even sometimes used synonomously, T. R. Schellenberg's summary of differences reveals disparities of function and, consequently, differing standards of relevance. Library materials are often chosen for their cultural significance; whereas the cultural significance of archival materials may be "incidental."[23] The archive exists to document a particular institution, not a large cultural configuration, and therefore all items are more closely related to one another than are those of a library, which tends to consist of discrete items "whose significance is wholly independent of their relationship to other items" (p. 17). Because the archive exists to preserve the shape and articulation of the particularized institution it serves, its significance lies in the preservation of structures, not single documents but the relationships of parts. Thus the arrangement of the archive must differ from that of the library. A library groups items "in accordance with a predetermined logical scheme," whereas the archive must preserve items in their context, using a "classification that is dictated by the original circumstances of creation." The librarian preserves discrete items, trying to keep likes together, but "the significance of a particular item will not necessarily be lost if it is not classified in a certain place" (p. 22). The librarian thus attributes an independent coherence and cultural

---

[23] T. R. Schellenberg, *Modern Archives: Principles and Techniques* (Chicago: University of Chicago Press, 1956), p. 17. Subsequent references are noted in the text.

significance to these discrete items. The archivist, in contrast, deals with units that "derive their significance, in large part at least, from their relation to one another" (p. 23).

The attempt at modern exhaustiveness that Wotton displays and Swift parodies has a generalizing aspect seemingly more in common with the library or the encyclopedia than with the limited institutional nature of the archive. Yet the modern concern for part-to-whole relationships resembles the conception of the archive. Wotton's understanding of a classical civilization that exists in dispersal and fragmentation but that can be brought to coherence through careful comparison and criticism of existing texts is an archival analogy. Texts are not so much independent and valued monuments as in Temple but pieces whose significance lies in the proper arrangement that will bring the historical order of classical civilization into clearer outline. Swift's parodic version of this conception represents it as a process that creates confusion and replaces existing wholeness with fragmentation, as in Bentley's destroying of the positions of Aesop and Phalaris in the canon. The rearrangements of the archive turn the discrete order of the library into a multiplicity that in Swift's version is a battle for dominance, not a move toward increased understanding. *A Tale of a Tub* parodies the archive of modernism, representing it not only in statement but also in its formal confusion, so stuffed with its own ambitions that nothing can be eliminated, its writing requiring even the "perusing some hundreds of Prefaces" (p. 45).

II

Richardson uses the archival conception that Swift parodies as a governing fiction for *Clarissa*: masses of documents, written for varying purposes, are all brought together for mutual illumination in service of the institution (ultimately the monument) that Clarissa makes of herself. In themselves the letters are fragments; in their arrangement a "history." But to Richardson's consternation, his archival fiction was interpreted in contradictory ways, thus calling into question the very sense of documentary completeness and objectivity that is advanced by the conception of an archive. Some aspects of these interpretive conflicts may be more clearly articulated through an examination of the concept of the archive itself in relationship to its constituting "traces" and its epistemological ambitions. The archive's contents are documents, the materials evoking and supporting a conception of the institution to which the archive is responsible. Only assertions warranted by the archival documents are considered valid. But as Paul Ricoeur points out, archives are also monuments, their contents consisting of what was thought worthy of being preserved, and thus already a product of an institutional conception or self-conception rather than its basis.[24] A differing understanding of the document may be acquired by placing it within a broadened and/or markedly different context from that in the archive, where the monumental function may exclude much. The document itself requires interrogation and interpretation; it can achieve its status as warrant only by means of the uncertainties and partialities of argument, not by any apparent self-evidence. Thus the document is a "trace," even when collected in an archive, having both an implicit intelligibility and the characteristic absence or partiality of context that thwarts interpretation. It implies absence (from knowledge as well as the present) but tantalizes with hints of recoverability. An archive is an organization of traces with the purpose of providing the mutual contextualizing that leads to documentary usefulness. It is like that "cabinet of curiosities" built by seventeenth- and eighteenth-century artisans to hold the artifacts of the virtuosi—each little compartment holding its own separate item, yet in an arrangement designed to shed light on them all, the classification system itself leading to understanding.[25] The monument, of course, proposes to depict finalities, whereas the "cabinet of curiosities" and the archive also have the possibility of constant rearrangement as contexts are altered or expand.

The limits of the monumental archive (of which *Clarissa* is a fictional example) and the kind of history to which it is related are discussed in Foucault's *Archeology of Knowledge*, which defines and rejects the critical history that moves from document/trace to totality (the history Wotton praised as a salient modern achievement). Foucault rejects history that has as its purpose the transformation of the monumental into the documentary through the interrogation of its biases and designs; instead "in our time, history . . . transforms *documents* into *monuments*" by rejecting the assumption that the documentary can be disinterred from its monumental function and converted into a link in an existing continuity.[26] The historian's ambition, in his view, should not be to overcome discontinuity but to make it a

---

[24] I am indebted in my discussion of monuments and traces to Paul Ricoeur, *Time and Narrative*, vol. 3, trans. Kathleen Blamey and David Pellauer (Chicago: University of Chicago Press, 1985), pp. 116–26.

[25] Amy Boesky, " 'Outlandish-Fruits': Commissioning Nature for the Museum of Man," *ELH* 58 (1991), studies the beginnings of the Ashmolean Museum, suggesting that "the collections or ' cabinets' of the sixteenth and seventeenth centuries were not so distinct from the great national museums of the eighteenth and nineteenth centuries" (p. 307). She argues that "every collection, however haphazard or random it may (anachronistically) appear, is in its own right an allegory—of salvage, of teleology, of the masterpiece, of classification" (p. 309).

[26] Michel Foucault, *The Archeology of Knowledge*, trans. A. M. Sheridan Smith (New York: Harper & Row, 1972), p. 7.

"working concept": discontinuity is an instrument as well as an object of research (pp. 8–9). As a consequence, the possibility of "total history" disappears and "general history" emerges. Total history is the ambition of the moderns, seeking as it does to "reconstitute the overall form of a civilization" (p. 9), whereas general history questions the possibility of connecting perceived discontinuities and takes the constitution of series, rather than filling in already established series, as its problem. The archives, then, are not for Foucault those "institutions, which, in a given society, make it possible to record and preserve those discourses that one wishes to remember and keep in circulation," but instead "the law of what can be said . . . *the system of its functioning*" (p. 129). Archival study is not properly "a question of rediscovering what might legitimize an assertion, but of freeing the conditions of emergence of statements" (p. 127). An implication of Foucault's views is that the apparent cacophony of voices within a culture cannot be validly ordered to show an underlying continuity of perspective or hierarchy of values but that, nevertheless, the very discords that constitute the cacophony are authorized by discourse; the conflicts of content are not resolvable in the monumental archive of documents but can be comprehended by the Foucaultian archive of discourse, in which is sought not the resolution of conflicts but the conditions that govern their articulation.

Foucault's analysis of the archive brings into relief the import of Richardson's attempt to make his fictional monument documentary. Making optimistic assumptions like Wotton's about the powers of a totalizing history, Richardson expects that which is fragmentary in itself to yield a full meaning in context. He obtrudes the fragmentation of both perspective and form: the writers have limited knowledge and letters themselves begin and end *in medias res*. Richardson's method, therefore, presupposes continuity as an end and an instrument of analysis, for if this presupposition is changed to discontinuity, the gaps within and between letters enlarge. If reduced from documents to traces, the letters raise questions about their grounding. In the context of other traces, a trace may document a much expanded conception of a "passing," yet the character or characteristics of the cause of the trace evade definition despite scrutiny of the effect, the mark.

The "passing" of Lovelace and Clarissa is evidenced by the collection of letters, but their precise relationship to their writings is never fully resolved. To argue that such questions about a fictional work must find resolution through asking questions of authors rather than of characters is to add another layer to the analysis but not to dissolve the questions themselves. In following the epistolary fiction of archival representation and reconstruction, Richardson himself recognizes the problematical relationship of writer to letter, of cause to mark. Such complexities are part of the fiction, not bracketed out by it. Designating Lovelace as a Proteus and subjecting Clarissa's feelings about him to sustained and contradictory analysis raise questions about the relationship of trace to cause, of letter to writer, rather than suppressing them. Foucault remarks that "making historical analysis the discourse of the continuous and making human consciousness the original subject of all historical development and all action are the two sides of the same system of thought," a system of thought Foucault rejects as an attempt at total history (p. 12). Richardson's project enmeshed him in the problematics of "total history," and many elements of the structure and content of *Clarissa* reveal the difficulties of making the archive yield continuity and human consciousness.

Clarissa's writing of letters includes the intention of preserving them to reify and thus vindicate her conduct after it and its occasions have vanished. The letters have other purposes too—ranging from ordinary instrumental uses to the expression and relief of feelings—but their monumental use is what requires their collection; if they are to serve as her monument, preserving and organizing are of equal importance with writing and sending. As has often been noted, the production of writing is a central topic of Richardson's fiction; *Clarissa* adds the duties of archivist to production. In *Pamela* too, it is true, letters require disposal, yet it is perhaps of significance that the major cache of Pamela's writing surrounds her person beneath her outer garments; whereas Clarissa's letters are far too voluminous and have too explicitly public a rationale for such presentation.[27] Clarissa herself functions in a significant way as archivist in the book. The demands on that role, however, expand, and ultimately Belford must undertake the increased collecting, arranging, and obtaining access that are required because of the need for multiple perspectives and multiple correspondences in the interest of completeness.

Clarissa frequently narrates her performance of the somewhat pedestrian tasks of collecting and ordering her letters. Even before she leaves Harlowe Place, she sends Anna Howe a substantial parcel of letters divided into three groups—one group containing new letters written over a period of time but not yet conveyed to Anna; a second group containing the letters and copies that record her interchanges with Anna since their last meeting, as well as an additional collection written on subjects "above me" that Anna may read now and Clarissa "review" later; and a third group containing her correspondence with Lovelace "since he was forbidden the house," his letters combined with

---

[27] Robert Folkenflik, "A Room of Pamela's Own," *ELH* 39 (1972), analyzes Pamela's resistance to Lord B's invasions of her privacy, including his attempts on the letters attached to her undercoat (p. 586).

copies of her responses.[28] Anna duly acknowledges receipt of the packet several days later (no. 74; pp. 291, 292). Despite Clarissa's apparent engagement with the material management of these letters, which suggests a kind of detachment from their content rather than a total identity with it, the letters themselves continue to retain a private orientation, maintaining their purpose of self-scrutiny by enabling limited but sustained communal analysis through the seeming stability and continuity of the written. But as Clarissa herself gains a sense of how little of her story has actually been part of her consciousness, she realizes that its truth will not become apparent through her own and Anna's narration and commentary alone. Lovelace's correspondence with her does not envelop his stratagems, which can only be understood if recounted in supplementary writings. Clarissa realizes that her story is to some degree already public, encompassing a multiplicity of passions and correspondences that will be documented only if there is a significant expansion of her archive of letters.[29] Very early in Clarissa's writing, her self-scrutiny is connected with the more public function of self-justification, Anna Howe's opening letter suggesting that Clarissa's account will enable her to exculpate herself if the violence incipient in the Harlowe family's situation erupts (no. 1; p. 40). This function for her letters remains subsidiary, however, until she realizes that her character has been damaged as a consequence of her confinement by Lovelace; furthermore, after the rape the exculpatory function is expanded to a quasi-judicial effort to expose fully the details of Lovelace's treachery.[30]

The process that leads to Belford's being appointed executor is inaugurated by Clarissa's recognition of his knowledge of essential supplements to her version of the story: while writing and speaking to Clarissa, Lovelace has written a parallel series of letters to Belford, explicitly defining some of the stratagems concealed by his communications to her. At first she appears only to want the information contained in relevant extracts, but her imagination finally extends to a far more imposing monument, a "compilement to be made

---

[28] Samuel Richardson, *Clarissa*, ed. Angus Ross (New York: Penguin, 1985), letter no. 69, p. 283. Subsequent references are to this text based on the first edition by letter and page number, except for one reference to a footnote Richardson added later.

[29] William Ray, *Story and History: Narrative Authority and Social Identity in the Eighteenth-Century French and English Novel* (Cambridge: Basil Blackwell, 1990), aptly defines Clarissa's changed response to constructing her story: "Permanently excluded from the story she once thought was her own [that of the 'virtuous daughter'], she will reassess the structure of history in general and take over the active management of her history in particular" (p. 177).

[30] Christina Marsdon Gillis, *The Paradox of Privacy: Epistolary Form in Clarissa* (Gainesville: University Presses of Florida, 1984), discusses the tension between isolation and community, concluding that Clarissa's faith "in her own collection or 'story' " implies that "letter texts are finally to be read, reliably, within context, by a community of readers" (pp. 3, 3–4).

of all that relates to my story" in two copies, one for Anna Howe, the other to remain in Belford's possession to be used for the satisfaction of her family (no. 507; p. 1418). Although this undertaking is too massive for Clarissa, she continues to participate in minor cycles of compilement, which will themselves eventually be incorporated into the monument. In expectation of her death, she provides for the conservation of uncollected letters by keeping "letters and copies of letters, disposed according to their dates" arranged in her drawer for her executor (no. 460; p. 1329). Like *Pamela*, much of *Clarissa* is taken up with the writing, sending, and hiding of letters, but far more than *Pamela*, *Clarissa* is taken up with the ordering of letters, with making them intelligible as a vast interlocking commentary on each other.[31]

Belford's efforts to establish Clarissa's story begin before he is appointed executor and extend well beyond the contribution suggested by the term "compiler."[32] On the occasion of Clarissa's false imprisonment for debt, he questions the culprits and takes evidence, providing portions of the narrative not otherwise accessible, and he also extends the narrative through his later visit to Mrs. Sinclair's death bed. He interprets the compiler's portion of his executor's task more broadly than the narrowly defined one of vindicating Clarissa's reputation, continuing it well past her death in the attempt to complete all aspects of the story and to give an understanding of Clarissa that includes more than the matters associated with her betrayal by Lovelace. He even commissions Anna Howe to write a character sketch of Clarissa that will extend beyond the boundaries of the already collected letters (nos. 528–29; pp. 1465–66), and he writes a "Conclusion" that rounds out the other characters' lives. His efforts at collection, completion, and resolution are

---

[31] William Beatty Warner, *Reading "Clarissa": The Struggles of Interpretation* (New Haven: Yale University Press, 1979), discusses, in chap. 4, "Building a Book into an Empire of Meaning," the power created by Clarissa's construction of her book: "After the rape Clarissa goes from being an agile tactician of self-representation to being a master-builder. By building a book, and putting her friends and adversaries *in* her book, she tries to assume a Godlike authority and dominion over them" (p. 75). To this assertion of Clarissa's power through her book, Terry Castle opposes a different perspective: "Clarissa is without force: as a woman she is without the kinds of power available to Lovelace. . . . Lacking such 'authority,' Clarissa is made to enact the fantasies of her persecutor" (*Clarissa's Ciphers: Meaning and Disruption in Richardson's "Clarissa"* [Ithaca: Cornell University Press, 1982], p. 25). Both perspectives surely have merit. It is difficult to deny that Clarissa becomes victor through her book. It is also difficult to deny that Lovelace faces few serious social obstacles to his manipulations of Clarissa, controlling as he does her sources of information and supporting his will by direct force and threats of force. It is perhaps worth noting that Clarissa's book can be prepared definitively only with the assistance of the power that Belford lends to her cause.

[32] Robert A. Erickson, *Mother Midnight: Birth, Sex, and Fate in Eighteenth-Century Fiction* (New York: AMS Press, 1986), comments on the relationship between Belford and Richardson: Belford becomes "a kind of ideal editor, the artistic role Richardson finds most congenial for himself" (p. 180).

indefatigible, resulting in the apparently full panoply of all relevant written documents being included, all however with the aim not only of exculpating Clarissa, but also of making an enduring presence of her virtue.

Before becoming *Clarissa*, Clarissa needs one more mediator—the editor. A vast collection of letters, erratically delivered, and circulated among a diversity of recipients by original and copy is brought toward coherence by the efforts of Clarissa and then completed by Belford when her efforts at compiling are apparently doomed to insufficiency. The letters themselves provide materials relevant to their own placement (selections of, and references to, pertinent documentation are defined within the letters themselves) and participants in the writing also comment on the process by which they raise and resolve questions by their own archival efforts. Yet such material is often repetitious, containing originals and copies variously circulated for varying purposes and repeating descriptions of the same events. Without the efforts of an information manager, this book would be even longer. And what mere reader could have the simultaneous grasp of the facts and implications of widely separated letters that is needed to arrive unescorted at a just understanding of every episode and implication, the objective truth that is assumed to emerge merely from archival completeness?

The editorial interventions in the text suggest changing views of the archival fiction—implicitly, the more intervention is needed, the less credence is allowable to the claim that self-evident truth emerges from the documentation or the traces themselves. Any generalizations about the editorial functions in *Clarissa* are risky because the functions are varied and do not alter in some precisely demarcatable fashion. Nevertheless, some major categories of editorial activity are definable and, in general, the intervention becomes more aggressive as the text proliferates. The editor starts as a mere facilitator of the reading of this massive correspondence, then enters and alters the text itself in the interest of making it less demanding, and finally insists on certain interpretive consequences of the text. These editorial activities are not discrete and all are at least incipient from the beginning; nevertheless, the more interventionist activities become characteristic of later stages of the book, the interpretive insistence becoming most evident after the publication of the first edition.[33]

---

[33] Warner studies Richardson's "much more aggressive use of the role of editor in the second and third editions of *Clarissa*" (*Reading "Clarissa,"* p. 130), and considers also the controlling effects of Richardson's index-summary of the novel that was placed in the second edition (pp. 180–96). Mark Kinkaid-Weekes, "*Clarissa* Restored," *Review of English Studies* 10 (1959): 156–71, shows that much of the material that Richardson claimed to be "restoring" to *Clarissa* in the second and third editions was in fact new composition designed to combat what he thought of as erroneous interpretations of the novel.

From the beginning to the end of the book the editor is a cross-referencer, indicating where in other letters information will be found that is relevant to topics in a particular letter. At first these notes point to future letters, but soon to past ones as well, as the reader's memory becomes less able to deal with a correspondence that requires crossing by memory the often large stretches of writing lying between the relevant letters. The cross-referencing is a kind of stitching, linking letter to letter, fragment to fragment, yet the increasing complexity of the annotation is an implicit acknowledgment of a fragmentation brought on by too large a context. Under the pressure of the rapidly increasing weight of the book, the editor cuts and pastes: for example, excerpts from Clarissa's letters are given, out of writing order, immediately after several of Anna Howe's letters, a reordering with the presumably benign intention of immediately satisfying the reader of Clarissa's response while relevant details are still fresh in the reader's mind (no. 151; p. 517).

An increasingly more interpretive, in contrast to a solely textual, version of the editor gradually emerges; the editor appears to be in control of a vast store of papers, deciding which are needed, which can be excerpted, and which left out: for example, a letter of Clarissa's is interrupted within the text by the editorial statement that "Mr. Lovelace's next letters giving a more ample account of all, hers are omitted" (no. 200; p. 644). The editor remains notably scrupulous in indicating textual provenience and defining any alterations, yet the interventions reach a complexity that from a reader's perspective might be thought to court obscurantism: for example, the editor places in inverted commas those passages in a letter by Clarissa that Anna Howe will later quote, the justification being "to avoid the necessity of repeating them when that letter comes to be inserted" (no. 359; p. 1115; the later letter where these sentences are not repeated is no. 373, which is cross-referenced to no. 359). Such alterations, while apparently maintaining the integrity of the substance of the book, influence its texture significantly, sometimes seeming to move it from the participants' provenience to that of the editor. At one point the editor tells us that Clarissa produced minutes to "help her memory" during a time when she was too debilitated to write. These minutes are then quoted only in part (no. 273; pp. 926–27) and later introduced at the bottom of the page as discrete glosses on assertions in one of Lovelace's letters; these comments by Clarissa are, however, introduced in the editor's words and sometimes quoted but also sometimes paraphrased (no. 276; pp. 932–36). Such alteration takes the minutes from their original context and introduces them into another that the editor finds more pertinent to his elucidating purpose.

Such editorial activity is a response to two sometimes incompatible pressures: the increases in sheer bulk and the fragmentation. Allowing all written comment to be presented in the text reduces fragmentation in one sense, as it permits the presentation of the full range of information. Nevertheless, the increase in quantity also inhibits full assimilation of the material, blunting the sense of coherence. But the editorial dispersal of the relevant fragments of Clarissa's minutes to strategic places in Lovelace's text, while reducing length and increasing coherence, presents its own dangers, tending as it does, to dissolve the archival fiction that is the premise of *Clarissa*, moving this archive of letters in the direction of a narrative presented by an authorial voice.[34]

As Clarissa's story moves toward its inexorable end, the defensive measures against the proliferation of documents increase. Clarissa's own writing is sometimes summarized or even reduced to headings, as when the editor interrupts with the statement "The lady next gives an account," followed by thirteen headings without amplification (no. 315; p. 1012). Mr. Brand's letters of recantation are mentioned but omitted "as this collection is run into an undesirable length" (no. 469; p. 1343). And there are implied demands for additional inclusions increasingly hovering in and around the text, those urged by Clarissa's "Meditations" for example, which appear in various letters but, like her minutes not in any systematic or authoritative form. Before her death, Clarissa herself prepares them as a book written in her own hand and willed to Mrs. Norton (no. 507; p. 1417). Richardson's press almost rose to the challenge when in 1750 it printed them, but, nevertheless, according to William Sale, allowed them to remain unpublished (*Master Printer*, p. 198).[35] And perhaps the most formidable challenge to the editor is Clarissa's bequest to Anna Howe of her entire correspondence completed before that destined for *Clarissa*, "a correspondence that no young person of my sex need to be ashamed of." She has arranged all that she has ever written and received according to dates (no. 507; p. 1417). What starts out as a

---

[34] Frank Palmeri makes a related distinction between the text that emphasizes controversy through the conflict between text and notes and the text that establishes "a seamless and coherent narrative': "These tendencies within the paradigm receive major emphasis in succession: skeptical criticism predominates from the 1690's into the 1730's; perspicuous narrative coherence predominates through the 1780's" ("Satiric Footnotes," p. 247). I suggest that exploring the question of the fragment in relation to a seamless narrative is a part of the novelistic project of the eighteenth century.

[35] Tom Kymer, "Richardson's *Meditations*: Clarissa's *Clarissa*," in *Samuel Richardson. Tercentenary Essays*, ed. Margaret Doody and Peter Sabor (New York: Cambridge University Press, 1989), provides a sustained study of the relationship of the *Meditations* to the "compilement" that is *Clarissa*.

struggle to collect letters essential to filling out the story, ends with an archival abundance demanding excision for coherence.

Both the editorial management in the interest of intelligibility and the complexity of the text itself motivate a suspicious reading of *Clarissa*. The notes that Richardson introduced in response to what he saw as misreadings have an occasional testy tone to them as the reader is chided for missing the obvious: "It is easy for such of the readers as have been attentive," reads a note added to highlight Lovelace's perfidy.[36] Such overt persuasions directed at the reader suggest that Richardson is finding not just his faith in the reader misplaced but also his faith in the text. The textuality of Richardson's work is so convoluted in itself and so excellently represented by Lovelace's simulations that letters which can, on the one hand, be conceived of as straightforward documentation of a crime also, on the other hand, appear more and more insulated from external experience and more and more enveloped in text that is difficult to ground.[37] Letter 473, for example, a letter from Belford to Lovelace, is in most respects unequivocal, having none of the difficulties of forgery and duplicitously intended meaning that can so easily make others of the letters more likely to raise than resolve arguments. Yet this letter is so layered with texts, so far removed from the epistolary crispness of one person writing to another, so inclusive of diverse audiences as well as writers, that it speaks of a textual world—an archive that represents itself. Belford addresses Lovelace, then interrupts the letter to have Anna Howe's letter to Clarissa transcribed and included verbatim as 473.1; following Anna's letter, Belford continues again, but interrupts his commentary to give a transcription of the response of Clarissa to Anna, 473.2, which response was written by Mrs. Lovell from Clarissa's dictation; the subscription is however in Clarissa's hand, whose waverings Belford in his transcription has "endeavoured to imitate"; Belford then writes his closing segment to Lovelace (pp. 1347–49). The exemplary reader is presumably being asked to comprehend this pastiche of correspondence in relation to what it means to each writer enclosed in Belford's text; in relation to to the correspondence between these enclosed writers; in relation to Belford, the encloser of it all;

---

[36] The text from which this note is cited is the Everyman edition, introduced by John Butt (New York: Dutton, 1932), no. 90, p. 463.

[37] John Preston, *The Created Self: The Reader's Role in Eighteenth-Century Fiction* (New York: Barnes & Noble, 1970), discusses the isolation from all but the reading and writing experience in *Clarissa*: "The event narrated is at a distance, the act of narrating is immediate, and inseparable from the act of reading. The only realities for the writers are those concerned with telling. And it is clear that the reader is in the same predicament. The words on the page are the scope of his experience, and the fictional perspectives of this novel lead him back constantly to confront that experience" (pp. 55–56).

in relation to Lovelace who receives, eavesdrops on, the individual letters; and finally in relation to the correspondence of Belford and Lovelace. And Belford's attempt to imitate Clarissa's subscription is the kind of thing that can only be distantly imitated by the press; consequently, the attempt suggests not authenticity but a doubled distance of the printed book from the actual documents seemingly but unsuccessfully being evoked.[38]

The print world of *Clarissa* intersects aspects of the satire of Swift's *Tale*; Swift reduced to absurdity Wotton's praise of the proliferation of modern books and of the modern devices for information management that allow the appropriation of such a vastly increased stock of books. Swift rejects modern claims to significant originality and defines a characteristic modern fragmentation that results from exhaustion. In Richardson this fragmentation is presented as the consequence of a minute view of human character in conflict. According to Richardson's view, then, the collecting of the fragments results in the construction of continuity rather than in contradiction. Those devices of arrangement and summary, which are seen by Swift as degenerative repetition, function in Richardson as enablers of an insight into the larger patterns of continuity and organization that enfold the fragments. Swift and Richardson share a "modern" world on which they have markedly different perspectives. Yet similar anxieties and ambiguities emerge from their differing perceptions of those threatening inundations of text that are evoked by the conflicting versions of modernity presented by Temple, Wotton, Swift, and Richardson.

In 1755 Richardson published *A Collection of the Moral and Instructive Sentiments, Maxims, Cautions, and Reflections, Contained in the Histories of Pamela, Clarissa, and Sir Charles Grandison* (London: Printed for S. Richardson). In Swift's terms this production is a recycling of old materials, an unneeded new book made from already existing ones. And it also exemplifies the self-praise that Swift so ridiculed as an attribute of the modern author: the preface "By a Friend" praises the moral instruction of "an author modestly *anonymous*" (p. v), and finally suggests, *"These Lives and Morals* will perhaps last as long, probably be as much admired, and certainly prove much more extensively beneficial" than Plutarch's *Lives* (p. ix). Richardson's modernism appears almost to be an instantiation of Swift's parody. Looked at from a different point of view, Richardson's effort is an attempt not to repeat but to provide access to the instruction contained in those enormous

[38] Terry Castle notes that the evocations of handwriting "have a curiously subversive effect on the real reader. . . . Instead of assuring us of the authenticity of what we read, they remind us precisely of the inaccessibility of *original* documents, and our separation from the realm of the 'History' itself" (*Clarissa's Ciphers*, p. 159).

volumes. The moral and instructive sentiments are "Digested under Proper Heads, with References to the Volume, and Page, both in Octavo and Twelves" (title page), thus producing a "*General Index* both of *Maxims* and of *References*" that will enable those who want not merely to read the sentiments but also to "refer themselves occasionally to the volumes for the illustrations of these maxims" (p. ix). The described possibilities of either merely reading the sentiments or of finding them illustrated in the stories implicitly raises an issue central to the differences between Swift and Richardson: Are these maxims grounded in the particularities of characters or are they an elucidation of common forms without regard to individuation? Swift's satire appears to support the common forms against what he found to be unsuccessful attempts at originality of self or writing, whereas Richardson's vast volumes exploring connections of self to text imply the individuation of the writing self.[39]

The issue of the individuation of the writing self is more fully raised by Richardson's *Letters Written To and For Particular Friends On the Most Important Occasions*, published in 1741 but begun before *Pamela*; it is a work designed to provide useful models of letters for those not accustomed to writing.[40] This task bears on the face of it the assumption that the occasions of letters and appropriate responses to these occasions can be reduced to a not extraordinarily extended paradigmatic compendium, thus implying that only relatively limited patterns of character and situation obtain among realistically conceived people. But the topics of the letters do not always appear to be what we would understand as the most usual occasions for writing: letter no. 42, for example, "To a Country Correspondent, modestly requesting a Balance of Accounts between them," appears to be rather widely adaptable and paradigmatically useful, whereas no. 11, "To a young Man too soon keeping a Horse," seems perhaps somewhat too particularized. Richardson's conception of the letters, however, is that they are to "inculcate the principles of virtue and benevolence; to describe properly, and recommend strongly, the social and relative duties; and to place them in such practical lights, that the letters may serve for rules to think and act by, as well

---

[39] John A. Dussinger, "Truth and Storytelling in *Clarissa*," in *Samuel Richardson: Tercentenary Essays*, ed. Margaret Anne Doody and Peter Sabor (New York: Cambridge University Press, 1989), examines the status of Clarissa's moral sentiments, concluding that "role-playing, as Clarissa discovers, is the requisite condition of being in the world, inescapable not only in talking to others but also in setting pen to paper" (p. 50). Dussinger analyzes several of the moral sentiments from the *Collection of Moral and Instructive Sentiments . . .* , showing differences between the listed sentiments and their novelistic instantiations.

[40] Samuel Richardson, *Letters Written To and For Particular Friends On the Most Important Occasions*, introduction by Brian W. Downs (New York: Dodd Mead, 1928).

as forms to write after" (p. xxvii). What he sees as the cohesive notion in the letters is their social morality, not unlike what Swift or his narrator denominates as the "common forms," including a responsibility to the social world that encompasses but exceeds narrowly defined questions of politeness. What makes the letters a compendium is the relatively comprehensive view of appropriate social morality that is exhibited in them rather than their isolation of the paradigmatic occasions for writing letters. It is their social vision, at least as much as their subjects for writing, that is conceived of as generally applicable.

But *Clarissa* reveals the failure of letters to create a social network uniting manners and morals: it shows Lovelace's virtuosity in using the common forms for individualistic purposes that destroy Clarissa.[41] On display is an archive of textual devices for manipulative deception, as if the *Familiar Letters* had been rewritten by a counterfeiter, who uses and recommends the forms for reasons unrelated to their ostensible purposes, delighting in textual deceit. Richardson and Clarissa finally establish a textually defined truth through Belford's compilement, yet despite Richardson's intentions and resistance, he saw in his readers' questions the muddling of that truth too. Lovelace is Richardson's version of the tale-teller, who, in Swift's parodic conception, links modern writing wholly to desire, eliminating any values beyond the self. As a consequence, this parodic version of the modern embraces any contradiction that will minister to his desires, thus eventually evacuating any self other than what inheres in appetite. Severed from a clear identity of person, textual meaning in the service of desire is evanescent, linked to no communal stabilities. Richardson counters by making text itself weighty, its convolutions supporting the illusion of self-groundedness.

Rejecting Lovelace is also presumed to be a repudiation of the fragmentation that occurs when no stable consciousness underwrites a text.[42] Richardson represents Lovelace as a forger who counterfeits both letters and

---

[41] Leopold Damrosch Jr., *God's Plot and Man's Stories: Studies in the Fictional Imagination from Milton to Fielding* (Chicago: University of Chicago Press, 1985), remarks on a radical change in assumption from *Pamela* to *Clarissa*: "*Pamela* had its origin in conduct books, including Richardson's own *Familiar Letters*, which were designed to help people integrate themselves into society. *Clarissa* stands utterly outside of such a structure" (p. 221).

[42] Terry Eagleton, *The Rape of Clarissa* (Minneapolis: University of Minnesota Press, 1982), describes eloquently the differing attitudes to text of Clarissa and Lovelace, implying his preference for Lovelace's relationship to text: "Lovelace's writing is mercurial, diffuse, exuberant. Clarissa's letters . . . brook no contradiction. Behind them stands a transcendental subject, apparently unscathed by her own slips and evasions, whose relationship to writing is dominative and instrumental. Lovelace, by contrast, lives on the interior of his prose, generating a provisional identity from the folds of his text, luxuriating in multiple modes of being" (p. 53).

himself, presenting versions of self that have no continuous existence external to the words from which they are inferred. He and the version of textuality that he exemplifies are rejected and associated with *A Tale of a Tub*, thus providing a defense of Richardson's archival fiction, which posits the stabilizing of meaning through completeness of documentation, individual aberration refuted by comparative analysis.

Swift appears in *Clarissa* as the author of "The Lady's Dressing Room," the *Travels*, and, most notably, the *Tale*.[43] The most directly antagonistic comment about Swift occurs in a note to Belford's description of his visit to the dying Mrs. Sinclair, which Richardson uses to congratulate himself on having presented a "not only more natural but more decent painting" than that in the "Lady's Dressing Room" (no. 499; p. 1388). Belford himself compares the "profligate woman" he describes to "one of Swift's Yahoos, or Virgil's obscene Harpies." References to the *Tale* are more frequent and primarily Lovelace's. He alludes to the *Tale* in warning Belford that if he interferes between him and Clarissa, he will "be a madder Jack than him in the *Tale of a Tub*" (no. 370; p. 1144). This warning comes after his ridicule of Belford's efforts at reforming him, which he compares to the interpretive efforts of the enthusiasts in a passage reminiscent of satire from the *Tale*: "As enthusiasts do by Scripture, so dost thou by the poets thou hast read: anything that carries the most distant allusion from *either* to the case in hand, is put down by both for gospel, however incongruous to the general scope of either." Rather than connecting Belford to the dissenters, however, such hermeneutical skepticism connects Lovelace to a blinding materialism.

[43] T. C. Duncan Eaves and Ben D. Kimpel, *Samuel Richardson: A Biography* (Oxford: Clarendon Press, 1971), state that "the prose writers [Richardson] mentions most often are, not surprisingly, Addison and Swift. Swift is almost always mentioned with great reservations" (p. 579). John Carroll, "Richardson at Work: Revisions, Allusions, and Quotations in *Clarissa*," in *Studies in the Eighteenth Century II: Papers Presented at the Second David Nichol Smith Memorial Seminar, Canberra, 1970*, ed. R. F. Brissenden (Toronto: University of Toronto Press, 1973), finds that "in both his letters and his novels, Richardson clearly stood on the side of the moderns in the battle of the books" (p. 65). Carroll notes additional direct criticism of Swift in the third edition of *Clarissa* when Anna Howe states that Clarissa chided Swift "for so employing his admirable pen, that a pure eye was afraid of looking into his works, and a pure ear of hearing anything quoted from them" (1751, viii, p. 214; p. 71). Richardson's antagonism to Swift appears to be at least in part a response to what W. Jackson Bate identifies as the burden of the past, a sense especially fostered by neoclassicism that the great achievements of the past leave little for the modern to do (*The Burden of the Past and the English Poet* [Cambridge: Harvard University Press, 1970]). In his satires Swift explicitly expresses the view that little remains for the modern to do, yet at the same time he exhibits his mastery of a kind of literature that subsequent moderns must also compete with. Harold Bloom, *The Anxiety of Influence: A Theory of Poetry* (New York: Oxford University Press, 1973), presents categories of characteristic responses to the burden of the past that illuminate some of the duplicity in Richardson's response to Swift, his use, as well as rejection, of the earlier writer.

Clarissa's subsequent ambiguous reference to her expected departure to "my father's house" where "I am bid to hope that he will receive his poor penitent with a goodness peculiar to himself" (no. 421.1; p. 1233) is read by Lovelace with a numbed univocality that is responsive only to his desires. His eventual suspicions about her meaning and his mistaken interpretation of it lead to a comparison of her figural use of her "father's house" to what "Gulliver in his abominable Yahoo story" calls "saying the *thing that is not*" (no. 439; p. 1271). This Gulliverian literalism is exemplified in his earlier perverse interpretation of her meditation "On being hunted after by the enemy of my soul": "She says she has *eaten ashes like bread*—a sad mistake to be sure!—*and mingled her drink with weeping*—sweet maudlin soul! should I say of anybody confessing this but Miss Harlowe" (no. 418; p. 1221).

Lovelace characterizes his deceptions of Clarissa as throwing "a tub to a whale" (no. 103; p. 412), and he justifies his deceit by paraphrasing "The Digression Concerning . . . Madness": "Are we not told that in being *well* deceived consists the whole of human happiness" (no. 218; p. 700). His allusions to the *Tale* take a formal turn as he describes Hickman's speech as Tubbian: "parenthesis within parenthesis, apologizing for apologies, in imitation I suppose of Swift's Digressions in Praise of Digressions" (no. 346; p. 1091). Possible, but scattered and less explicit allusions to *The Battle of the Books* also occur, a reference to Phalaris and his bull, and a comparison of Clarissa's counterplotting to "a spider . . . spinning only a cobweb" (no. 252; p. 865: no. 256; p. 879). But more important than the bare allusive references is Richardson's fascinated construction of one for whom writing is not presence, nor presence any more definitive than writing, one who is a threat to the conception of text that Richardson valorizes.[44]

Lovelace is characterized as unfixed, a reference to his being unanchored to religious and moral principles, a failure that is also related to his protean qualities, his persistent role-playing that is not reducible to a consistent substratum or essence. Clarissa is able to locate the nature of Lovelace's threat relatively early although not immediately: "He is very various, and there is an *apparent*, and even an *acknowledged* unfixedness in his temper. . . . Hence it is that I have always cast about . . . what ends he may have in view from *this* proposal, or from *that* report" (no. 117; pp. 445, 446). Lovelace acknowledges three "passions" reminiscent of those in the "Digres-

---

[44] In a now well-known letter to Sophia Westcombe in 1746, Richardson writes: "While I read [your letter], I have you before me in person. . . . Who then shall decline the converse of the pen? The pen that makes distance, presence; and brings back to sweet remembrance all the delights of presence; which makes even presence but body, while absence becomes the soul" (*Selected Letters of Samuel Richardson*, ed. John Carroll [Oxford: Clarendon Press, 1964], p. 65).

sion Concerning . . . Madness" of the *Tale*: "Love, revenge, ambition, or a desire of conquest" (no. 223; p. 719). These are, however, drives without any very specific content, rather than motives in an explicit sense. Clarissa's perception of Lovelace is verified for the reader not only by his behavior but also by his self-conception as it is displayed in letters. His failure of consistency is sometimes presented not so much as a matter of hypocritical design—a purposive deception—as an inability to persist in some consistent role: "Do not despise me, Jack, for my inconsistency—in no two letters perhaps agreeing with myself—Who expects consistency in men of our character?—But I am mad with love—fired by revenge—puzzled with my own devices" (no. 216; p. 694). It is particularly difficult to use language as a predictor of the motives of someone whose conduct and language are radically volatile and inconsistent. He sometimes glories in the power of his unsubstantiated words, once calling himself a "name father" who speaks "by virtue of my own single authority" and gives preferments and degredations: "What a poor thing is a monarch to me!" (no. 174.2; p. 569). At other times he appears to respond to his own actions as if they were a reality out of his control, as if his words and behavior preempted *him*: "Was the devil in me! I no more intended all this ecstatic nonsense than I thought the same moment of flying in the air!" (no. 138; p. 493).

Lovelace is in some respects a composite of Peter and the tale-teller, exhibiting an appetite that consumes all voluntary restraints and loses coherence. "I will draw out from this cursed letter an alphabet," is Lovelace's preface to forgery, a statement exhibiting the overt domination of meaning that the brothers of the *Tale* attempt to conceal as they reassemble the alphabet of their father's Will (no. 229; p. 754). Lovelace's encroachments on others' meanings are evident throughout, but reach a notable involution when he annotates his own letter to Belford, "that I may not break in upon my narrative" (no. 233; p. 774). His machinations have reached a complexity that cannot be easily contained in narrative, an excess that perhaps implies that such doubling of text in narrative and commentary cannot easily be grounded in a unitary consciousness. When Lovelace's climactic attempt at domination, the rape, fails to achieve his end, he is left without any rationale for an incoherent self that has only its craving for power over others as its structuring object: "I will take an airing, and try to fly from myself—Do not thou upbraid me on my weak fits—on my contradictory purposes—on my irresolution" (no. 274; p. 930). Clarissa conceives of her rape as having occasioned a multiplication and loathing of self: "Once more have I escaped—but alas! *I*, my *best self*, have not escaped. . . . What a tale have I to unfold!—But still upon *self*, this vile, this hated *self*" (no. 295; p. 974). She, however, moves from textual fragmentation toward unity and coherence as she constructs the archive that will define her story.[45] Lovelace in contrast increasingly manifests the textual incoherence that is presupposed by his radical selfishness. Lovelace conceives of his plotting as narration—as turning bits and pieces into a story that has the shape required by his desires. His letters, thus, represent his plots more closely than by analogy alone. Writing to Belford of his elaborate charades at Hampstead, he boasts: "Now, Belford, for the narrative of narratives. I will continue it as I have opportunity; and that so dextrously, that if I break off twenty times, thou shalt not discern where I piece my thread" (no. 233; p. 767). But when his plotting fails, his narration does also, and he increasingly replicates the narrative failures of Swift's tale-teller. He convicts himself of writing upon nothing: "Wilt thou, or wilt thou not, take this for a letter? There's quantity, I am sure—How have I filled a sheet (not a shorthand one indeed) without a subject!" (no. 321; p. 1024). He sees his writing as an escape from the burdens of a self that is no longer ordered by his pursuit of Clarissa: "I am ashamed of my ramblings: but what wouldst have me do?—Seest thou not that I am but seeking to run out of myself in hope to lose myself; yet, that I am unable to do either?" (no. 472; p. 1347). Lovelace's verdict on his own recently written letter late in the book is that it borders on insanity: "Were I to have continued but one week more in the way I was in when I wrote the latter part of it, I should have been confined, and in straw the next" (no. 512; p. 1431).

Belford has earlier placed his own and Lovelace's character in relation to the foundational texts of their culture—the Bible and the classics. He transcribes one of Clarissa's "Meditations"—a paraphrase of verses from *Job*—as part of an attempt to obtain a reorientation of Lovelace's values toward Clarissa and scripture, which she reworks in relation to her own experience, much in the manner of Bunyan. In this same letter to Lovelace, Belford cites an accidental encounter with Anthony Blackwall's *The Sacred Classics Defended* (no. 364; p. 1126), which is a two-volume work subtitled *An Essay Humbly offer'd towards proving the Purity, Propriety, and true Eloquence Of the Writers of the New Testament*.[46] Blackwall's procedure is to find in

[45] Jonathan Lamb, "The Fragmentation of Originals and *Clarissa*," *Studies in English Literature* 28 (1988), discusses two uses of repetitive fragments—pleonasm or "fragment on fragment" and tautology or "fragment as fragment." Pleonasm can be "the consoling mockery of ruin—pieces on pieces," whereas tautology is "ruin itself—pieces as pieces." After her rape, "nine of Clarissa's written fragments are continuous with destruction, fragments as fragments; but the tenth, consisting of ten fragments of poetry, makes fragments of [on?] fragments by matching each bit of wreckage with a quotation" (p. 453).

[46] Anthony Blackwall, *The Sacred Classics Defended and Illustrated*, 2 vols. (London: printed by J. Bettenham for C. Rivington, 1725, 1731). Richardson printed the second edition of the first volume and the first edition of the second volume, as well as the fourth edition of Blackwall's *An Introduction to the Classics*.

ancient classical authors passages and usages comparable to biblical ones, thus making of the classics a standard that the Bible is shown to exceed. Belford expresses his newly awakened regrets for his former admiration of "less noble and less natural beauties in pagan authors; while I have known nothing of this all-excelling collection of beauties, the Bible!" He implicitly characterizes himself and Lovelace as classically educated rakes who have not recognized the extent of their own ignorance, examples of what Blackwall describes as "young scholars, taking the charge of solecisms, blemishes and barbarisms in these sacred authors for granted" and thus having "either neglected to read those inestimable treasures of wisdom and genuine eloquence" or having "read them with a careless indifference and want of taste" (p. 13). Characterizing the Bible as superior to the classics is not unusual and often coexists (in Blackwall among others) with admiration of ancient learning. Yet it also appears that Richardson is using Belford's almost casual citation of Blackwall to forward his rejection of Swift and the ancients. In an image reminiscent of *The Battle of the Books*, Belford remarks, "We choose to derive the little we know from the undercurrents, perhaps muddy ones too, when the clear, the pellucid fountain-head is much nearer at hand and easier to be come at" (no. 364; p. 1125). Swift's image is of Wotton attempting to drink too far from Helicon and drawing up mud rather than inspiration; while Belford associates the mud with the classics and the "pellucid fountain-head" with the Bible.

In Richardson's scheme, debility of text is to be regarded as symptomatic of Lovelace's character and thus without reflection on Clarissa's text, which is at least sometimes associated with scripture. In one case, the writing is grounded on a principled character and in the other on an appetitive consciousness. If one accepts that view, the meaning of Swift's *Tale* must be relegated to the disorders of the tale-teller and not applied to the modern consciousness that is exemplified in the writing of what we now know as the novel. The tale-teller and Lovelace are to be contrasted to Clarissa, whose story is to be connected to those "common forms" that provide a stability of character to underwrite a unitary text. Yet both Clarissa and Lovelace are examples of radical subjectivity, her writing the product of sustained and intense self-scrutiny and, as much as the tale-teller's, a product of almost physiological need. Some who confuse the simplicity of Swift with simplemindedness may see the attack of the *Tale* as a limited one on the obvious deficiencies of Temple's enemies. The implications of the *Tale*, however, are not easily confined to those modern examples that Swift cites (Vaughan, Dryden, Wotton, Bentley, and so on); he seems more generally to be denominating what Pope later described as "the Itch of Verse and Praise" ("Epistle to Dr. Arbuthnot," 1.224), an obsession with text that is associated with narcissism, an obsession Swift too suffered from and made into an "other" by calling it Grub Street.[47] *Clarissa* stands as an exemplification of the modern consciousness that Swift parodically represented in the *Tale*; Richardson diverts Swift's indictment to Lovelace, with whom he associates Swift.

In 1759 Richardson printed Edward Young's *Conjectures on Original Composition. In a Letter to the Author of Sir Charles Grandison*, a work he had helped Young revise.[48] *"Know thyself"*; *'Reverence thyself,"* commands Young: "dive deep into thy bosom; learn the depth, extent, biass, and full fort of thy mind; contract full intimacy with the stranger within thee; excite, and cherish every spark of Intellectual light and heat" (p. 879). Not unexpectedly for someone expressing such sentiments, he admires Richardson's writings and uses Swift as an opposing example of failure. Swift's was "an Infantine Genius; a Genius, which, like other Infants, must be nursed, and educated, or it will come to nought" (p. 876). But the kind of genius Young admires "has ever been supposed to partake of something Divine" and does not require learning (p. 875). Any modern inferiority to the ancients derives, in Young's view, from imitating them rather than from not knowing them. Originality is for him the preeminent quality: "Born *Originals*, how comes it to pass that we die *Copies*? That medling Ape *Imitation*, as soon as we come to years of *Indiscretion* (so let me speak), snatches the Pen" (p. 878). In his view, Swift's negative judgments on human capabilities are inimical to the true possibilities of the moderns, who as "heaven's latest editions of the human mind may be the most correct, and fair" (p. 883). But in making the Houyhnhnms superior to mankind, Swift "blasphemed a nature little lower than that of Angels" (p. 881). "Some are of Opinion," Young writes, "that the Press is overcharged"; he, however, believes that within the restraints of virtue "the more Composition the better" (pp. 871, 872).

This late salvo in the ancients and moderns controversy brings Swift and Richardson, satire and the novel, to the center of the controversy where the

---

[47] C. J. Rawson, *Gulliver and the Gentle Reader: Studies in Swift and Our Time* (London: Routledge & Kegan Paul, 1973), characterizes the *Tale* as follows: "The *Tale's* whole marathon of self-posturing cannot be entirely accounted for by its ostensible purpose, which is to mock those modern authors . . . who write this sort of book straight. For the *Tale* has at the same time a vitality of sheer performance which suggests that a strong self-conscious pressure of primary self-display on Swift's own part is also at work" (p. 2).

[48] The text of Young's work is quoted from *Eighteenth-Century English Literature*, ed. Geoffrey Tillotson, Paul Fussell Jr., and Marshall Waingrow (New York: Harcourt, Brace & World, 1969), a text based on the first edition but including substantive variants from the second edition. In *Samuel Richardson: A Biography*, T. C. Duncan Eaves and Ben Kimpel discuss the extent of Richardson's influence on Young's work, Richardson having read a draft in response to which he made relatively extensive suggestions to Young (pp. 432–36).

printing press has been at least since Wotton. But the press that Young evokes duplicates originals that come into being without essential reference to one another. In this view, books exert no pressure on one another if they proceed from an individual genius. There is thus no need for the accumulative efforts of indexes, summaries, and encyclopedias, the detritus of modernism. The anxieties of comprehension are at this later stage replaced by the anxieties of influence. Where Swift saw repetition, Young saw the originality of self that might be contaminated by engagement with the proliferations of the other. The inundations of text continue but, for the true modern, the need to acknowledge them has been dissipated.

CHAPTER 4

The Machine of Narrative:
Tom Jones and *Caleb Williams*

The narration of *Tom Jones* (1749) is notoriously self-reflexive; the narrator's commentaries on his procedures are on occasion extended to the point of self-acknowledged tediousness.[1] Fielding is concerned both to guide the reader's interpretations and to rationalize his own narrative techniques, which are inconsistent with his sense of the modern romance and also depart significantly from the classical writings he claims as antecedents. This display of authorial control over the carefully ordered plot has suggested to many critics that Fielding's literary work is designed to be an analogue to a providentially controlled world.[2] Yet the systematically displayed self-conscious

---

[1] Glenn W. Hatfield, *Henry Fielding and the Language of Irony* (Chicago: University of Chicago Press, 1968), differentiates between Richardson and Fielding on the basis of their different kinds of reflexiveness: "In *Pamela* it is the writing of the *journal* which is part of the action, not the writing of the *novel*, which is never overtly acknowledged by Richardson at all. It is rather Fielding . . . who truly makes the writing of the novel a part of its action" (p. 199).

[2] The question of a providential reading of *Tom Jones* has occasioned a wide range and shading of views. Martin Battestin, *The Providence of Wit: Aspects of Form in Augustan Literature and the Arts* (Oxford: Clarendon Press, 1974), presents one of the more influential arguments for the view that the plot of *Tom Jones* is an analogue to a divine order imposed by "a benevolent Diety whose genial Providence governs all contingencies" (p. 141). Leopold Damrosch Jr., *God's Plot and Man's Stories: Studies in the Fictional Imagination from Milton to Fielding* (Chicago: University of Chicago Press, 1985), differentiates the nature of Fielding's providential narrative from the preceding Puritan tradition: "When Defoe asserts providential pattern we may protest that we see his hand behind the arras. . . . But Fielding openly admits that his hand is behind the arras, and offers the great structure of *Tom Jones* as an analogue of God's structure, not as a literal instance of it" (p. 289). C. J. Rawson, *Henry Fielding and the Augustan Ideal under Stress* (London: Routledge & Kegan Paul, 1972), finds that Fielding

and sometimes laborious concern with new departures for telling a story *and* for understanding the "nature" authorizing it tend to undermine the claim that an author is analogous to the creator of the universe. Fielding shows us that there are many ways to shape a story, depending on a narrator's goals, and that truth emerges only through the reader's vigilance and the good will of at least some of those who bear witness, including narrators like his in *Tom Jones*. Although some truths are not available to even the best and brightest, this novel implies that it is possible to reach probable understandings that are for the most part adequate. Such careful, if not fully systematic, inquiry does not greatly resemble the imposition of divine order but seems rather to be related to human epistemology of a guardedly skeptical, but nevertheless practical, character.

In an important analysis of *Tom Jones*, Alexander Welsh argues that Fielding conceives of his presentation as conforming to a courtroom model in which the narrator, like a prosecutor or judge, evaluates contradictory testimony as well as circumstantial evidence and recommends a verdict that takes account of the available evidence. Characters like Allworthy must reach judgments within the story as must the reader outside; however, "both the reader and the judge within the story are obliged to await the inspiration of the narrator, who marshals all the evidence and presents it in the order most likely to bring conviction."[3] Welsh links this forensic model to a kind of narrative that dominated in the West from the mid-eighteenth through the nineteenth centuries: "In this period, narrative consisting of carefully managed circumstantial evidence, highly conclusive in itself and often scornful of direct testimony, flourished nearly everywhere—not only in literature but in

---

exemplifies a mid-eighteenth-century ambivalence in which even the "limited harmonies" of a residual assuredness were perceived to be threatened, resulting in "a sense of beleaguered harmony, of forms preserved under stress, of feelings of doom and human defeat ceremoniously rendered" (p. ix). J. Paul Hunter, *Occasional Form: Henry Fielding and the Chains of Circumstance* (Baltimore: Johns Hopkins University Press, 1975), p. 186, suggests that although Fielding may endorse a providential view, *Tom Jones*, nevertheless, sometimes shows a "simplistic rigidity in the face of growing personal doubts." Leo Braudy, *Narrative Form in History and Fiction: Hume, Fielding, and Gibbon* (Princeton: Princeton University Press, 1970), urges a strongly antiprovidential reading and emphasizes the force of contingency within the novel: "No matter how sincere its basis and how respectable its spokesmen outside the novel, the providential view in *Tom Jones* is at best supererogatory and at worst ignorantly or meretriciously self-serving" (p. 163). Andrew Wright, *Henry Fielding: Mask and Feast* (Berkeley: University of California Press, 1965), posits a version of Fielding in which such questions may be evaded or left unresolved: "Wherever, in *Tom Jones*, the moral pressure threatens to destroy the light and festive tone of the novel as a whole, Fielding interposes in one or more of several ways and, by the act of linguistic prevention through embellishment, preserves the tone entire" (p. 190).

[3] Alexander Welsh, *Strong Representations: Narrative and Circumstantial Evidence in England* (Baltimore: Johns Hopkins University Press, 1992), p. 57.

criminal jurisprudence, natural science, natural religion, and history writing itself" (p. ix). But if one takes history writing, rather than the courtroom, as the more inclusive model for the trials of *Tom Jones*, the narrator of Fielding's novel appears less authentically figured as judge, and rather assumes the more ambiguous role of author, someone whose authority must be garnered from a reader who questions the implicit coincidence of the narrative with an evidentiary base. The narrator's claimed status of judge (who demands the concomitant societal authority) may appear to be a rhetorical ploy for dissembling occasional tampering with the evidence, rather than an accurate assessment of a figure whose judgments ought to be law; neither the judge nor the historian is supposed to be altering the evidence, although both are empowered to produce narratives that marshal the evidence toward a particular end. The complexly ordered narrative of *Tom Jones* may speak either of the ordered creation—the harmony that exists in God's created structure—or of the usurpation of the divine position by an author whose created pattern does not appear in either the circumstantial evidence or the testimony.

When Fielding's narrator claims historical status for his narrative ordering, we are brought back to the question of providence, not merely to the human authority of the judicial system. A narrative so complexly ordered as *Tom Jones* implies that in some sense it imitates an order underlying the apparent disorder of human vicissitudes, an order beyond testimony and, as Hume later showed, beyond the possibility of confirmation by circumstances. Departures from probability may, however, indicate romance rather than providence. J. Paul Hunter notes that the narrational acceleration of the final chapters of the book make prominent the coincidences that appear elsewhere: thus the "radical symmetry of *Tom Jones* at once asserts the absolute order and calls all into doubt" (p. 191). Fielding may be conceiving of the writing of the book as analogous to a divine ordering of the world (thus in some ways replicating and revealing the forms that the providential order takes), yet the focus on narrative procedures and epistemological questions also exposes the processes of narrative construction, suggesting their sometimes deep implication in human deception, including self-deception.

Tom Jones claims a foundation in history while at the same time somewhat defensively asserting the limitations of the many kinds of history that are incompatible with its fictional ordering of the flux of human events.[4] Fielding's fictional narration claims a truth that he wishes to found on

---

[4] Philip Stevick, "Fielding and the Meaning of History," *PMLA* 79 (1964), argues that Fielding did not believe that history revealed any "particular pattern of decline or ascent" (p. 563), but that, nevertheless, contrary to Bayle's view, it "coheres in endless and intersecting chains of cause and effect" (p. 564). John J. Burke Jr., "History without History: Henry

humanist history—the history that claims to expose the large patterns of universal significance in human events, a meaning applicable to all times. This history is the kind that Temple and Swift supported in opposition to what they thought of as the pedantry of Bentley and the antiquarians. The humanists supported an exemplary history teaching the necessary lessons of civic virtue, as opposed to a history dedicated to a scrupulous erudition that values exactitude over scope and usefulness. Yet the narratives of humanist history are vulnerable to the charge that they distort the truth to fit the demands of exemplarity. Fielding's narrator openly displays his narrative ordering and selectivity of detail, which are essential to a persuasive presentation of events and a meaningful construal of their meaning. But such powers within narrative may not only enhance history by bringing it to apparent significance rather than relegating it to a recital of mere events, but may also ally history with romance by allowing the formation of meanings that are responsive only to the narrator's and reader's desires. In *Tom Jones* Fielding exposes the possibilities of narrative manipulation, allowing us to comprehend the perils in the construal of meaning through narrative but also revealing the poverty of an interpretation that stops short of "nature," that is, of principles that connect and order the seemingly evanescent events of existence.[5]

Tom Jones catches in its web a number of versions of representation that claim historicity, ranging from the extremes of an allegory that aims to reconcile described events to a totalizing preexistent meaning or text (as in *The Pilgrim's Progress* and the Bible) to an annalistic version of experience that lists events without regard to purpose, connection, or importance. Although Fielding's fiction is closer to allegory than to annal, it also distinctly rejects allegory as its historical mode, choosing instead to insist on explanation by second causes in terms that will as much as possible conform to

Fielding's Theory of Fiction," in *A Provision of Human Nature: Essays on Fielding and Others in Honor of Miriam Austin Locke*, ed. Donald Kay (University: University of Alabama Press, 1977), comments on "Fielding's burlesque of the compositional methods of historiographers, ancient and modern," but concludes that "the main target of Fielding's scorn was not the unreliable methods of historians, but the very subject matter of history, the affairs of the great" (p. 49). I would add, however, that shifting the subject matter of history also involves Fielding in significant evidentiary questions.

[5] Leland E. Warren, "History-as-Literature and the Narrative Stance of Henry Fielding," *Clio* 9 (1979), argues that Fielding wished to define "a role in which he could simultaneously make a convincing case for his views of reality and rouse his audience to question the propositions he asserted" (p. 98). Three distinct roles for the historian are discernible: "the authoritative historian as a valuable source of knowledge and guidance, the historian as demagogue whose influence is to be feared, and the historian whose authority is real but must be discounted through irony" (p. 99).

probability. Fielding's human world has an insistent specificity, in distinction to being folded into a world of constant experience that is susceptible to unified interpretation. His version of historical uniformitarianism relies on "nature" as its persisting foundation, a nature construed as exhibiting divine ordering but also allowing human freedom and variation. Nature thus requires a panoply of human interpretive programs for its understanding, even if its patterns are ultimately providentially controlled.

The narrator's complex rationalizations of his procedures respond to the need he perceives for true history to keep in view the larger patterns of meaning, while at the same time remaining responsive to the minutiae and diversity of observed experience. Fielding does not, however, present this difficulty in maintaining both pattern and specificity merely as one of epistemological and hermeneutical balance—of maintaining whole and part relationships—but as a difficulty in representation as well, keeping us aware that narration and event are separable from each other. Reader and narrator engage in a joint venture of interpretation, the narrator having to interpret an event as the reader interprets its representation. The narrator is conceived of as having resolved many of the problems in the interpretation of events prior to the narration, yet he also takes on the task of educating the reader in the essentials of understanding the potential deceptions in the representation of these events.

The figural possibilities within *Tom Jones* have often been remarked. Tom is a neotype of Adam, cast out of Paradise Hall for his errors: "*The World*, as *Milton* phrases it, *lay all before him*; and *Jones*, no more than *Adam*, had any Man to whom he might resort for Comfort or Assistance" (VII, ii, 331).[6] Yet despite his very real errors, he is being cast out by a deceived ungodlike Allworthy on the basis of impressions fostered by the snake Blifil and his supporter Thwackum. When Tom finally returns to Paradise Hall, it is not only because of his reformation but also because others' lies and errors of judgment are rectified. The narrative pattern is, as the Miltonic allusion suggests, that of a pilgrim in a fallen world, yet the concern is with this world and the possibilities of knowledge and activity within it, not with its possibilities for subsumption into the biblical anagogical narrative. Like *The Pilgrim's Progress*, *Tom Jones* foregrounds interpretative concerns, but they are not resolved through a deep understanding of a Bible that introduces a totalizing reality, but by a broad mixture of secular learning and experience in addition to sacred learning. When Fellamar woos Sophia by declaring, "That if he was

---

[6] Henry Fielding, *The History of Tom Jones: A Foundling*, 2 vols., ed. Martin C. Battestin and Fredson Bowers (Oxford: Clarendon Press, 1974). All references are to this text, which is paginated consecutively over both volumes.

Master of the World, he would lay it at her Feet," she responds: "I promise you, Sir, your World and its Master, I should spurn from me with equal Contempt" (XV, vii, 797). The allusion to Satan's temptation of Christ is almost explicit, yet the effect is not of great spiritual issues being contested, but of an inept line being trumped. The biblical figures are part of Fielding's construction of an artistic and moral pattern, but they don't pretend to subsume the narrative; they crop up in it.

The nature of the inquiry that is *Tom Jones* demands that the addressed reader be skeptical of narrative and not passively grant authority to the account of a presumedly beneficent narrator. The power of narrative lies in its ability to connect disparate events into signifying wholes: significance arises not from the isolated event but from its relationship to other events. Thus stories may be told in many ways, depending on what meaning or interest they serve. The narrator of *Tom Jones* wishes to claim his meaning as nature's and his interest as truth, claims that can only become persuasive in the world of this novel after they have survived contestation. The narrator's attempt to create a unified narrative must confront the skepticism about narrative that is displayed even within the novel.

Plausible but false narratives abound in *Tom Jones*. The story begins with the search for a plausible narrative to explain the infant Tom's appearance in Allworthy's bed. This attempt at the construction of a narrative has more requirements than simply ascertaining the identity of Tom's parents; Tom's mother must not merely appear but be made to appear in a narrative that also includes all the other known facts relevant to the sudden presence of a child between the sheets of the widower Squire Allworthy. Jenny Jones's history plausibly satisfies the requirements of time, place, and motive, and when accused she confesses. She will not by herself, however, flesh out the narrative, which needs to include a father for full persuasiveness. The father is plausibly supplied by the accusation of Partridge's wife, Partridge having been Jenny's master. This story is authorized by Allworthy's condemnation of its errant participants, but it is, of course, false; Jenny's story is a hoax and Partridge is an innocent bystander. But the neighborhood has also concocted other false versions of the narrative and continues to do so, believing (not entirely erroneously) that Allworthy must in some way have a prior connection to a baby found between his sheets. The true connection of Allworthy to this story in which his presence is seemingly contingent appears only much later when a very different set of events is connected to Tom's appearance. For another example of the importance of narrative linkings, the maturing Tom's fall from grace at Paradise Hall is hastened by the clever narrative constructions of his enemies, who link the episodes of the poached partridges and the sold horse and Bible to Tom's procurement of sex with Molly, the gamekeeper's daughter. When these episodes are linked, even the well-disposed Allworthy finds it plausible that they indicate Tom's sensual corruption rather than his generosity to Black George the gamekeeper (IV, xi, 196), although there is no necessary connection among them (and the narrator has already exculpated Tom for the reader).

Nor are deliberate deceit and profound ignorance the only sources of narrative distortion; the personal involvement of even honest narrators results in inadvertent bias. When Tom tells his story to the barber Benjamin, who turns out to be his putative father Partridge, the barber cannot believe that Allworthy would have turned away someone so little to be blamed. The narrator of *Tom Jones* comments:

> For let a Man be never so honest, the Account of his own Conduct will, in Spite of himself, be so very favourable, that his Vices will come purified through his Lips. . . . For tho' the Facts themselves may appear, yet so different will be the Motives, Circumstances, and Consequences, when a Man tells his own Story, and when his Enemy tells it, that we scarce can recognize the Facts to be one and the same. (VIII, v, 420)

The deceptiveness encountered in narrative explanations is not limited to articulated narratives but also appears in the informal narratives through which meaning is attributed to observed events. Mr. Fitzpatrick, seeing Tom leaving his wife's house and being reminded of his earlier suspicion of Tom at Upton, immediately challenges Tom to a duel, although Tom neither was nor is improperly interested in Mrs. Fitzpatrick (XVI, x, 871–72). Fitzpatrick's concatenation of events creates a narrative that demands of him a life-threatening action.

Fielding's narrator explores a series of narrative possibilities and constraints as he attempts to validate his own narrative, a story containing within itself many other narratives, erroneous or true to varying degrees. Included among the truths that history tells are the views of the participants in events, which may not appear to be truthful at all from a later perspective. Yet a history that excludes the possible perceptions of participants must remain incomplete, unable to comprehend the motivations of their actions. Attempts at understanding past understandings are, however, hazardous: much behavior, even much narration, does not accurately portray, or even betray, its motives. Consequent on this realization, a myriad of narrative foci offer themselves, ranging from the most restrained and limited of external views (which may give little useful insight), through various degrees of inferential judgment, to the internal access that a writer of fiction conventionally claims. Such claimed internal access is not easily restricted to fiction, however; a memoirist writing about people who are well known through personal experience might attempt something of the same perspective. Nevertheless, the historian who approaches an internal view without characterizing its speculativeness is affronting conventional boundaries. The narrator of a "history" of "private" life, the claimed, perhaps oxymoronic, task of the narrator of *Tom Jones*, is confronted by problems of plausibility: after all, how much *external* information can possibly be available about the seeming inconsequentialities of even recent events of daily living?

These problems of determining validity—or, more precisely, of creating plausibility—are much of the substance of Fielding's narrator's commentary on his procedures. He exposes what we might call the novelistic in his narration, and he distinguishes the evidentiary rationale for the seemingly more conventional historical narration. Yet such distinctions also tie some Gordian knots. Since the claimed evidentiary basis for a statement nearly always involves at least some kind of inference, is he not then constructing a merely probabilistic narrative? And what is the status then of events that seem to be fully verified, yet improbable? And as what is accepted as probable has altered over time, the supernatural having once been regarded as probable, must he adapt probabilistic interpretation to the audience of the present alone? And if truth is properly established according to the audience's changing criteria of probability, in what sense can history claim truth? Such is the tangle of issues raised as the narrator tests the boundaries of historical and fictional (that is, romance) narration in *Tom Jones*.[7]

The narrator of *Tom Jones* sometimes appears to be commenting opportunistically, nudging a particular rhetorical effect from a narrated episode rather than exposing systematic principles of interpretation and representation. Without denying the opportunism of many of his comments, however, one may also notice the repeated principles that are inculcated in the reader to guide interpretation and the reiteration of discussions that foreground a cohering set of problems about the book's representations. The following analysis is intended to expose this systematic side of *Tom Jones* without arguing that every aspect of the narrator's often tauntingly manipulative style can, or should, be reconciled to a system.

The earliest introduced and most fundamental of the narrator's announced principles for guiding interpretation and representation is "nature," which is later implicated in his discussion of "probability," the latter concept appearing as a persuasive, but not necessarily always definitive, guide for

---

[7] The fullest situation of *Tom Jones* within the romance tradition occurs in Henry Knight Miller, *Henry Fielding's "Tom Jones" and the Romance Tradition*, English Literary Studies (Victoria, B.C.: University of Victoria Press, 1976). My argument emphasizes the interactions of romance and history.

understanding the former. The opening "Bill of Fare" (I, i) designates the subject of the book as *"Human Nature,"* which is then characterized as virtually inexhaustible. Behind the amusing but not always illuminating analogies to cooking in this chapter lie the ambiguities, even contradictions, of neoclassical views of representation and of the uniformitarian conception of human nature. If nature is the same in all times and places, then seeming alterations in people occur only in manners, which if understood properly can be resolved into the unchanging principles of nature of which they are only particularized manifestations. Where then is the space for a new province of writing? Fielding appears to be conceding the potential repetitiousness of a modern rendering of nature when he argues that "the mental Entertainment" of the subject consists in the author's presentation of it, not in its material. But he later also claims a "prodigious Variety" for human nature. Presumably the new species of writing is needed not only to represent changing manners but also to explore more fully this "prodigious Variety" in human nature (I, i, 32), filling in omissions of previous writing.

But "nature" also functions as an interpretive principle as well as a definition of the normative object of representation. It is "nature" to which the "prodigious variety" of human behavior is to be referred for consolidation and comprehension. In this respect "nature" is a principle of simplicity, allowing the bewildering multiplicity of behavior to be understood as well as described. Here is where the conception of "probability" becomes both a solution and a problem for the writer. The natural is, of course, by definition probable, yet conceptions of probability are notorious for changing from age to age. Using probability as a guide to the interpretation and representation of events is, then, accepting the limitations of a particular time and place rather than appealing to what is true in every time and place. For someone like Fielding, who claims historical truth and also wishes to connect such truth to a uniformitarian nature, probability is in some respects a temptation to adhere to the prejudices of a time and place rather than accepting his responsibility to the best available evidentiary grounding.

In his chapter on the marvelous, Fielding explores potential uses of the conception of the probable. He first eliminates the impossible from the arsenal of the writer who follows nature, finding the miracles in Homer to be explicable only on the grounds that he wrote to "Heathens, to whom poetical Fables were Articles of Faith" (VIII, i, 397). But if one focuses on man rather than the gods, the humanly possible is all that is allowable, and for the poet, as Aristotle suggested, the probable rather than the possible is the preferred limit. But the writer of history "is obliged to record Matters as he finds them; though they may be of so extraordinary a Nature, as will require no small Degree of historical Faith to swallow them" (p. 400). Here Fielding appears to be succumbing to the kind of history he is repudiating—a history that repeats previous accounts, however much they violate the truths of nature. But he then defines a softened version of this fidelity to sources, suggesting that facts central to the story may not be omitted or altered, but less consequential facts "tho' ever so well attested, may nevertheless be sacrificed to Oblivion in Complaisance to the Scepticism of a Reader," citing as an example of an omittable story that of the ghost of George Villiers in Clarendon's *History of the Rebellion* (p. 401). He subsequently states a principle as rigorous as the one Hume adopts in "Of Miracles": "To say the Truth, if the Historian will confine himself to what really happened, and utterly reject any Circumstance, which, tho' never so well attested, he must be well assured is false, he will sometimes fall into the Marvellous, but never into the Incredible" (pp. 401–2). Urging the historian's obligation to truth, not just to the repetition of an evidentiary foundation, Fielding supports a critical use of evidence, obliging the historian to judge the evidence by the standard of nature but without necessarily allowing the narrower criterion of probability to prevail over testimony. Improbabilities (but not impossibilities) may be included if well attested.

But this rational solution is then further modified to reflect the difficulties of the historian of private life, who has no "publick Records, with the concurrent Testimony of many Authors" to support an account that is not probable. Trajan and Antoninus, Nero and Caligula, however improbably good or evil, "have all met with the Belief of Posterity" (p. 402), but the historian without comparable documentary evidence needs "to keep within the Limits not only of Possibility, but of Probability too" (p. 402). This kind of private history must then be restricted in its representations of events, able to include only what can be interpreted according to the canons of the probable. But the Fieldingesque narrator can, of course, present a critique of those canons that allow only certain reductive versions of probability, as when he defends a conception of love that is not reducible to appetite, thus allowing some actions to be probably motivated by love even if they do not reflect appetite alone (VI, i, 270–72).

In his discussion of the marvelous, Fielding introduces one of the more complex, even vexed, perhaps dubious, categories of *Tom Jones*: "Conservation of Character"—actions must not just be humanly probable but probable for a particular character (p. 405).[8] Fielding, in fact, appears not to accept the most obvious interpretations of this concept, especially since most of his

---

[8] John S. Coolidge, "Fielding and 'Conservation of Character,' " in *Fielding: A Collection of Critical Essays*, ed. Ronald Paulson (Englewood Cliffs, N.J.: Prentice-Hall, 1962), pp. 159–62, discusses the background and application of this doctrine. This essay first appeared in *Modern Philology* 57 (1960): 245–59.

fictional creations are not accorded a visible and categorical character analogous to the figures in the dramas that are the literary-historical basis for the concept. Nor can character and deeds be identical in quite the same way as the concept implies, unless one is dealing with an unvarying behavior that is unresponsive to motivational variation and is thus foreign to Fielding's novelistic constructions. Yet significant portions of the metanarrative of *Tom Jones* are related to the ramifications of this doctrine, which "requires a very extraordinary Degree of Judgment, and a most exact Knowledge of human Nature" (p. 405).

Fielding's use of the concept of "conservation of character" participates in the conflict of romance with history that forms the basis of his claim to the establishment of a new province of writing. The narrator of *Tom Jones* alternately, sometimes simultaneously, adopts the roles of historian and of romancer or novelist as he explores the limits of both kinds of representation. In history the concept of conservation of character is a useful aid to interpretation, whereas in fiction it limits what may be plausibly represented. Thus this concept facilitates Fielding's exploration of the boundary shared by novel and history.[9]

In his role as writer of fiction, Fielding explains the possibilities for inspiring attention while not quite violating probability; he sometimes appears to be engaged in stretching the limits that he evokes. The ending of the discussion of probability applies "conservation of character" to the literary drawing of character, not to its interpretation, and the narrator appeals to the audience's desire for delight, not for instruction: "If he thus keeps within the Rules of Credibility, the more he can surprize the Reader, the more he will engage his Attention, and the more he will charm him" (p. 406). (I take the meaning of this potentially ambiguous statement to be that the more surprises that can be managed within the limitations imposed by the need for credibility, the more the reader will be engaged.) The narrator warns against achieving probability by merely repeating what everyone has already experienced: neither characters nor incidents should be what "may be met with in the home Articles of a News-Paper" (p. 407). Subsequently, still speaking as a creator of characters, the narrator tells the "Reptile of a Critic" that the

---

[9] Ronald Paulson, "Fielding in *Tom Jones*," in *Augustan Worlds: Essays in Honour of A. R. Humphries*, ed. J. C. Hilson, M. M. B. Jones, and J. R. Watson (Leicester: Leicester University Press, 1978), sees Fielding as adapting the methods of the Abbé Banier in *The Mythology and Fables of the Ancients, Explain'd from History* to expose the differing roles of historian, poet, and mythographer: "The poet mythologizes historical facts, the historian tries to establish what really happened, and the mythologist analyses the myth in the light of history." In *Tom Jones*, Fielding simultaneously demonstrates the "construction and explanation of myth, showing how it is produced by poets out of historical events" (p. 180).

categorization of characters must not destroy their individuality; to preserve the characteristics of a class "and at the same Time to diversify their Operations" and "to mark the nice Distinction between two Persons actuated by the same Vice or Folly" are the talents of a good author (X, i, 525). Furthermore, characters should not be consistently good or evil: "If thou dost delight in these Models of Perfection, there are Books enow written to gratify thy Taste; but as we have not, in the Course of our Conversation, ever happened to meet with any such Person, we have not chosen to introduce any such here" (p. 526). And he goes on to argue the moral utility of mixed characters, whose contrasts make good emulable and the effects of evil regrettable (pp. 526–27). In this discussion the emphasis gradually shifts from the creation of the delightful by means of probable fictions to the need for accuracy in imitation, ending with a rationale for the moral usefulness of truthful imitation. The discussion appears to be a gradual departure from any rigorous standard of "conservation of character," rather than a vigorous defense of the concept.

The other role of the author in Fielding is that of historian, and thus interpreter of character, as opposed to creator. In his attempts at separating his fiction from romance, Fielding claims that his created characters are allied with history in that they are founded on existing, not literary or represented, character: "Though as we have good Authority for all our Characters, no less indeed than the vast authentic Doomsday-Book of Nature . . . our Labours have sufficient Title to the Name of History" (IX, i, 489). Asserting throughout the need for the writer of his new species of book to be learned, Fielding also insists that conversation and experience must be added to learning. These additional elements are enabling to "historical Writers, who do not draw their Materials from Records" (p. 489). The "Genius" needed is one that is "capable of penetrating into all Things within our Reach and Knowledge" (p. 490). Learning, Fielding suggests, is necessary to the historian because "Nature can only furnish us with Capacity, or . . . with the Tools of our Profession; Learning must fit them for Use, must direct them in it; and lastly, must contribute, Part at least, of the Materials" (pp. 491–92). (I take "learning" to refer to the literary part of the historical enterprise, the reading needed to create an appropriate representation.) But without conversation and experience added to learning, the historian fails, because conversation is necessary "to the Understanding the Characters of Men" (p. 492); and only from experience "can the Manners of Mankind be known" (XIII, i, 687).[10]

---

[10] Nicholas Lenglet-Dufresnoy, *A New Method of Studying History* . . . , 2 vols., trans. Richard Rawlinson (London: Charles Davis, 1730), summarizes qualities conventionally

In defining this new province of writing, then, Fielding brings together the imitation or creation of character with its interpretation in both fictional and historical contexts; he combines a theory of literary construction and historical reconstruction in the interests of a fuller history than can be provided without fiction and a truer fiction than can be provided without history. Fielding's understanding of the nature of character emphasizes the difficulties of its interpretation, difficulties resulting from a cluster of his assumptions about behavior: although behavior is visible, it can only be properly evaluated in the context of motivations, which are not easily understood; the motivations of behavior are often literally complex, as characters are not limited to a single relationship to any event and, furthermore, are usually neither wholly good or bad; although behavior is ordinarily visible to someone, evidence about it is often not direct but is conveyed through narratives and judgments that are themselves behavior and are thus subject to the pressures of interest and require motivational analysis. Given the opaque world of *Tom Jones*, a uniformitarian interpretation of character is available only at the end of the narrative, when the narrator is able to represent all characters in relationship to those fundamental aspects of human nature that are found in all nations at all times. Such finality is, however, the province of fiction, as it assumes a totality that is only partially assimilable to the conventions of history; history purports to be a representation of only a portion of an ongoing story in which it participates but must, nevertheless, borrow the fictional categories of beginning, middle, and end to delimit its story and its purpose.

Trying to situate himself within the boundaries of history while surpassing romance in his new province of writing, Fielding includes the perceptions of those within the story even if they do not support the anticipated final perspective; in representing what was perceptible then, he sometimes temporarily omits from the representations of character factors essential to its final comprehension and also includes factors that are accidental rather than essential from the standpoint of the outcome. A representation of the process by which meaning is generated must inevitably include a full emphasis on the particularities—the manners—that are limited to a time and place.

---

demanded of historians, which correspond roughly to Fielding's categories, although Lenglet-Dufresnoy does not demand all qualifications of all historians: "We should prefer an Historian, in whom we find these three Perfections, a natural Facility to write History, hard Study, and a great Experience of Affairs" (p. 276). In subsequent discussion Lenglet-Dufresnoy explains that valuable history may be written by those who combine two of these qualities without necessarily having all three. He applies "Study" both to historical research and to a knowledge of the classics of history.

Thus, while Fielding holds out a uniformitarian theory to order interpretation, his representation of character sometimes temporarily thwarts such theoretical conclusiveness in the interests of including the evidentiary base from which he must form the shape that fiction lends to history.

The interactions between historiography and fiction are further developed in Fielding's consideration of the difficulties of predicting a person's behavior as opposed to defining character on the basis of past behavior. Commenting on his procedure of allotting narrative time in proportion only to the importance of events, the narrator consigns twelve of the early, less eventful years of Tom Jones's life to the reader's care, suggesting that the reading of the preceding part of *Tom Jones* is sufficient qualification for such participation in the narration. This seeming confidence in the reader is coupled with an exhortation on the usefulness of being able to predict behavior: "It is a more useful Capacity to be able to foretel the Actions of Men, in any Circumstance from their Characters; than to judge of their Characters from their Actions. The former, I own, requires the greater Penetration; but may be accomplished by true Sagacity, with no less Certainty than the latter" (III, i, 117). This statement appears to mean that if circumstances are defined and character is known, behavior can be foretold by the truly sagacious. What is not being suggested is that actions will be the same whatever the circumstances. While there is, in the narrator's view, a fixity in character, character can manifest itself in markedly different but not unforseeable ways as circumstances alter. (This is a version of Fielding's complex view of "conservation of character.") Given, however, the vast possibilities for the adaptations of character to multiplicities of circumstance, even the latter and easier task, telling character from action, is itself formidable. Furthermore, the more difficult task—foretelling action from character—is dependent on the easier task of telling character from past actions (there is no Momus glass in Fielding). These two categories may be referred to the narrator's fictional and historical roles, showing how they too are interconnected. The historian's judgments are based on ascertained actions, whereas the writer of fiction makes character visible in action—in a sense defining actions that are appropriate for a character in changing, not past, circumstances. Yet the historian must also have this fictionalizing sagacity to some degree. The inferential reasoning needed to ascertain motivation and evaluate behavior in changing circumstances is just such a predictive capacity: the persistently insufficient historical record of behavior must be supplemented by an understanding of how a certain character is likely to act, thus authorizing an algebra that allows motivation to be deduced if behavior and circumstances are known or circumstances to be deduced if behavior and motivation are known.

The actual interpretations of character by the actors within *Tom Jones* often show little of the "sagacity" needed either to predict behavior or even to judge character on the basis of past behavior. Although fellow characters do sometimes understand each other partially and slowly, making judgments that in the long run are creditable, a large number of the judgments within the book are mistaken, often seriously so. The narrator, alternately assuming the notes of historian and fictionist, sees events from the perspective of their end (conclusion *and* goal) and is able to create a structure allowing the reader to achieve partial but valid understandings that are gradually linked, eventually making the total pattern visible. Such guidance is not available to the characters. As Allworthy pronounces his unjust sentence on Tom, which we know is based partially on the false narratives of Blifil and Thwackum, the narrator states: "The Reader must be very weak, if, when he considers the Light in which Jones then appeared to Mr. *Allworthy*, he should blame the Rigour of his Sentence" (VI, xi, 311). This insistence that the reader must comprehend the situation from the perspective of the character, distinguishing the reader/narrator's position from the limited view of the character, is repeated when Mrs. Whitefield treats Tom Jones disdainfully after hearing a grossly distorted version of his disgrace. Tom concludes that her response is the characteristic one of a landlady to a customer who has little money to spend (a conventional way of judging character in accord with an occupational category). But although both Jones and the Landlady are wrong, their views are justified, neither having the appropriate knowledge to judge differently:

> She was perfectly well-bred, and could be very civil to a Gentleman, tho' he walked on Foot: In Reality, she looked on our Heroe as a sorry Scoundrel, and therefore treated him as such, for which not even *Jones* himself, had he known as much as the Reader, could have blamed her; nay, on the contrary, he must have approved her Conduct, and have esteemed her the more for the Disrespect shewn towards himself. (VIII, viii, 434–35)

Even Sophia with all her prepossessions in favor of Tom is impelled to reject him because he has spoken improperly of her in public places, an erroneous conclusion deriving primarily from Partridge's presumptuous speeches, not Tom's. But here again the narrator remarks, "She had sufficient Reason for her Opinion; since, I believe, every other young Lady would, in her Situation, have erred in the same Manner" (XII, viii, 652).

There is a procedural logic and test implicit in these estimations of what is an appropriate judgment for the character, as opposed to the narrator or the reader, that goes beyond a mere forgiveness of them for their ignorance but even imposes an obligation on them to act as they do: to act without accord to the available evidence would be improper. Knowing Thwackum's character as we do, it seems insufferable that Allworthy keeps him around and even relies upon him. Yet the narrator rebukes any tendency in the reader to blame Allworthy:

> [As Thwackum's] Infirmities . . . seemed greatly over-balanced by his good Qualities, they did not incline Mr. *Allworthy* to part with him; nor would they indeed have justified such a Proceeding: For the Reader is greatly mistaken, if he conceives that *Thwackum* appeared to Mr. *Allworthy* in the same Light as he doth to him in this History; and he is as much deceived, if he imagines, that the most intimate Acquaintance which he himself could have had with that Divine, would have informed him of those Things which we, from our Inspiration, are enabled to open and discover. (III, v, 135)

In such considerations we have the benefits of the fictional and historical character of this new province of writing set side by side. The "Inspiration" of the narrator has enabled a full understanding that would not be possible at the time and, in some respects, perhaps not ever possible to a participant. But such "inspiration" also imposes its own kind of limitation. We must not only be able to separate *then* from *now*, but also the unmediated understanding possible to a participant from the enhanced understanding acquired from fiction. The narrator requires of the reader the doubled understanding brought about by both history and fiction. We must bring to comprehension not only the justification for a past error but also the impropriety *then* of the view we *now* understand to have been a correct one. Such a complete view if possible would truly surpass the limits of what Herbert Butterfield called Whig history.

Fielding is wary of the "inspiration" that belongs to the romance—exceeding as it does the limitations of ordinary human nature. The context in which he makes prominent his inspiration also includes a call for the sober assistance of history. Fielding, in fact, induces his narrator to plead ignorance, sometimes facetiously of course, more often than he urges inspiration. For example, the narrator remarks that Dr. Blifil impressed Allworthy by a "great Appearance of Religion" and immediately stifles the careful reader's suspicion of that "Appearance" by which Allworthy is pleased: "I am not possessed of any Touch-stone, which can distinguish the true from the false" (I, x, 61). Although this external view is only one of the narrator's stances, it represents his sense of the limits of ordinary human perception, limits surpassable but not usually with certainty. When Squire Western, roaring with rage at Tom, sees that Sophia has fainted in Tom's arms, he immediately calls for water and ignores Tom, at which the narrator remarks: "Indeed, I believe, the present Circumstances of his Daughter were now the sole Consideration which employed his Thoughts" (VI, ix, 302). His "I believe" is a refusal to claim direct access to Western's thoughts, even as it announces a plausible account of his state of mind. Such restraint, however, coexists with occasional definitive inner views of characters, as when Blifil spots Tom secreting himself with Molly: "*Blifil* knew *Jones* very well . . . ," yet "thought proper to conceal it, and why he did so must be left to the Judgment of the sagacious Reader: For we never chuse to assign Motives to the Actions of Men, when there is any Possibility of our being mistaken" (V, x, 258). The difference between access to Blifil's concealed knowledge and his concealed motive is to be found in a tension between the roles of fictionist and historian that involves not just the source of their respective knowledge but also the differing kinds of authority accorded them. As fictionist, the narrator knows what his creature Blifil saw, even if Blifil will not testify to it, but he refers the interpretation of Blifil's motives to less arbitrary systems of thought that are common to both audience and writer.

Despite his "liberty" as "Founder of a new Province of Writing" to make any laws he wants to, the narrator announces his plan to be a constitutional monarch, rather than a "*jure divino* Tyrant" (II, i, 77), extending the anti-Jacobite politics supported by the book into its narrative procedures too. Readers are granted the privilege of assenting to meanings, rather than required to accept them, even if the narrator of this book knows far more about its world than the reader does. Although the narrator is in charge of the plot, his authority must be exercised for the benefit of the reader. Thus his commentary seeks to function within the bounds of an understanding that is not unique but shared by the community. Needing to gain community assent for his evaluations, he is usually confined to probability. Without persuasive documentation for his private history, it is only the reading community's sense of appropriate standards of interpretation that enable his private materials to acquire the status of history. The narrator may reason with, even cajole and threaten, the reader in an effort to extend and refine the community sense of what deserves assent, but he must, nevertheless, appeal to standards of plausibility and judgment that are not confined to any individual, however insightful. His narrative procedure of limiting what the reader can know at any particular time is also related to this necessary reliance on community understanding. The reader and narrator often exercise their interpretive abilities on what is generally known rather than on what a privileged or hypocritical character may know, and thus they judge within the confines of the possibilities open to the general community, without, nevertheless, acceding to the malice and stupidity that frequently govern community judgment.

It is in the context of this attempt to function not only as an author of a fiction but also as an interpreter who accepts the constraints of community evaluation that we must understand the narrator's seemingly blatant misstatement that "it is our Province to relate Facts, and we shall leave Causes to Persons of much higher Genius" (II, iv, 87). The search for causes forms, in fact, a large part of the subsequent narrative. Without attempting to purge from the narrator's statement the provocative irony that invites the reader's resistance, there remains a defensible point to this division between "Facts" and "Causes"; facts are in his province because he controls the plot, whereas the interpretation of causes, a process that demands the participation of the reader, must be validated by a larger community than the author. He nags the reader to interpret without expecting authorial direction: "Indeed I shall seldom or never so indulge him, unless in such Instances as this, where nothing but the Inspiration with which we Writers are gifted, can possibly enable any one to make the Discovery" (I, v, 47). That the interpretation preceding this statement hardly seems to require inspiration emphasizes the narrator's undependability without diminishing the sense of his control over the narration.

The vast metanarrative apparatus of *Tom Jones* is used to encourage the reader's belief that the book works in accord with a defined plan demanding not only compliance but also participation. It is this shared labor that explains the narrator's claim not to be responsible for interpretation, despite his acceptance of the responsibility for making events meaningful: "I am not writing a System, but a History, and I am not obliged to reconcile every Matter to the received Notions concerning Truth and Nature" (XII, viii, 651). After this assertion, which implies that his responsibility is only to events, the narrator canvases the distorted views aroused by Sophia's blaming of Tom for his demeaning uses of her name. Instead, however, of then abandoning the notion of community interpretation, he validates the opinion in question—Sophia's erroneous opinion of Tom—by asserting its conformity to another version of community standards of judgment: "I believe, every other young Lady would, in her Situation, have erred in the same Manner" (p. 652).

However often the narrator defines his responsibility as being primarily to event, his evaluation of other histories is antithetical to such a constriction of focus. The narrator particularly eschews the method of the annalist, who lists events without regard to a plot, placing them only in relation to each designated unit of time. In contrast, this narrator will "spare no Pains nor Paper to open [any extraordinary Scene] at large to our Reader; but if whole Years should pass without producing any thing worthy his Notice, we shall not be afraid of a Chasm in our History; but shall hasten on to Matters of Consequence, and leave such Periods of Time totally unobserved" (II, i, 76). As the narrator understands very well, importance is not inherent but relative: designating something as notable or the reverse requires purposiveness, a theme or subject. Much history, even history that is not strictly annalistic, fails by the narrator's standards: if the present history were not of matters of an "extraordinary Kind," the reader might just as well "travel through some Pages, which certain droll Authors have been facetiously pleased to call *The History of England*" (I, iii, 38).[11] He excludes from his history events that are of equal importance with those found in the "weekly Historians of the Age" (III, i, 117), having a standard of relevance that is known only retrospectively and in relation to a defined and emplottable purpose.

The narrator's dubious opinion of much history is indicated by his treatment of the reading of two not very highly regarded characters, Mrs. Western and Mrs. Fitzpatrick. Both are readers of romance and history, yet neither enjoy the balance implied by that combination. Mrs. Fitzpatrick's frantic reading during her unhappy marriage includes "*Daniel's English History of France*; a great deal of *Plutarch's* Lives; the *Atalantis, Pope's Homer, Dryden's* Plays, *Chillingworth*, the Countess *D'Anois*, and *Lock's* Human Understanding" (XI, vii, 596–97). Mrs. Western, also an avid reader, "had not only read all the modern Plays, Operas, Oratorios, Poems, and Romances . . . but had gone thro' *Rapin's* History of *England, Eachard's Roman History*, and many *French Memoires pour servir a l' Histoire*; to these she had added most of the political Pamphlets and Journals, published within the last twenty Years" (VI, ii, 272–73). As Battestin's notes indicate, these lists contain writings of varying value in Fielding's view. While perhaps part of the reason for establishing these patterns of incongruously diversified reading is that Fielding finds the notion of a woman attempting to become truly educated innately comic, there is also in these lists an implication that history and romance do not by themselves sufficiently complete each other. The reading of these women does not adequately remedy the absence of that wide range of experience, of conversation, that Fielding demands of the true historian. Both women know something of the world of fashion and intrigue but have a very small sample of the "inexhaustible variety" of nature that *Tom Jones* attempts to purvey. In this treatment of reading as related to character, Fielding both writes a critique of history and implicitly validates his new

[11] See Battestin's note in *Tom Jones* for commentary on the possible references of this statement. Fielding may intend Thomas Carte's recently published *General History of England*.

province of writing, which not only combines features of history and romance but also claims to represent a wider variety of nature than is found in more conventional versions of either.

The inexhaustible variety of nature evident in *Tom Jones* demands not only inclusion but also exclusion. The incommensurability of linear narrative with the multiplicities and simultaneities of actions is often evident as the narrator pursues relevance at the expense of completeness: "To describe every Particular, and to relate the whole Conversation of the ensuing Scene, is not within my Power, unless I had forty Pens, and could, at once, write with them all together, as the Company now spoke" (VII, xii, 377). The kind of narration that proceeds without purposive exclusion is parodied in Partridge, whose interest in every detail thwarts meaningfulness and sometimes threatens even intelligibility. Purporting to bring news of Sophia, Partridge gives so many details irrelevant to this main purpose that Tom finally cries out: "What News . . . you have not mentioned a Word of my *Sophia*," to which Partridge responds, "Bless me! I had like to have forgot that" (XV, xii, 830). During the Man of the Hill's spare narration, Partridge irritatingly interrupts with questions eliciting information obviously relevant to a fuller representation but not to one serving the thematic, philosophical, and historical interests favored by the Man of the Hill's own narrative choices. Telling of meeting with his depraved gambling friend, Mr. Watson, shortly before taking arms with the Duke of Monmouth, the Man of the Hill states: "Here I will not trouble you with what past at our first Interview: For I would avoid Prolixity as much as possible"; to which Partridge responds, "Pray let us hear all . . . I want mightily to know what brought him to *Bath*" (VIII, xiii, 474).

Fielding's exposure of the hiatuses at the heart of intelligibility does not serve to make all purposive exclusion innocent, for we see that the narratives produced by Tom Jones, Mrs. Fitzpatrick, and others conceal wrongdoing by their exclusions. The narrator's own indications of necessary exclusions are sometimes a validation of his sparer account; by a figure of paradox, we are told what is excluded. Yet his motives for exclusion are sometimes far from the necessities of intelligible historical narration. Episodes are left unnarrated because unpleasant, dull, or controversial, thus emphasizing the shaping hand of the narrator as much as the intractability of truth. Inclusions, too, are narrative choices, not impositions by nature. When Mrs. Miller is introduced at some length, the narrator notes that her importance must now be assumed, "As our History doth not, like a News-Paper, give great Characters to People who never were heard of before, nor will ever be heard of again" (XIII, v, 705). This process of purposive exclusion and inclusion sometimes gestures toward narrative's power to make the meaning a narrator did not find.

On his trek to London, Tom Jones finds himself "upon a wide Common where were several Roads" and stops "to consider which of these Roads he should pursue" (XII, v, 635). During this interval a drum is heard, which Partridge takes as a sign of the imminent arrival of the army of the Pretender but turns out to emanate from a puppet show. This scene is rich with literary associations, the puppet show perhaps connecting with Ginés de Pasamonte—criminal, autobiographer, and puppetmaster of *Don Quixote*— whose chivalric puppet-world deceives the Don as the Stuart pretender may be deceiving England. From our perspective, the roads look forward and back—back to the Oedipus who killed a man where three roads met and forward to *Tristram Shandy*, whose narrator in his frustration with the demand to tell several stories simultaneously, says: "O ye Powers . . . which enable mortal man to tell a story worth the hearing. . . . I beg and beseech you . . . that where-ever . . . three several roads meet in one point . . . that at least you set up a guide-post, in the center of them, in mere charity to direct an uncertain devil, which of the three he is to take" (III, xxiii, 244–45).[12] This scene in *Tom Jones* links questions of narrative to the confusion of public and private realms that confounds history and fiction.

The persistent interpretive methodology of *The Pilgrim's Progress* is the clarification of human history through its connection to biblical patterns, but *Tom Jones* signals the limits of this biblical figural by its evocations of the Oedipal myth, a myth treated in this novel as a shadowy, obscure, unrationalizable force.[13] Tom's unknown parentage allows the narrator to raise groundless fears of inadvertent incest, eventually permitting the Mrs. Waters of Tom's Upton sexual adventure to be designated as his putative mother Jenny Jones. Mrs. Waters/Jenny Jones puts us at rest about Tom's parentage, yet the identification of Bridget Allworthy as his real mother does not merely exculpate Tom but reinstitutes an incipient Oedipal pattern of the early part of the book, when the warmth of Bridget's liking for Tom persuades Thwackum and Square to be "greatly jealous of young [twenty-year-old] *Jones* with the Widow" (IV, v, 170). Bridget's feeling is explicitly sexual, becoming apparent only when Tom is handsomely and pleasingly adult: "When *Tom* grew up, and gave Tokens of that Gallantry of Temper which greatly recommends Men to Women, this Disinclination which she had discovered to him when a Child, by Degrees abated, and at last she so evidently demonstrated her Affection to him to be much stronger than what she bore her own Son" (III, vi, 139). The narrator carefully exculpates Tom

---

[12] Lawrence Sterne, *The Life and Opinions of Tristram Shardy, Gentleman*, ed. Melvyn New and Joan New, 3 vols. (Gainesville: University Presses of Florida, 1978). Cited by volume, chapter, and page number of the text of the novel.

[13] William Park, "Tom and Oedipus," *Hartford Studies in Literature* 7 (1975): 207–15, describes the many Oedipal and incestuous patterns in the novel.

from having any sexual interest in Bridget (IV, vi, 174), yet the eventual revelation of Bridget's maternal relationship makes the reader recur to the incestuous passions of this lubricious woman. Incipient incest seethes within the book. For example, when Mrs. Waters/Jenny Jones announces to Allworthy the identity of Tom's true mother ("your Sister was the Mother of that Child you found between your Sheets"), the figuration of Bridget's child between Allworthy's sheets flirts with metonymic accusations of incest (XVIII, vii, 941).[14] We know by now, of course, that Summers, for whom Allworthy was surrogate father, is Tom's father, but this attributed parental relationship of Allworthy to Bridget's paramour arouses another potential fibrillation of the faux-incest motif. Although all has been rendered harmless by the outcomes of the story, its narration is not precisely innocent. We may even notice Oedipal besmirching (as well as other kinds) in Tom's relationship with the considerably older Lady Bellaston, whom Tom attempts to pass off to his landlady Mrs. Miller as "my near Relation" (XIV, iii, 750).

These Oedipal patterns point toward the dark side of Tom Jones, where suggestiveness evades elucidation and where the narrator sometimes declares himself unwilling to exercise his usual process of inferential interpretation. Yet the story of Oedipus itself has two sides—the seemingly clear truth of terrifying, inexorable logic, and the murky side of private knowledge and motivation, of staged blindness and willed ignorance. The narrative treatment of the noxious Blifil evidences both a seeming hard clarity and disdainful obscurity in its representation of the unsavory materials of perversity. Blifil was despised by a mother who displayed her attraction to the bastard in the family when he had achieved young adulthood. Abandoned to the twisted Thwackum and Square, Blifil was pitied by Allworthy, who attempted to compensate for motherly indifference (III, vii, 140). Allworthy's efforts, however, never have any apparent effect on Blifil's devious mentality or deviant sexuality; Allworthy's trust only enabled Blifil's frauds. The narrator marks unequivocally not only Blifil's objective frauds but also his internal perversity, shrinking from analysis but not from explicit reference: "Nor was his Desire at all lessened by the Aversion which he discovered in [Sophia] to himself. On the contrary, this served rather to

---

[14] Martin C. Battestin, "Henry Fielding, Sarah Fielding, and 'the dreadful Sin of Incest,'" Novel 13 (1979): 6–18, suggests biographical reasons in Fielding's relationships with his sisters for the incestuous patternings found in his novels. He also remarks on the "incest motif" in Sarah Fielding's writings, suggesting "her horrified awareness of how easily, and with what destructive consequences, an innocent friendship between sister and brother may be construed as a 'criminal' relationship" (p. 14). This material may be found in slightly shortened form in Martin C. Battestin's biography of Fielding, Henry Fielding: A Life (New York: Routledge, 1989).

heighten the Pleasure he proposed in rifling her Charms, as it added Triumph to Lust: nay, he had some further Views, from obtaining the absolute Possession of her Person, which we detest too much even to mention" (VII, vi, 346). Although unwilling to linger for an exploration of these polluted depths, the narrator is uncharacteristically committed to an unnuanced judgment on Blifil, not providing the customary exculpatory circumstances (available in Bridget's disdain and Square and Thwackum's distorted tutelage) or alternative possibilities of less damning motivation, but insisting on the absoluteness of the inner view that he elsewhere suggests is not humanly accessible. When, for example, Tom pities Blifil after his perfidy has been finally discovered, the narrator intones of Blifil's tears:

> Not in such Tears as flow from Contrition, and wash away Guilt from Minds which have been seduced or surprised into it unawares, against the Bent of their natural Dispositions, as will sometimes happen from human Frailty, even to the Good: No, these Tears were such as the frighted Thief sheds in his Cart, and are indeed the Effects of that Concern which the most savage Natures are seldom deficient in feeling for themselves. (XVIII, xi, 967–68)

The judgments on Blifil are absolute, the results not only of his apprehended conduct but also of his author's fiat.

In contrast, or seeming contrast, to the obscurity of these perversities is the most public history of *Tom Jones*—the intersection of the narrative with the events of the 1745 Jacobite Rebellion. On the one hand, material of a secretive nature is brought into only partial light, and on the other, an invasion that occurred in recent history is made a part of the story in a manner consistent with documented events. In his excellent analysis of *Tom Jones*, Homer Obed Brown argues the thematic interconnectedness of the two sets of events on the basis of a "genealogical disturbance . . . of particular relevance to the immediate historical situation of the 1745 Jacobite Rebellion."[15] The claims of the Stuarts to the throne now occupied by the Hanoverians rest on their legitimacy by birth; these claims are rejected in *Tom Jones*, just as Blifil's claims of legitimacy are displaced by Tom's claims of worth. In the narration of the Man of the Hill, the current Jacobite revolt is brought into relationship to the rebellion of Monmouth (the bastard of Charles II), who was then executed by his uncle James II. The Old Man, who fought for the bastard Monmouth, is astounded that the Stuart cause sur-

[15] Homer Obed Brown, "*Tom Jones*: The 'Bastard' of History," *boundary 2* 7 (1979): 204–5.

vives after James's public demonstrations of autocracy that ended in the Glorious Revolution (VIII, xiv, 477–78). Tom's later encounter with the gypsies is the occasion for the narrator's rejection of any arguments in favor of Stuart absolutism: the king of the gypsies is both a wise and absolute ruler of his people, but their form of government is not one to be emulated by the British. Although absolute government is capable of achieving great perfection, it is almost impossible to find a monarch who is equal to the task (XII, xii, 672). After pointing out the imprudence of altering a settled government for the sake of an absolutism that has had happy results in only a few cases in all history, Fielding contrasts a "pernicious Doctrine"— evidently Divine Right theory of government and, perhaps, the doctrine of passive resistance—to the interests of "honest Lovers of Liberty" (XII, xiii, 673).[16]

In these references public history is persistently brought into relationship with private history, most notably in the arguments of Squire Western and his sister; the Jacobite squire and his Whig sister introduce their political obsessions directly into familial living, the metaphors of government and family easily converting into each other.[17] Sophia is turned into an instrument of state and of business by the Whiggish Mrs. Western, for whom marriage should be considered as "a Fund in which prudent Women deposit their Fortunes to the best Advantage" (VII, iii, 332) or as an analogue to "Intermarriage between Kingdoms, as when a Daughter of *France* is married into *Spain*" (p. 335). But her Jacobite brother sees his daughter Sophia's resistance not as something to reason about but as a fundamental rebellion against constituted authority: "You have made a Whig of the Girl; and how should her Father, or any body else, expect any Obedience from her" (p. 336). Both of course act from motives of private interest and power, and the Whiggish sister ignores the criterion of liberty as much

[16] Martin C. Battestin, "Tom Jones and 'His *Egyptian* Majesty': Fielding's Parable of Government," *PMLA* 82 (1967), argues that Fielding is following an already established comparison in contrasting England's inability to sustain absolutism to what was possible in ancient Egypt. Furthermore, he suggests that "there was precedent for the explicit satiric comparison of Jacobites and gypsies" (p. 73). Manuel Schonhorn, "Fielding's Ecphrastic Moment: Tom Jones and his Egyptian Majesty," *Studies in Philology* 78 (1981), believes that "Fielding has, in the gypsy king, brought before his reader a model of authority and order" (p. 308). The episode, as I read it, presents a society for which an absolute ruler is appropriate and provides an admirable form of government, but, unfortunately, one that is totally unsuitable for England despite any theoretical arguments in its favor.

[17] Peter J. Carlton, "*Tom Jones* and the '45 Once Again," *Studies in the Novel* 20 (1988), argues that "the novel does support an allegorical interpretation along political lines" (p. 361), and he interprets a substantial number of events and characters of the novel in relation to Whig and Jacobite oppositions.

as her Jacobite brother, except when her own rights are threatened because of sex discrimination.

The dispersion of political ideology through areas of personal as opposed to national interest is a feature of the novel that appears especially in the seeming alliances of the lower classes with Hanoverians or Jacobites. Partridge's consistently held but rarely exercised Jacobitism seems designed by Fielding only to show how easily political allegiance can be muted in conformity to convenience. A landlord who mistakes Sophia for Jenny Cameron, Charles Stuart's companion, debates the advantages of flattering or betraying her, and finally determines that the rumors of French military support for the Pretender favor the course of flattery: "the *French* are our very best Friends . . . the People who are to make old *England* flourish again" (XI, vi, 594). A landlady so admires Sophia that under the misapprehension that she "attended *Jenny Cameron*, became in a Moment a staunch *Jacobite*" (XI, iii, 580). A puppeteer decides he can sustain the Jacobites' return of England to Catholicism as he could not sustain a return to Presbyterianism, "for they are Enemies to Puppet-shows" (XII, vii, 647). But a Hanoverian exciseman asserts forthrightly that he will not be "bubbled out of my Religion in Hopes only of keeping my Place under another Government"; his reason for this fidelity, however, is that though excisemen might be needed under a new government, his friends would then be out of office "and I could expect no better than to follow them" (p. 648).

Fielding's ironic dissolutions of nominal ideological categories in the acid of private interest or infatuation is a demonstration of the inevitable connections of public and private history. The full history of Jacobite and Whig, of the rebellion of 1745, includes analogues of Squire Western and Partridge, Tom Jones and the exciseman, not just the theology of Protestant and Catholic and the political commitments to constitutional monarchy or Divine Right. The unmilitant, although bombastic, country Jacobitism of Squire Western may be as relevant to the defeat of the Stuart cause as the movements of the Duke of Cumberland's army. In this foregrounding of individual behavior and private motivation, Fielding is not, however, merely demonstrating the need for a different kind of history but also, to at least a limited degree, a skepticism about the possibilities of writing history. Fielding's new province of writing shows the way to a kind of history that can only be fully achieved (or, more precisely, simulated) in the novel. This skepticism is, however, only partial, for Fielding also establishes an interpretational norm that frequently relies only on the possibilities in an external, communally accessible view, accepting probabilities without demanding certainties, and circumscribing areas of meaning without insisting on singleness of interpretation. The narrator is thus entrusted with the task of exploring

the boundaries between existing histories and this new one—the new conceived of as addressing the possibilities for including the narration of private
life that is essential to the truth of history but not always available to it. Thus
the explorations with the reader of what is communally derivable from
narrated actions and what can be understood only on the authority of the
interpretive privilege accorded the narrator are an attempt to constitute
the boundary between history and the novel—an extension of the limits of
history until the border between it and the novel are violated. That history is
a "fiction" in the sense of being organized with a beginning, middle, and
end—a structure whose incidents are chosen and ordered with a cognitive
and affective purpose—is never in question in Fielding. All narration orders
information to reveal meaning to a reader, and the reader is implicitly invited
to consider the narrator's representations not only of events but also of the
possibilities for interpreting a given sequence of events. Fielding's narrator
keeps before the reader his purpose to gather these interpreted events into
a single large pattern that will constitute the whole of the history. The
possibilities for achieving this goal rest on the adequacy of the tentative
epistemological assumptions agreed on by narrator and reader; their adequacy is tested by the plausibility with which the various events of the book
are drawn into one unified and consistent pattern.

II

The narrator of *Tristram Shandy* creates a great, almost perpetual motion
machine by his narration: "I have constructed the main work and the adventitious parts of it with such intersections, and have so complicated and
involved the digressive and progressive movements, one wheel within another, that the whole machine . . . shall be kept a-going these forty years, if
it pleases the fountain of health and life to bless me so long with life and good
spirits" (I, xxii, 81–82). His control of the narration is exuberantly celebrated,
not just acknowledged, although at other times he rebels against the burden
imposed on him by his story. Like Fielding he recognizes that meaning must
be represented through narrative arrangement and that description cannot
transparently reveal event. But the Shandy exuberance also points to another
element of narration, its potentiality to create self-serving coherence. The
great machine of *Tom Jones* may represent either a providentially ordered
world or a literary world representing only its author's desires. Fielding
includes this questioning of narrative within his own narration by liberally
illustrating the potentialities for narrative distortion—a questioning of narrative that continues even as he works out his vision of a comic world arriving

at coherence through a communal understanding of truths that exceed the limitations of any single character. A more sinister interpretation of the powers of narrative is given in William Godwin's *Things as They Are* (1794), later renamed after its narrator *Caleb Williams*. Godwin's post–French Revolution novel thematizes the functions of narrative in creating justifications for tyrannies of many kinds, public and private.

The eponynomous narrator defines the essential feature of his mind as a persistent tendency to what we might call narrative concatenation—an insistent connection of events in a tight causal sequence that is illustrated by, or analogized to, mechanics and natural philosophy, as well as literature:

> The spring of action which, perhaps more than any other, characterised the whole train of my life, was curiosity. It was this that gave me my mechanical turn; I was desirous of tracing the variety of effects which might be produced from given causes. It was this that made me a sort of natural philosopher; I could not rest till I had acquainted myself with the solutions that had been invented for the phenomena of the universe. In fine, this produced in me an invincible attachment to books of narrative and romance.[18]

Caleb's subsequent narration attributes infallibility to his ordering of events through this narrative understanding. He is able to connect apparently unrelated events into revelatory trains:

> I shall interweave with Mr. Collins's story various information which I afterwards received from other quarters, that I may give all possible perspicuity to the series of events. To avoid confusion in my narrative, I shall drop the person of Collins, and assume to be myself the historian of our patron. To the reader it may appear at first sight as if this detail of the preceding life of Mr. Falkland were foreign to my history. Alas, I know from bitter experience that it is otherwise. (pp. 9–10)

Caleb writes of this reconstruction as if it were an inexorable causality embedded in the world:

> Hitherto I have spoken only of preliminary matters, seemingly unconnected with each other. . . . But all that remains is rapid and tremendous.

---

[18] William Godwin, *Caleb Williams*, ed. David McCracken (London: Oxford University Press, 1970), p. 4. Karl Sims, "Caleb Williams' Godwin: Things as They Are Written," *Studies in Romanticism* 26 (1987), argues that Caleb attempts "to trace a variation of effects, which in turn are to be found in other narratives" (p. 347).

The death dealing mischief advances with an accelerated motion, appearing to defy human wisdom and strength to obstruct its operation. (p. 37)

While the first volume consists of Caleb's reconstruction of the underlying meaning of events that occurred before he enters the story, the second volume consists of his construction of a story confirming of conclusions about Falkland's guilt that he has already reached. For example, when Falkland as justice of the peace has to hear evidence against an accused murderer, Caleb "conceived the possibility of rendering the incident subordinate to the great enquiry which drank up all the currents of my soul" (p. 126). And as expected, when Falkland perceives himself being closely observed by Caleb he is deeply shaken and the two "exchanged a silent look by which we told volumes to each other" (p. 126). The desire embedded in Caleb's obsessed narrative construction of Falkland's guilt reaches a feverish intensity that is finally rewarded by Falkland's confession but is then also immediately punished by Falkland's making Caleb the object of a surveillance similar to that to which Caleb had subjected him.[19]

Yet what Godwin shows is that Caleb's truth is and is not true. Caleb's narrative starts with his announcement of his life as "a theatre of calamity" because of his enemy's persecution (p. 3) and reaches an ending just before the proposed final confrontation with Falkland. Its purpose is to be a "precaution," should the truth not then emerge and he no longer be able to

---

[19] A number of critics have commented on the fallacies of Caleb's claims to truth. Eric Rothstein, *Systems of Order and Inquiry in Later Eighteenth-Century Fiction* (Berkeley: University of California Press, 1975), remarks on Caleb's failure to give us a "sober body of notes and attestations, such as a real Collins could have provided for him," and concludes that "no one should be surprised . . . to find him shaping events in terms of the structures he knows best, those of novels that he has read" (p. 211). Andrew Scheiber, "Falkland's Story: *Caleb Williams*' Other Voice," *Studies in the Novel* 17 (1985), argues that "the 'truths' embodied in the Falkland story are institutional and deductive, antithetical to the individualistic and experiential brand of knowledge pursued by Caleb" and concludes that "Caleb . . . is caught between an old, defunct order of sentimental beliefs and a sterile, materialistic incoherence of facts" (pp. 257–58, 265). Caleb's obsessed surveillance has also been commented upon. Gary Kelley, *The English Jacobin Novel, 1780–1805* (Oxford: Clarendon Press, 1976), points out that Caleb shares his name with the biblical figure who spied out the land of Canaan (p. 204). Robert W. Uphaus, "Caleb Williams: Godwin's Epoch of Mind," *Studies in the Novel* 9 (1977), links Caleb's curiosity to a particular kind of rationality: "Secrets must become public, not merely to satisfy Caleb's curiosity, but to defend Caleb's obsessive attachment to the idea that all human activity is rationally accessible, just as he believes human problems to be soluble" (p. 282). James Thompson, "Surveillance in William Godwin's *Caleb Williams*," in *Gothic Fictions: Prohibition/Transgression*, ed. Kenneth W. Graham (New York: AMS Press, 1989), connects spying in *Caleb Williams* to the political atmosphere resulting from the suppression of the English Jacobins (pp. 176–77).

deliver it (p. 316). Godwin and Caleb, however, then conclude the narrative with a "Postscript" that repudiates the prior narrative, not on the factual basis of Falkland's guilt but on its presumption of Caleb's innocence: "I began these memoirs with the idea of vindicating my character. I have now no character that I wish to vindicate: but I will finish them that [Falkland's] story may be fully understood" (p. 326).

Godwin repudiates the claims for scientific narrative construction found in Caleb's main narrative. He shows that Caleb's confidence in, and obsession with, its inexorability is misplaced, not on a limited factual level but on the level of understanding, because of Caleb's deep involvement with "self, an overweening regard to which has been the source of my errors" (p. 325).[20] Godwin writes a critique of aspects of the Fieldingesque narrative with its ability to dispose of all events in a grandly persuasive and logically unimpeachable manner; such narrative needs to be underwritten by confidence in the socially validated system of verifying truth that *Caleb Williams* rejects.

Caleb Williams represents a late stage in the eighteenth-century process of constraining figural interpretation. Godwin's narrative recognizes the continuing influence that the structures of feeling associated with the figural have on characters and culture, but it opposes the implications of the figural, attempting to displace the biblical master narrative that in Godwin's view authorizes earthly tyranny by analogy to a theology of divine omnipotence and human worthlessness. In effect Godwin not only secularizes the situation of Christian in *The Pilgrim's Progress* but also reverses its meaning, finding that total absorption into the figure of the journey and absolute rejection of the earthly city as urged by *The Pilgrim's Progress* in fact implicitly recommend that one submit to the tyrants of the earth, not replace them by some otherworldly alternative. The repetition that is implicit in the figural is in Godwin's view associated with the *ancien régime* and its claims for the authority of tradition, whereas a narrative of truth is individual and immediate.

In a discussion from *Political Justice* of the possibilities of cooperation in the uncoerced society of the future, Godwin ventures the startling observation that he cannot imagine that musical and dramatical performances of the kind presently given will persist, as few would then value a repetition of the words and music of others: "All formal repetition of other men's ideas seems

---

[20] Gay Clifford, "*Caleb Williams* and *Frankenstein*," *Genre* 10 (1977), states that "Godwin saw that a world of plurality constantly encompassed individuality, and that the hero or heroine who constructed a self without constant recourse to that world was deceived" (p. 606). Jerrold E. Hogle, "The Texture of the Self in Godwin's *Things as They Are*," *boundary 2* 7 (1979): 261–81, shows that Caleb's self is largely constructed from texts.

to be a scheme for imprisoning, for so long a time, the operations of our own mind. It borders perhaps, in this respect, upon a breach of sincerity, which requires that we should give immediate utterance to every useful and valuable idea that occurs."[21] But in a broad sense language and musical notation are *in themselves* repetition, although they permit diversity within their systemic limitations. What Godwin appears to be struggling toward in at least some of his formulations is a presence that dispenses with the contingencies of the medium and transforms language into pure interpersonal communication unconstrained by the situational limits of circumstance and history. The situation of *Caleb Williams*, however, is one of "things as they are" in which allusion and the figural show the imbrication of a literary work in a texture of prior texts. Caleb struggles to find his own voice, but his narrative shows the overwhelming social and historical constraints that inhibit the actualizing of that voice.

Caleb asserts the invincibility of expressed truth despite repeated evidence that "truth" is determined by power: "Virtue rising superior to every calumny, defeating by a plain, unvarnished tale all the strategems of vice, and throwing back upon her adversary the confusion with which he had hoped to overwhelm her, was one of the favourite subjects of my youthful reveries" (p. 160). Fraudulently accused of theft by Falkland, Caleb responds: "Why have we the power of speech, but to communicate our thoughts? I will never believe that a man conscious of innocence, cannot make other men perceive that he has that thought. Do you not feel that my whole heart tells me, I am not guilty of what is imputed to me?" (p. 171). But Forester reduces this claim to "dexterity," which "will avail little against the stubbornness of truth" (p. 172). The situation resonates with those interchanges of *The Pilgrim's Progress* in which Christian asserts the unchallengeable authority of the combination of book, heart, and tongue; yet the difference here is that Caleb is undocumented, having no book or certificate to vouch for him and consequently resembling Ignorance in his mistaken confidence and obstinacy. Persisting in his belief in the power of truth within his society, Caleb eventually moves from defense to offence, resolving to tell the full story about Falkland, not just about himself: "I will tell a tale—! The justice of the country shall hear me! The elements of nature in universal uproar shall not interrupt me! I will speak with a voice more fearful than thunder!" (p. 314).

In the published ending Godwin confirms Caleb's faith in the power of the word, while at the same time also reiterating the burden of the prior

---

[21] William Godwin, *Enquiry Concerning Political Justice and its Influence on Modern Morals and Happiness*, introduction by Isaac Kramnick (London: Penguin, 1976), p. 760.

narrative that seeming institutional verifications of truth are merely putative—at best irrelevant, at worst self-serving perversions grounded in an
unjust social system. Falkland concedes his guilt in response to Caleb's
speech: "The artless and manly story you have told, has carried conviction to
every hearer. All my prospects are concluded" (p. 324). But the magistrate is
irrelevant to Caleb's seeming success; there is no effort to test the story by
the evidentiary criteria of the law.[22] And furthermore the public exposure of
Falkland that is entailed by the presence of an audience does not vindicate
Caleb, it reveals his corruption. Caleb now sees his appeal to institutional
justice as an immoral concession to a corrupt society and his destruction of
Falkland as unforgivable. Thus the power of the word is vindicated but only
to the degree that it rises above its social and historical restrictions and
becomes purely communicative. In the rejected original ending of the novel
no such vindication of the truly told story occurs. There Caleb speaks with
"energy, fervour, and conscious truth" (p. 328); demanding justice, he is,
nevertheless, eventually silenced by the magistrate: "Do you believe you can
overbear and intimidate us? We will hear none of your witnesses. We have
heard you too long" (p. 330). In this draft Falkland is unrelenting and persists
in his persecution of Caleb, following the amply demonstrated pattern of the
book in which truth is determined by power, not power by truth.[23]

The published ending shows Falkland as well as Caleb to be the victim of
the social/political system—"things as they are"—that perpetuates structures
of power in opposition to individual worth (in McKeon's formulation the
book mediates a "question of virtue" and a "question of truth"). Both characters are implicated in an apparent pursuit of truth that is exposed as ideological, an epistemology whose aim is power. Falkland under Caleb's
surveillance is described as "a fish that plays with the bait employed to entrap
him" (p. 109), and when the situation is reversed, Caleb describes Falkland's
"vigilance" as "a sickness to my heart" (p. 143). In the "Postscript" Falkland
attributes his past evil course to his need to "protect [himself] against the
prejudices of [his] species" (p. 324), and Caleb belatedly acknowledges that

[22] Kenneth W. Graham, "Narrative and Ideology in Godwin's *Caleb Williams*," *Eighteenth-Century Fiction* 2 (1990), argues that the last hearing is no more an instrument of justice than previous ones: "Falkland's guilt is established not in Caleb's eloquent testimony but in Falkland's confession. Thus, institutionally, things remain as they are" (p. 222).

[23] The endings of the book have aroused considerable comment. Mitzi Meyers, "Godwin's Changing Conception of *Caleb Williams*," *Studies in English Literature* 12 (1972), argues that the ending first written was unsatisfactory because it tended to endorse Caleb's perspective, while in the published ending "Caleb achieves recognition of the guilt implicit in his own selfish egoism" (p. 624). B. J. Tisdahl, *William Godwin as Novelist* (London: Athlone Press, 1981), remarks that in the published ending Caleb "realises that he has not only been buffeted by an evil world; his own mind has been invaded by its destructive modes of thinking" (p. 39).

if he had "opened [his] heart to Mr. Falkland" (p. 323), telling his tale privately rather than under threatening circumstances, the catastrophe would have been avoided. This thematization of surveillance and the will to dominate others in *Caleb Williams* shows Godwin's resistance to those aspects of eighteenth-century culture that Bender calls "novelization." In James Thompson's words, "The continuing power of [this] novel owes much to Godwin's uncanny recognition of the new form of the state and state punishment. . . . [S]urveillance in *Caleb Williams* should be seen . . . in larger terms of the function of an authoritarian state, the professionalization of the police force, and the development of the penitentiary" ("Surveillance," p. 179). Godwin exposes the complicity of language and literature with this society.

The preferable alternative to social coercion that Godwin imagines is not, however, a renovated government but reason, rational anarchy being in his view something to move toward, though not directly achievable in the present. Godwin looks forward to the time when a jury (like the Houyhnhnms) will exhort rather than condemn, and then to the time when no jury will be needed (*Political Justice*, pp. 553–54). He also attempts to preserve the possibility of escaping from the domination of a state that "intrudes itself into every rank of society" ("Preface" to *Caleb Williams*), urging the maintenance of an efficacious individual speech as exercised somehow outside the context of government and the surveillance the government not only practices but also insinuates into the minds of its citizens. Leland E. Warren argues that Godwin to some degree participates in an "idealization of good talk" among gentlemen that denies a voice to those excluded from this social milieu; it is only through writing as opposed to speech that the "excluded individual [is enabled] to shape his part of the larger social discourse."[24] Warren then exposes the problematic of Godwin's going on to write "as if writing . . . could eradicate the conditions that brought it into existence" (p. 68). Despite his less pessimistic theories, what Godwin shows in his writing is the perhaps inevitable enmeshing of language in a history that he regards as repressive and restrictive.

The ideal of a purity of individual speech that will redeem society places literature itself in an anomalous position. (The Houyhnhnms, we recall, have no written language and very little history, as their society is unvarying and

---

[24] Leland E. Warren, "*Caleb Williams* and the 'Fall' into Writing," *Mosaic* 20 (1987): 68. Jacqueline T. Miller, "The Imperfect Tale: Articulation, Rhetoric, and Self in *Caleb Williams*," *Criticism* 20 (1978), argues that from *Caleb Williams* "emerges an idea of language that equates words and things, defining the self and the world as basically linguistic constructs which are shaped, manipulated and controlled by those who possess the most powerful language" (pp. 366–67).

their literature oral, primarily commemorative.) Godwin recognizes the implication of Caleb's written narrative in the compromised culture that it rejects. Caleb's construction of a book that would function as verification of his view of his journey, the written text that will underwrite his heart and tongue (to summon up the verification processes of *The Pilgrim's Progress*), is identified as a mistaken effort. It has little merit in its form as a self-justifying interpretation and is efficacious only to the limited extent that it bears witness to a history of human errors, thus preventing the world from hearing and repeating the "half-told and mangled tale" otherwise extant (p. 326).

Caleb Williams confronts the figural as a kind of repetition that implicates action in past error, denying the possibility of rational freedom. The tyranny represented by a biblical master narrative is also attributed to other literary and social forms when they assume authority over present life. This topic of repetitive error is brought up implicitly when Caleb and Falkland debate the merits of Alexander the Great. Caleb summons up the opinion of "Doctor Prideaux," who "says in his Connections that [Alexander] deserves only to be called the Great Cutthroat" (p. 110). Prideaux's work sheds light on the subsequent dialogue and also on the topic of figural repetition generally.

The work referred to is *The Old and New Testament Connected in the History of the Jews and Neighboring Nations* (1716–18) by Humphrey Prideaux, D.D., dean of Norwich, who explains his purpose in the "Preface" to the first volume: "the clearing of the sacred history by the profane, the connecting of the *Old Testament* with the *New* by an account of the times intervening, and the explaining of the prophecies that were fulfilled in them."[25] This attempt is part of an enterprise often encountered in the eighteenth century in which the historicity of scripture is taken seriously in the sense that it and other authoritative historical accounts are assumed to be reconcilable. Intertestamental history is also a needed supplement to the Bible because it demonstrates the historical meaning of certain biblical prophecies and provides a missing historical context for Christ. This effort exemplifies the transition in biblical interpretation as defined by Hans Frei: eighteenth-century historicism motivated a movement from the adaptation of secular history to the biblical narrative to the subjection of the biblical narrative to verification and explanation by secular history.[26] Prideaux's work

[25] Humphrey Prideaux, *The Old and New Testament Connected*, 7th ed., 2 vols. (London: R. Knaplock & J. Tonson, 1720), 1:v.

[26] Hans Frei, *The Eclipse of Biblical Narrative: A Study of Eighteenth- and Nineteenth-Century Hermeneutics* (New Haven: Yale University Press, 1974), p. 130.

accepts the authority of the biblical narrative, yet also relies on secular history to determine the Bible's meaning and, implicitly, to confirm its authority, thus insinuating the possibility of a delicate equilibrium between the two interpretive stances:

> To make this History the more clear, I have found it necessary to take in within its compass the affairs of all the other eastern nations, as well as those of the *Jews*, the latter not being thoroughly to be understood without the other. And as far as the *Grecian* affairs have been complicated with those of *Persia*, *Syria*, or *Egypt*, I have been obliged to take notice of them also. And without doing thus, I could not lead the reader to so clear a view of the completion of those prophecies of the *Old Testament*, which I have in the ensuing history explained. . . . [H]ow could the fulfilling of the prophecies, which were delivered of *Alexander*, his swift victories, and his breaking by them the power of *Persia*, (*Dan*. vii.6. and *ch*. viii.5,6,21. and *ch*. x.20. and *ch*. xi.3,4.) be brought into a clear light, without laying before the reader the whole series of those wars whereby it was effected? (p. xxiv)

Biblical history appears here to be qualitatively central, yet too limited in scope to be adequate even for Christian understanding.

The debate between Caleb and Falkland over Alexander's merits focuses on issues of moral judgment rather than on biblical *figurae*, yet Prideaux hovers over significant portions of the debate. While Caleb represents accurately Prideaux's judgment on Alexander as "cutthroat" (p. 110; Prideaux, 1:387), that judgment is not the only connection to the *Connections*. Godwin shows Falkland's bondage to a system of chivalry that has brutal power at its heart and thus makes Alexander's brutality an acceptable model, whereas Alexander himself acts in accord with precedents or types representing his desires rather than his rationality. Falkland's defense of Alexander is founded on the conqueror's nobility of ambition: "He formed to himself a sublime image of excellence, and his only ambition was to realise it in his own story" (p. 110). In effect Falkland compares Alexander to himself, both of them exhibiting nobility of ambition. Yet that ambition is not self-generated but a form of imitation of past deeds and codes—Falkland's outmoded chivalry and Alexander's emulation of legends of the pagan gods and heroes. Throughout his account, Prideaux iterates Alexander's bondage to patterns established by legendary predecessors:

> The old *Greek* ballads, and the fables of their ancient heroes, were the patterns from which he formed most of his conduct. This made him drag *Betis* round the walls of *Gaza*, as *Achilles* had *Hector* round those of *Troy*.

This made him make that hazardous expedition into *India*; for *Bacchus* and *Hercules* were said to have done the same. And this made him, in imitation of the former, make that drunken procession through *Carmania* on his return. . . . And the same was the cause of that ridiculous affectation, whereby he assumed to himself to be called the son of Jupiter. (1:410)

Caleb's attack on Alexander derives from these details of the conqueror's destructiveness and cruelty, and it includes reference to his being a "sort of madman," among other things for "marching his whole army over the burning sands of Lybia, merely to visit a temple, and persuade mankind that he was the son of Jupiter Ammon" (p. 111).

Prideaux's objective is to place Alexander within the divine plan of Christianity while showing the futility of his own willful patterning of himself on pagan models: "But God having ordained him to be his instrument, for the bringing to pass of all that which was by the prophet *Daniel* foretold concerning him, he did by his providence bear him through in all things for the accomplishing it, and when that was done, did cast him out of his hand" (I, 410). Godwin, however, is not validating one of these repetitive patternings over the other but rejecting both pagan and Christian typology as tyrannical rationalizations of injustice.[27] Just as Alexander assumes and enforces a fraudulent divinity through his cruel exercise of power, Falkland too gives himself the attributes of a malign god, a parodic version of the god of the Calvinists: "You might as well think of escaping from the power of the omnipresent God, as from mine! If you could touch so much as my finger, you should expiate it in hours and months and years of a torment of which as yet you have not the remotest idea!" (p. 144). This pseudo-divine tyranny is not alone a reflection of Falkland's inflated imagination of himself but also acquires power through the providential imagination of someone like the servant Thomas, who converts Caleb's charges against Falkland into evidence of Caleb's gross impiety: "I should expect the house to fall and crush such wickedness! I admire that the earth does not open and swallow you alive!" (p. 176). We are reminded that in preparation for writing *Caleb Williams* Godwin testifies that he read portions of "'God's Revenge Against Murder,' where the beam of the eye of Omniscience was represented as

---

[27] Pamela Clemit, *The Godwinian Novel: The Rational Fictions of Godwin, Brockden Brown, Mary Shelley* (Oxford: Clarendon Press, 1993), pp. 50–51, surveys the allusions to historical characters in *Caleb Williams*, noting the tendency of heroes to become villains: Falkland's name associates him with the Civil War royalist hero Lucius Cary, Viscount Falkland; Tyrrel recalls Sir James Tyrrel, murderer of the princes in the Tower in *Richard III*; Alexander the Great is compared to Jonathan Wild; Raymond, the outlaw leader, appears to be patterned on the scholar Eugene Aram, who had killed his own friend.

perpetually pursuing the guilty, and laying open his most hidden retreats to the light of day" (*Caleb Williams*, p. 340). Caleb is brought fully to understand that Thomas's appropriation of such pieties constitutes one arm of Falkland's tyranny and that such insidious ideological tyranny is backed by more literalized force: Falkland "exhibited, upon a contracted scale indeed, but in which the truth of delineation was faithfully sustained, a copy of what monarchs are, who reckon among the instruments of their power prisons of state" (p. 177).

But it is simplistic to reduce the attack on the figural in *Caleb Williams* to an unmasking of the tyrannical uses of structures of feeling embedded in religious tradition. These structures of feeling are also exploited by the book to create its peculiarly urgent rhetoric.[28] Falkland's Gothic intensity is partially derived from his implied relationship to the tyrant god; the perpetual feelings of frustration created by Caleb's helplessness are communicated through references to a religious ideology that appears to produce the invincible blindness characteristic of Caleb's seemingly righteous oppressors. In the poet Clare, Godwin figures this fundamental ambivalence of literature— its power to cleanse the language of false mythologies yet its tendency to remain implicated in those same mythologies. Clare shows the participation of literature in both the promise of a future in which the untrammeled word will create justice, and its ties to this present world where it creates an affective bondage to things as they are and as they have been. The eminent poet returns to the place of his birth with a literary and moral authority that is unquestioned: "His remonstrances produced astonishment and conviction, but without uneasiness in the party to whom they were addressed" (p. 24), and he possesses "a richness of conception which dictated spontaneously to his tongue, and flowed with so much ease, that it was only by retrospect you could be made aware of the amazing variety of ideas that had been presented" (p. 24). Yet his reading of Falkland's "Ode to Chivalry" verges on ventriloquism—lending his own to Falkland's already large powers and insinuating the dangerous values of chivalry through his repetition: in Clare's reading "The pictures conjured up by the creative fancy of the poet were placed full to view, at one time overwhelming the soul with superstitious awe, and at another transporting it with luxuriant beauty" (p. 26). Clare later warns Falkland of the destructive propensities of his chivalric values; on this earlier occasion, nevertheless, he is able and willing to present a poem that

---

[28] Rudolph Storch, "Metaphors of Private Guilt and Social Rebellion in Godwin's *Caleb Williams*," *ELH* 34 (1967), argues of *Caleb Williams* that "the psychic energy for social criticism is derived from rebellion against parental authority, which in its turn is linked with guilt finding its expressive language in Calvinist obsession with divine persecution" (p. 190).

"would probably have been seen . . . with little effect" in a manner that "carried it home to the heart" (p. 26).

Godwin's alteration in the second edition of the name of Jones—who becomes Falkland's principal tool for the persecution of Caleb—to Gines (a rather unlikely name for an Englishman in realistic fiction until one imagines its anglicized pronunciation with the "i" lengthened) is a mordant comment on the imbrication of literature and a defective society. Ginés de Pasamonte of *Don Quixote*, chained and on his way to the galleys, is writing his own life, a work that he believes will put him in rivalry with Lazarillo de Tormes (bk. I, chap. xxii). Freed by Quixote, he then leads his fellow convicts to pelt their liberator with stones (in response to Quixote's demands that they carry chivalric messages to Dulcinea), an action of ingratitude that is compounded by Ginés's later theft of Sancho Panza's donkey. The pattern of chivalric lunacy that Quixote exhibits in freeing these criminals who might perhaps be best employed on the galleys is repeated when Quixote later meets Ginés, who is disguised as Peter the puppetmaster. When the virtuous puppet of Ginés's show, Lady Melisendra, is in danger of being overtaken by evil puppet Moors, Don Quixote saves her by hacking apart the entire puppet show (II, xxvi). In his interactions with Quixote and in his identities as picaresque autobiographer and puppetmaster, Ginés enacts repetitious narrative patterns, the romance narratives conflicting with the self-serving picaresque narratives.

Godwin transforms Gines into a more sinister character who, understanding the lies society tells itself, preys on it with impunity as both thief and thieftaker (Jonathan Wild and Peachum lie somewhere in his background). Gines's narrative, unlike that of Cervantes' character, is not of himself but of Caleb. His version of Caleb's life, *The Wonderful and Surprising History of Caleb Williams*, asserts Caleb's criminality and takes precedence over any protests of the living Caleb, much as the spurious continuation of *Don Quixote* threatened to absorb the so-called true Quixote (p. 301). When this false story first appeared in London, Caleb's self-alienated state is already apparent. Disguise upon disguise had deprived him of any authentic voice, and his expedient of survival through writing leads him to repeat the fictitious criminal lives embodied in the picaresque: "I retailed from time to time incidents and anecdotes of Cartouche, Gusman d'Alfarache and other memorable worthies, whose career was terminated upon the gallows or the scaffold" (p. 259). He recognizes the potential autobiographical reference of these stories—"a retrospect to my own situation"—even if undeserved (p. 259). When finally he narrates his own story, hoping that it will vindicate him from these stories of others, he discovers that, whatever his intentions, he repeats their disastrous pattern: "It is only now that I am truly miserable" (p. 325).[29]

Quixotism is given a malevolent cast in *Caleb Williams*: Falkland's love of chivalry, like Burke's in Godwin's view, is repressive and aggressive in its application, while Caleb's belief in the vindication of truth by law is danger-ously foolhardy in practice and destructive as an ideal. Godwin's respelling of his plain Jones as Gines in the second edition places this dark quixotism more prominently in relationship to the rejected figural. The incident of Caleb's leaving jail only to be assaulted by the thieves led by Gines is a conflation of *Quixote* with the parable of the Good Samaritan: stripped of his clothes and left nearly dead, Caleb is rescued by a samaritan who turns out to be the leader of the gang of thieves by whom Caleb had been assaulted (pp. 207–16).

Just before this assault, Caleb engages in his own version of quixotism. Rejoicing in his escape from the injustice of civil society, he declares himself ready to face the rigors of a state of nature: "Let me hold [life] at the mercy of elements, of the hunger of beasts or the revenge of barbarians, but not of the cold blooded prudence of monopolists and kings" (p. 210). This bit of grandiosity is shortly followed by the vicious attack of Gines and his fellows, who thus display some of the disadvantages of living outside the restrictions of civil society and in retrospect recall Quixote's foolish freeing of the convicts. But when the kindly leader of the thieves rescues him, Caleb's view of the possibilities of life outside the confines of society appears to be resuscitated, succor having been granted by an outcast, not by priests and Levites. Yet the ambiguity implicit in both the aggressors and rescuer being thieves is used to give the parable another turn. Caleb finds that the defini-tive positioning of the thieves outside of society produces an inevitable viciousness in them, accustomed as they are "to consider wounds, and blud-geons and stabbing, as the obvious mode of surmounting every difficulty" (p. 218). Their activities are "injurious to their own interest" as well as "incom-patible with the general welfare" (p. 226). The benevolence of their chief, the Good Samaritan, remains undiminished toward Caleb, yet his activities as thief go against the grain of his own understanding, and his status outside society is compelled as much as chosen. Gines provides a connection of the

---

[29] Donald R. Wehrs, "Rhetoric, History, Rebellion: *Caleb Williams* and the Subversion of Eighteenth-Century Fiction," *Studies in English Literature* 28 (1988), argues that Collins's story of Falkland "follows the conventions, echoes the themes, and re-stages scenes familiar to any reader of Richardson, Fielding, Goldsmith, and Burney," while Caleb's questioning of that story "places in doubt the 'naturalized conventions' that underlie Falkland's representation of him-self." Wehrs concludes that Caleb, however, "cannot conceive of his own 'story'" outside the context of eighteenth-century fictional norms (p. 499).

parable to the thieves of *Don Quixote*, allowing neither faith in society as it is constituted nor in groups organized in mere opposition to it. Perhaps on a more general level, Godwin suggests that there is no possibility of social redemption in the repetition of old narrative patterns, whether chivalric or biblical.

As *Caleb Williams* explicates its own deep roots in the narratives it rejects, it does not, nevertheless, sever its relationship to things as they are, which things are and must be its very means of articulation. In *Caleb Williams*, Godwin shows the difficulties, or rather perhaps the impossibility, of writing that stands against itself and advances a utopianism based on the presence of the word—views he sometimes appears to be advocating in *Political Justice*. Godwin's narrative exposes and rejects the validity of the master narratives that underwrite his book, yet it cannot avoid, any more than Sprat's description of his ideal language can, the implication in history of both language and audience.

Godwin's use of Burke's theory of the sublime illustrates this complicity of the text with materials that it attempts to purge. It would be foolish to treat every echo and instance of the common stock of the imagery of the sublime in Godwin as if derived from Burke, yet there are enough patterns of commonality between *A Philosophical Enquiry into the Origin of Our Ideas of the Sublime and Beautiful* and *Caleb Williams* to make one an apt commentary on the other.[30] Godwin sometimes contests, but also often exemplifies, Burke's conceptions of the sublime. Physical appearance, curiosity, isolation, and sympathy are themes prominently taken up in both books. Falkland's fall may be described in Burke's terms as a movement from the beautiful to the sublime—the small, handsome, and sociable man moving to the isolated, feared, and physically distorted figure of the later portions of *Caleb Williams*. For Burke the "first and the simplest emotion which we discover in the human mind, is Curiosity,"[31] a seemingly benign emotion that is extended by Godwin into a destructive obsession, the "restless propensity" that "often does but hurry us forward the more irresistibly, the greater is the danger that attends its indulgence" (p. 113). Solitude occupies a feared

[30] There is considerable commentary on the relationship of *Caleb Williams* to Burke's writings and politics. James T. Boulton, *The Language of Politics in the Age of Wilkes and Burke* (Toronto: University of Toronto Press, 1963), argues that "in Falkland Godwin was not only presenting the ideal of honour, of the *ancien régime* . . . he was providing an imaginative presentation and assessment of [their] supreme advocate . . . Edmund Burke" (p. 229). See also David McCracken, "Godwin's *Caleb Williams*: A Fictional Rebuttal of Burke," *Studies in Burke and His Time* 11 (1969–70): 1442–52, and Marilyn Butler, "Godwin, Burke, and *Caleb Williams*," *Essays in Criticism* 32 (1982): 237–57.

[31] Edmund Burke, *A Philosophical Enquiry into the Origin of Our Ideas of the Sublime and Beautiful*, ed. J. T. Boulton (London: Routledge & Kegan Paul, 1958), p. 31.

position in both writers. For Burke "absolute and entire *solitude* . . . is as great a positive pain as can almost be conceived" (p. 43), and in Godwin's novel the punishments of Tyrrel, Falkland, and Caleb are all versions of solitude; in one form or another, in explicit or implied ways, they suffer and fear this intolerable condition, although Caleb believes himself to be the most profound sufferer: "Solitude, separation, banishment! These are words often in the mouths of human beings; but few men, except myself, have felt the full latitude of their meaning. The pride of philosophy has taught us to treat man as an individual. He is no such thing. He holds, necessarily, indispensibly, to his species" (p. 303) For Burke sympathy is one of the "principle links" to be found "in the great chain of society," operating by preventing us from being "indifferent spectators of almost anything which men can do or suffer" (p. 44). Caleb, however, discovers that power can cut even that link, an implication that society is less benign than Burke suggests: "Sympathy, the magnetic virtue, the hidden essence of our life, was extinct" (p. 308). However much Godwin modifies the Burkean sublime, it remains a powerful aspect of his book's emotional appeal.

Godwin's politics are, nevertheless, in opposition to Burke's view that awe and fear are essential to the maintenance of stability. For Burke the sublime is always "some modification of power," since it is "impossible to be perfectly free from terror" while in the presence of that which may inflict pain or death (pp. 64, 65). People possessing virtues of the "sublimer kind, produce terror rather than love," such sublime virtues turning "principally on dangers, punishments, and troubles" (pp. 110, 111). Neal Wood connects Burke's aesthetics and politics, defining Burke's view that "in the case of the civic ruler, fear, awe, and respect must come before love"; "Ties of love and affection are never potent enough even in the family, to check the an-archic, egoistic tendencies of the essential man."[32] Out of this Burkean sublime, Godwin makes a recipe for human bondage and failure, in a sense treating Burke's analysis of the psychology of the sublime as an accurate description not of nature but of perverted nature. Falkland's movement toward the sublime is also toward despotism and injustice, not toward a beneficial order.

Despite Godwin's opposition to Burke, the sublime provides an opening to a conception of a transhistorical language that serves Godwin's conception of a word that is not enmeshed in contingencies. Burke believes that signifi-

---

[32] Neal Wood, "The Aesthetic Dimension of Burke's Political Thought," *The Journal of British Studies* 4 (1964): 57. Ronald Paulson, *Representations of Revolution (1789–1820)* (New Haven: Yale University Press, 1983), finds in Burke's views both a true and false political sublime: "The true sublime in government is a mixture of fear and awe or admiration, whereas the false sublime . . . generates only fear and a grotesque energy" (p. 66).

cant portions of our emotional responses are derived from our common physical natures. While agreeing with Locke that much behavior is derived from the accidents of association, Burke also argues that accidental associations are not to be considered as the necessary basis of our affective responses: "It seems to me, that an association of a more general nature [than Locke argues in regard to darkness], an association which takes in all mankind may make darkness terrible; for in utter darkness, it is impossible to know in what degree of safety we stand" (p. 143). Burke is here arguing against Locke's derivation of a fear of darkness from the arbitrary accidents of our experience, such as a nurse's tales. Godwin uses Burke's theory of the sublime to construct a narrative that illustrates the appeal of the master narratives that underwrite our bondage even as he suggests that our affective manipulation by them need not necessarily prevent our looking toward a world that can dispense with these apparently communal narratives, the nurse's tales that inform our mind-forged manacles. We are not at the total mercy of our particularized histories—our associations—and may thus look toward a "more general nature" to authorize our narratives. Burke's sublime is used to support affect while simultaneously allowing critique.

Godwin's *Caleb Williams* is a critique of the architectonic novel as represented by *Tom Jones*, which is itself a critique of more limited narratives. *Tom Jones* seeks to expose and subsume the biases of individual narration and reach the consensus of community in its large and authoritative narrative. *Caleb Williams* finds that the sweeping narrative concatenation of a book like *Tom Jones* is itself misleading because of its failure fully to acknowledge the powerful institutions that govern even its consensual truths. But as his antidote to the truths contaminated by the community's history, Godwin looks toward an escape from history. He is in this respect the heir to the French Revolution as interpreted and opposed by Burke, who foresees the destruction of society in the French attempt to make all things new. While Godwin rejects revolution in favor of evolution, he nevertheless argues for a rational understanding that is freed from its bondage to history.

Burke's view of society as a continuously evolving system too complex to be radically altered without unforeseeable deleterious results authorizes history alone to comprehend the social order. The constitution itself can only be understood "in our histories, in our records, in our acts of parliament, and journals of parliament."[33] And liberty becomes imposing through being connected to "its gallery of portraits; its monumental inscriptions; its records,

---

[33] Edmund Burke, *Reflections on the Revolution in France*, ed. Conor Cruise O'Brien (Harmondsworth: Penguin, 1969), p. 117.

evidences, and titles" (p. 121). Burke, however, is not recommending the critique of history that these materials might imply; history is too important to be absorbed by historiography. For him, history is constantly present, preserved in tradition, and when he states that "in history a great volume is unrolled for our instruction" (p. 247), he refers to the reading of history as if metaphoric, as if one could overleap the small printed volume to its referent, the great one. He is not delayed by reflections on the opacity of the medium.

Thus both Burke and Godwin in their different ways question certain aspects of the project of the eighteenth-century novel, Burke implicitly finding danger in its evidentiary skepticism and Godwin looking forward to an emancipation of language from history that would render the novel irrelevant. Yet both also endorse aspects of the novel's project, Burke finding its assumption of history as the arena in which meaning must be found to be a foundational truth, and Godwin finding its critique of its own and history's narrative procedures to be essential if history is to be loosened from the grip of repetition.

CHAPTER 5

From Personal Identity to the Material Text: Sterne, Mackenzie, and Scott

Historical time lies somewhere between time as we experience it in our daily lives and a cosmological time that is incommensurable with our mortality. We inscribe our existences in historical narratives as a way of connecting ourselves to a less limited time, extending our lives into as much of the past as can be meaningfully configured in relation to a present. Paul Ricoeur identifies "reflective instruments" that make possible the needed mediations among these times: a *calendar*, which uses some designated founding event from our histories in conjunction with regular intervals derived from cosmic phenomena to bring all other occurrences, including our lives, into definable temporal relationships; and the *succession of generations*, which provides a biological basis for historical time through its conceptualizing of a human chain that embodies memory and continuity.[1] Thus we have an extension of individual memory into the memories of a *we* that includes our predecessors. But this personalized memory changes character as it recedes into the past and increasingly derives from *archives*, *documents*, and *traces*. These too yield up and become part of our history, but they represent it in a way that is both increasingly public and increasingly problematical. As David Lowenthal states in *The Past Is a Foreign Country*, the basis of all awareness of the past is memory, which is our confirmation of the existence of the past, yet history is collective rather than personal.[2] Because much of memory is private and

---

[1] Paul Ricoeur, *Time and Narrative*, vol. 3, trans. Kathleen Blamey and David Pellauer (Chicago: University of Chicago Press, 1988), chap. 4, "Between Lived Time and Universal Time: Historical Time."

[2] David Loewenthal, *The Past Is a Foreign Country* (Cambridge: Cambridge University Press, 1985), pp. 193–214.

cannot be corroborated, history is both more and less than memory—more because communal and less because severely selective.

In *Time, Narrative, and History*, David Carr construes our formation of a personal identity as a narrativization of our experience, a configuration of the multiplicities of our past into patterns that are meaningful in, and include, the present.[3] But personal identity also includes group identity; the many groups we acknowledge our participation in—for example, familial, ethnic, religious, political, class, occupational—also structure personal identity. These groups can, of course, conflict with one another and are adhered to or resisted with varying degrees of urgency through changing circumstances. Indeed, Carr suggests, "many of the moral conflicts and dilemmas facing individuals have their origin in the individual's sense of belonging to different groups at the same time" (p. 155). The identities of these groups are also narrative constructions, often formulated by leaders whose rhetoric "unites the group and expresses what it is about, where it has come from, and where it is going" (p. 156); through such a shared narrative account, in Carr's view, the "group achieves a kind of reflexive self-awareness as a 'subject' that is analogous to . . . the individual" (p. 157). But groups may also have conflicting narratives representing different versions of group identity, and, as with individuals, these narratives must then be revised and recomposed to accommodate dissonances in experiences, goals, and self-conceptions.

Such intersections of the narratives of self and community interject the self into another temporality, as the time of the group often does not coincide with that of the individual: it is not unusual to use "we" when referring to events that happened to the group long before our birth. And the story of the group intersects with that of many other groups, putting us into relationships with a history that at first glance may appear irrelevant to us: "The proximate communities to which we belong . . . are situated for us within the larger panorama of history reaching back into the remotest regions and times" (p. 174). Carr's view is, then, that the historian as professional enters a world that is already saturated with historical narrative: the historian does not "reconstruct the past *ex nihilo* by applying rules of evidence to a heap of documents or ruins" but "functions in a context in which an account already exists before he or she begins" (p. 169). The historian's narrative has a cognitive aim that differentiates it from many of the narratives by which we construct ourselves or our groups, yet, nevertheless, all of us, historians or not, are, "*in* history as we are *in* the world: it serves as the horizon and background for our everyday experience" (p. 4).

[3] David Carr, *Time, Narrative, and History* (Bloomington: Indiana University Press, 1986), esp. chap. 3, "The Self and the Coherence of Life."

The attempts of Ricoeur and Carr to connect the time of the individual to historical time are complemented by Hume's discussion, "Of contiguity, and distance in space and time," from the *Treatise of Human Nature* (II, iii, vii).[4] Hume recognizes the location of the self in a present as an impediment to, as well as a precondition for, any comprehension of the past: "The imagination can never totally forget the points of space and time, in which we are existent; but receives such frequent advertisements of them from the passions and senses, that however it may turn its attention to foreign and remote objects, it is necessitated every moment to reflect on the present" (pp. 427–28). Hume canvases the various difficulties of overcoming this present-referring propensity of the human imagination, finding that we can more easily project ourselves into a future that may be ours than into a past that is growing increasingly more distant from us: "We advance rather than retard our existence; and following what seems the natural succession of time, proceed from past to present and from present to future. By which means we conceive the future as flowing every moment nearer us, and the past as retiring" (p. 432). While the self's connection with the present dominates, Hume regards a movement from past to present to future as a "natural succession," a judgment that is glossed by his earlier comment on the "order, which seems most natural" as one "passing from one point in time to that which is immediately posterior to it" (p. 431). Thus a time in closest proximity to the present is most powerfully conceived, and a succession forward in time, toward the self's position in a present, is more accessible to the imagination than one that goes backward. This view of the affective power of temporal relationships accounts for Hume's remark on the temporal order favored by historians: "Nothing but an absolute necessity can oblige an historian to break the order of time, and in his *narration* give the precedence to an event, which was in *reality* posterior to another" (p. 430).

Hume assumes, of course, that the historian establishes a temporal position in the past and then, having done so, moves regularly forward toward the present, without repetitive leaps forward followed by successive returns to the past, temporal leaps that might conceivably be made in deference to the present-referring imagination that does not allow continuously sustained concentration on the past. Presumably Hume is describing a decorum of history that suppresses the more radical pressures of the present, hoping that the forward motion of the narrative will be sufficient to divert the more immediate concerns of the self. This procedure appears to contradict Hume's analysis of our conceptions of distance in space: "When we reflect,

---

[4] David Hume, *A Treatise of Human Nature*, ed. L. A. Selby-Bigge and P. H. Nidditch (Oxford: Clarendon Press, 1978). In-text citations are by book, part, section, and page number.

therefore, on any object distant from ourselves we are oblig'd not only to reach it at first by passing thro' all the intermediate space betwixt ourselves and the object, but also to renew our progress every moment; being every moment recall'd to the consideration of ourselves, and our present situation" (p. 428). And when explaining why we venerate knowledge and artifacts of former times even more than those merely from distant places, Hume explains that the severe conceptual difficulties of overcoming temporal difference give us a sense of triumph when we succeed: "The imagination moves with more difficulty in passing from one portion of time to another, than in a transition thro' the parts of space; and that because space or extension appears united to our senses, while time or succession is always broken and divided" (II, iii, viii, 436). We here seem to be given reason to believe that the mind is perhaps even more driven to recoil to the present while conceiving of temporal as opposed to physical distance; the tendency of historians to keep the narration sequential might then be regarded as a technique designed to suppress or mitigate the brokenness of succession, thus thwarting their readers' propensities toward continual referrals and deferrals to the present. We may also recall Hume's practice in composing the *History of England*, his writing the account of the Stuarts in chronological order from James I to James II, then the Tudor volumes, and finally the earlier reaches of English history.

It is not surprising that Hume thought *Tristram Shandy*, "bad as it is," the best of recent English novels, exploring as it does so many of the issues of temporality and the writing of history that he had taken up earlier.[5] Sterne places his narrator and historian Tristram in the foreground of the narration and thus makes the present-referring propensities of self part of the narrative, rather than suppressing them. The past is persistently seen as needing both to be understood in relation to a differing present and to be narrated in a way that acknowledges the temporal complexities submerged in a consistently forward-moving account. With several strands of his story underway, all relevant but needing to be acknowledged and represented as temporally discrete, Tristram cries out in frustration: "O ye POWERS . . . who preside over this vast empire of biographical freebooters . . . I beg and beseech you . . . that where-ever . . . three several roads meet in one point, as they have done just here,—that at least you set up a guide-post, in the center of

---

[5] *The Letters of David Hume*, ed. J. Y. T. Greig (Oxford: Clarendon Press, 1932), 2:269. The context is a letter to the publisher Strahan in which Hume vetoed any Englishman as a possibility for writing a continuation of the *History of England*: "For as to any Englishman, that Nation is so sunk in Stupidity and Barbarism and Faction that you may as well think of Lapland for an author. The best Book that has been writ by any Englishman these thirty Years (for Dr Franklyn is an American) is Tristram Shandy, bad as it is" (Letter 482, 30 January 1773).

them, in mere charity to direct an uncertain devil, which of the three he is to take" (III, xxiii, 244–45).[6]

Tristram's book's title, *The Life and Opinions of Tristram Shandy, Gentleman*, defines him as an autobiographer, yet his sense of his identity as formed by a group, which was itself formed by events that occurred before his time, also turns him into a biographer who includes prominently his Uncle Toby as well as other family members and acquaintances. The structure of the book foregrounds this conflict between biography and autobiography, beginning with a search for the moment of conception of the narrator/object, who was born in 1718, and ending with an account of Uncle Toby's courtship of the Widow Wadman, following the Treaty of Utrecht in 1713. The events culminating in that courtship are shown to be connected to significant events of public history, including King William's War, which is the occasion of Toby's wounding, and Marlborough's campaigns in the War of the Spanish Succession, which are partially represented by Toby on his bowling green. The book makes no consistent backward movement, although its seemingly erratic movements may be systematic: the relatively recently wounded Toby is introduced in the second volume and the courtship is recounted in the ninth volume after many intervening post-courtship references. Tristram himself looks back on the principal characters of his book and life after their deaths and also confronts his own impending death in the course of his narration.

The many temporalities of *Tristram Shandy* call attention to a present in which the attempt to place events in meaningful patterns—to configure them—is at stake. The story must be constructed through connections that are the historian's responsibility: "What I have to inform you, comes, I own, a little out of its due course;—for it should have been told a hundred and fifty pages ago, but that I foresaw then 'twould come in pat hereafter, and be of more advantage here than elsewhere.—Writers had need look before them to keep up the spirit and connection of what they have in hand" (II, xix, 169). This foregrounding of problems of narrative configuration inevitably places the reader's temporality within the book, because the reader must unite all other temporalties. Having introduced and then parted from the midwife who is intended to deliver Tristram, the narrator Tristram reminds the reader of her, knowing she will be left behind once again: "But as fresh matter may be started, and much unexpected business fall out betwixt the reader and myself, which may require immediate dispatch;—'twas

[6] Laurence Sterne, *The Life and Opinions of Tristram Shandy, Gentleman*, ed. Melvyn New and Joan New, 3 vols. (Gainesville: University Presses of Florida, 1978). Hereafter cited in the text by volume, chapter, and page numbers of the text of the novel.

right to take care that the poor woman should not be lost in the mean time"
(I, xiii, 39).

Perhaps uncomfortably aware that such overt narrative manipulation may
lead to the charge that he willfully creates the perplexities of his narrative
rather than exposes those inevitably there, Tristram takes up the evidence
for his story in the immediately succeeding chapter, implicitly responding to
the challenge to tell his story straightforwardly according to its sources.
Tristram's apparent point is the rather simple one that it is impossible to
know when a story with the complications that his exhibits will be finished.
Yet the view emphasized, even if it is only implicit, is that no reprieve from
the obligation to construct the story is to be found in the seemingly rote
repetition of documents: "Could a historiographer drive on his history, as a
muleteer drives on his mule . . . he might venture to foretell you to an hour
when he should get to his journey's end;—but the thing is, morally speaking,
impossible" (I, xiv, 41). What is perhaps willful in Tristram's view is his
unwillingness to separate the narration about the making of the story from
the story. Tristram and Sterne appear to agree that the process of the story's
formation is part of the configuration, not a dispensable element. Tristram
begins the chapter by noting that he found a relevant detail about his
mother's marriage settlement after searching only a day and a half but that
it might have taken him a month. He regards the temporality of these
researches as constitutive of his story: the historiographer "will have views
and prospects to himself perpetually solliciting his eye, which he can no
more help standing still to look at than he can fly. . . . To sum up all; there are
archives at every stage to be look'd into, and rolls, records, documents, and
endless genealogies, which justice ever and anon calls him back to stay the
reading of" (pp. 41–42).

Tristram's displayed historical method combines in a sometimes disconcerting fashion the seeming formalities of research with private recollections
and intimate reflections: his invasion of his parents' bedroom on the very
night on which he may have been begotten succeeds by means of his
combination of two anecdotes delivered to him by Uncle Toby and family
tradition with his own sagacious interpretation of a memorandum from his
father's pocket-book (I, i, iii, iv). Tristram frequently founds elements of his
story on artifacts and documents that promise to transcend individual life,
fixing its instabilities and extending it into the past and future. But these
extensions of self sometimes stubbornly retain their own opacities, raising
questions about the validity of contemporary historical interpretation.[7]

---

[7] Stuart Peterfreund, "Sterne and Late Eighteenth-Century Ideas of History," *Eighteenth-
Century Life* 7 (1981): 25–53, argues that "Sterne felt the need to articulate an idea of history
in the dearth of any adequate idea available to him" (p. 26). He sees Sterne as responding
to concerns similar to those of Gibbon, Hume, and Kant, who "repudiated the hope . . . of

Tristram Shandy alludes to a broad range of scholarly activities connected to textual criticism by incorporating into itself a number of seemingly digressive documents—Yorick's sermon, the consultation of the doctors at the Sorbonne, the curse of Ernulphus, Slawkenbergius's tale, for some examples—and evaluating the texual authority of these interpolations, commenting on questions of provenience, transmission, and translation. With its temporal gaps and seemingly extraneous documents, Sterne's novel creates itself before our eyes, assembling itself as a book in the way that a textual editor might disassemble one. As Tristram makes the process of composition part of his narration, he does not cover up the seams of the narration—the leaps in time, the alterations of voice, the digressiveness—but exposes them to scrutiny. As we are close to his consciousness, the book emphasizes presence and presentness, but this emphasis coexists with an equally strong concern with the recovery of a dead or dying past—the immediate past of his family and also the more distant historical past of some of the interpolated documents. These digressive insertions represent the documentary evidence on which the book is founded, but this evidence itself requires evaluation, thus leaving in question the validity of the foundation. Sterne's novel self-consciously struggles to recover the past for a present moment and to extend its own presentness for a later reader; however, the attempt reveals both the subjectivity of the consciousness that appropriates the past and the ultimate evanescence of the medium in which the past is represented.

Sterne's book displays a shift in emphasis from the "being" represented *in* a text to the "being" *of* the text, map, or model. In this it follows the lead of a satiric masterpiece that is one of its sources—Swift's *Tale of a Tub*.[8] Swift's attacks on the great textual scholar Richard Bentley and more generally on the "modern critic" derive some of their force from his persuasion that they separate medium from meaning, creating a specious material of the medium

---

pursuing the study of history with total detachment and objectivity, and complete authority in meaning" (p. 33).

[8] Ronald Paulson, *Satire and the Novel in Eighteenth-Century England* (New Haven: Yale University Press, 1967), pp. 248–62, places *Tristram Shandy* in the context of eighteenth-century satire, pointing out changed directions in Sterne's work. Melvyn New, *Laurence Sterne as Satirist* (Gainesville: University Presses of Florida, 1969), deals with *Tristram Shandy* as a variant of eighteenth-century satire, especially of *A Tale of a Tub*. New has again taken up specific connections between the two works in "Swift and Sterne: Two Tales, Several Sermons, and a Relationship Revisited," in *Critical Essays on Jonathan Swift* (New York: G. K. Hall, 1993), pp. 164–86. Martin Battestin, *The Providence of Wit: Aspects of Form in Augustan Literature and the Arts* (Oxford: Clarendon Press, 1974), sharply contrasts the two works, despite the later work's use of formal aspects of the earlier: "In *A Tale of a Tub* the image of madness projected implicitly declares the nature of sanity and the value of rational order; in *Tristram Shandy* the mind is presented as an autonomous, irrational mechanism preventing rather than promoting knowledge of any objective reality" (p. 216).

and infusing it with their own desires. Swift frequently satirizes the reduction of scripture to an object, as when the brothers of the *Tale* manipulate the letters of their "father's will" or when Jack burns an inch of it under his nose to cure illness. Satiric details reminiscent of the *Tale* appear repeatedly in *Tristram Shandy*. Nature having "sown the seeds of verbal criticism" in him, Walter Shandy uses his penknife to alter some letters in a dialogue by Erasmus in order to arrive at a more satisfactory meaning than the "strict and literal interpretation" (III, xxxvii, 272, 271). Perhaps even more Swiftian is the incident in which Phutatorious, a hot chestnut having dropped into his breeches, is advised to wrap his burnt member in a "soft sheet of paper just come off the press"—"provided, quoth *Yorick*, there is no bawdry in it" (IV, xxviii, 386–87).

Sterne's attitude toward the materiality of an intellectual production is somewhat less satiric and more rueful than Swift's. *Tristram Shandy's* emphasis on the process of its own construction implies a material basis that might be relevant for any text, however valuable. Furthermore, Tristram's exultations in his authorial powers suggest on some occasions at least a limited victory for the moderns, whose authority over the past is exemplified in Tristram's masterful assimilations and revisions of earlier texts. Sterne sometimes hints at the inevitability of authorial egoism, accepting to some degree what Swift attempted to turn into the hated *other* of modernism. Sterne exposes claims of historical objectivity as failures to recognize the subversive forces of authorial subjectivity, and he also mocks the pretensions of scholarly researches, which often fall short of the narrative configuration needed to create meaning. But in identifying the text so completely with its author, Sterne also emphasizes the implication of text in human mortality: human death is not mitigated by a dying text.

The treatment of the text of the sermon inexplicably found by Trim in the leaves of a book by Stevinus is a parody of textual criticism and an example of the often vanishing textual foundation in *Tristram Shandy*. On stylistic grounds Walter attributes the sermon to Yorick (harbinger of death as his Shakespearean original suggests), a conjecture confirmed the next day when Yorick sends a servant to claim the sermon (pp. 165–66). But we are then further teased by the question of how this sermon of Yorick, if *then* claimed, came to appear verbatim in the book we are *now* reading:

Ill-fated sermon! Thou wast lost, after this recovery of thee, a second time, dropp'd thro' an unsuspected fissure in thy master's pocket, down into a treacherous and a tatter'd lining,—trod deep into the dirt by the left hind foot of his Rosinante, inhumanly stepping upon thee as thou falledst;— buried ten days in the mire,—raised up out of it by a beggar, sold for a halfpenny to a parish-clerk,—transferred to his parson,—lost for ever to thy own, the remainder of his days,—nor restored to his restless *Manes* till this very moment, that I tell the world the story. (II, xvii, 166)

So elaborately detailed and improbable an establishment of the provenience of the sermon subjects the very process of tracing provenience to the stresses of comedy. Furthermore, this sermon had already been preached and published by Sterne *in propria persona*.

The Yorick to whom the sermon is so definitively and yet ambiguously attributed is himself earlier given a precise lineage that gradually vanishes in indefiniteness and humor. From "a most antient account of the family, wrote upon strong vellum, and now in perfect preservation," Tristram learns that Yorick's name was spelled as it now is for nine hundred years (I, xi, 25). Drawing back from this assertion as an improbability, Tristram nevertheless finds that through the "religious preservation" of family records, he can trace Yorick's ancestry to Denmark's court. And because many of Shakespeare's plays "are founded upon authenticated facts" (p. 26), he concludes that the dead jester of *Hamlet* was Yorick's ancestor. Recognizing that this assertion doesn't quite establish the authenticity of Shakespeare's historical details, Tristram comically truncates the regression: "I have not the time to look into *Saxo-Grammaticus's Danish* history, to know the certainty of this;—but if you have leisure, and can easily get at the book, you may do it full as well yourself" (p. 26). We are left with a parody of historical method that does not yield even the appearance of the expected certainties.

The uncertainties of historical method as shown in *Tristram Shandy* are specifically linked to biblical criticism in Tristram's comparison of his father to Job, a figure whose very existence had been called into question: "*Now* my father had a way, a little like that of *Job's* (in case there ever was such a man—if not, there's an end of the matter)" (V, xiii, 441). Although an interpretation of the character of Walter is rather ineffectually bolstered by pursuing questions about the existence of a biblical prototype, Tristram decides not to abandon Job: ". . . because your learned men find some difficulty in fixing the precise aera in which so great a man lived;—whether, for instance, before or after the patriarchs, &c.—to vote, therefore, that he never lived *at all*, is a little cruel" (p. 442). The allusion here is to a specific controversy about the historicity of *Job*, in which William Warburton was a major participant.[9] Although Warburton specifically states that Job existed, his interpretation of the biblical account is a dismissal of any literal view of its historicity.

---

[9] William Warburton, *The Divine Legation of Moses Demonstrated*, 4 vols. (London: Fletcher Gyles, 1741; facsimile ed., New York: Garland Publishing, 1978).

Warburton and the controversy over Job appear to have occupied a more important place in Sterne's imagination than these rather brief remarks on Job might indicate. Walter Shandy is compared repeatedly to Job and, as Melvyn New has shown, Warburton's *Divine Legation of Moses*, in which Job is discussed, appears in *Tristram Shandy* in repeated allusions.[10] In addition to these internal references, a plausible, although secondhand, account of Sterne's early plan for *Tristram Shandy* suggests that it was to be a satire like *The Memoirs of Martinus Scriblerus*, with Dr. William Warburton as tutor to Tristram, and including an allegory on recent interpretations of *Job* in which Warburton was to be Satan and three attackers of his theories about Job— Richard Grey, Leonard Chappelow, and Charles Peters—were to be Job's comforters.[11] Sterne's interest in the Job story itself is attested by the two sermons on Job printed for the *Sermons of Mr. Yorick*.

This controversy over *Job*, limited as it appears to be, expresses vividly the anxieties about scripture that were generated by eighteenth-century historicism. The commentators were attempting both to save some kind of historical reference for *Job* and to acknowledge its apparent literary structure. Allusions to the controversy may have served Sterne's interests in a number of ways. He was no doubt interested in discomfiting Warburton as has been suggested, recalling for his audience not just Warburton's reading of the Job story in *The Divine Legation of Moses* but also his theory that the Old Testament gives no indication of the Hebrews having any conception of an afterlife, a theory that offended some Christians and motivated a series of controversial writings. But the concerns in *Tristram Shandy* with history and the limits of its methods suggest that the larger outlines of the controversy may have held an interest for Sterne beyond any specific personal concerns. Certainly there is much in these writings to indicate the uncertainty of the critical methods of contemporary scholarship and thus support some of his jokes at the expense of what he considered pedantry. Perhaps, however, the aspect of the controversy most relevant to *Tristram Shandy* is the attempt on the part of the analysts of *Job* to reconcile its clear manifestation of literary shaping to some version of historicity—a concern relevant to central issues in Sterne's book.[12]

[10] Melvyn New, "Sterne, Warburton, and the Burden of Exuberant Wit," *Eighteenth-Century Studies* 15 (1981–1982): 245–74.

[11] See Arthur H. Cash, *Laurence Sterne: The Early and Middle Years* (London: Methuen, 1975), pp. 278–80. Martin C. Battestin, *The Providence of Wit: Aspects of Form in Augustan Literature and the Arts*, surveys the issues in the controversy over Job in his chapter on *The Vicar of Wakefield* (esp. pp. 200–205).

[12] Jonathan Lamb, "The Job Controversy, Sterne, and the Question of Allegory," *Eighteenth-Century Studies* 24 (1990), argues that Sterne's rejection of Warburton's position is a rejection of those who "read unredemptively in pursuit of single meanings" rather than pursuing the

Warburton, constructing an allegorical interpretation to save the histori-cal reference of a book whose literal statements he cannot accept, concludes that *Job* was probably written by Ezra and that it is an allegory of the difficulties of Judah after the return from the Babylonian captivity (*Divine Legation*, 2:482–542). Warburton is driven to this historical allegory in order to preserve some element of historical reference for a work that he recog-nizes as essentially literary, with the structure of a drama. Although there are historical truths within the story, Warburton believes that the described events have an allegorical meaning and that the work's structure and descrip-tions are governed by literary criteria.

Before reviewing some of the views of Warburton's adversaries, it may be useful to look at what one of his supporters found useful in this allegorical theory. John Garnett in his *Dissertation on the Book of Job* praises Warburton's views because they give the story significance without demand-ing any literal historicity of it.[13] *Job*, he finds, is full of absurdities if taken as history, but Warburton's solution of seeing it as drama and allegory saves it from any literalistic historical demands: "But once suppose the book allegorical as well as dramatical, all those difficulties vanish and the rules of probability and decorum become the sole standards, of judging of the whole scope and propriety of the performance" (p. 303). Garnett dispenses with the historicity of the book to a degree that might have made Warburton uneasy, interpreting it almost exclusively in literary terms. Persistently he expresses his admiration for the book in ways that might apply to any literary masterpiece:

> The *drama* opens with such rage and fury, and runs all along upon such high passions and incidents, that it seems to threaten nothing less than a tragic conclusion; but then this contributes only to enhance the surprize, as it should, when at last we find all the parties reconciled, and the whole dispute among them, terminated to the satisfaction of all parties. Thus it is, that the Orestes of Euripides is conducted, it opens with all the

---

elusive reciprocations of the literal and allegorical (p. 19). This view is also central to Lamb's *Sterne's Fiction and the Double Principle* (Cambridge: Cambridge University Press, 1989), in which he characterizes *Tristram Shandy* as a " 'book of books' [III, xxxiii] in which originals and copies perpetually circle one another, and parallels accompany each other to infinity" (p. 76). The "double principle" of Lamb's title is the Addisonian perception that "the most complex and powerful sentiments arise from a coalition of an impression and an idea which cannot conceal the imperfection of their union, but can exploit it" (p. 5). From this doubleness arises the emphasis on pleonasm, which induces us to attribute multiple meanings to repetitions of similar language.

[13] John Garnett, *A Dissertation on the Book of Job* (London: M. Cooper, 1749), p. 11.

rage of despair . . . and yet in the winding up of the *drama* at the catastrophe . . . the sentence pronounced upon Orestes is superseded. (p. 249)

The allegory in Warburton's interpretation is for Garnett a way of removing *Job* from the demands of historicity rather than a way of reintroducing historicity into the poem. Warburton's opponents read him in much the same way as Garnett did, but they oppose Warburton because they are unwilling to give up the historicity of the book.

Warburton's opponents argue for a historicity that is not dependent on allegoresis. Richard Grey, who had earlier written on *Job*, answers Warburton by asserting that the poem is *both* "dramatical" and "founded upon true history."[14] The poem needs an interpretation (like his own) that (in contrast to Warburton's allegorical one) "neither requires in the sacred *Author* of it [Moses], a Degree of Art and Refinement unknown to the Simplicity of the earliest Ages, nor represents the Actors in it as lost and bewilder'd in an intricate Dispute" (p. 52). He is essentially arguing that Warburton's allegorical interpretation is itself unhistorical, unsuited to the simpler literary milieu of the work. This view gives at least some weight to the literary aspects of *Job* but refuses to see literature and history as necessarily in opposition at that early time. Both Leonard Chappelow and Charles Peters take a more strident view of *Job*'s historicity, occasionally acknowledging literary aspects but subordinating them to a literal factuality.[15] Clearly both fear the effects of allowing literary criteria to compete with, in their views, the absolute claims of historical truth. For Chappelow, "The history of Job and his sufferings, is not a studied parable, or an artfully contrived drama; but a matter of real fact and truth" (I, xiv–xv). Charles Peters acknowledges literary aspects of the book while denying that its historicity is seriously vitiated: "The Book, though a Poem, is in the main Historical, and probably *Job* himself the Writer of it" (p. 3).

The predilection for the historical in opposition to the literary is perhaps most fully exhibited by Peters, who finds that the categories of the literary and historical chafe against each other. His *Critical Dissertation on the Book of Job* dismisses Warburton's arguments for allegory because of *Job*'s likeness to history: *Job* is in "Order of Narration" like history; "is not a plain and orderly Relation of Facts, History?" (p. 102). But taken as an "Allegoric

---

[14] Richard Grey, *An Answer to Mr. Warburton's Remarks* (London: J. Stagg, 1744), p. 28.

[15] Leonard Chappelow, *A Commentary on the Book of Job*, 2 vols. (Cambridge: J. Bentham, 1752); and Charles Peters, *A Critical Dissertation on the Book of Job* (London: E. Owen, 1751).

Fiction . . . Times and Persons" in *Job* are jumbled and "the Truth of History is Destroyed" (p. 47). The advantage of an older date than Warburton's is that even apart from its "Authority as an inspired Writing" a more ancient *Job* is "one of the most instructive, and most valuable Books, that the World has ever seen" (p. 38), giving "Evidence to the History and Doctrines of the most ancient Times" (p. 81). The book has greater authority "the nearer it was written to the Times wherein the Events happened" (p. 103); Job, consequently, is the most satisfactory author, for then "all objections to the Historical Truth of it vanish at once" (p. 125). In addition to believing in the historical circumstances conveyed by the book, Peters also uses it as a talisman. Its message, whatever its intrinsic value, is touched by and conse- quently touches us with a time long past, thereby extending our time (even if not our exact knowledge): "The oldest Writings, like the largest and best Diamond, are of a Worth superior to all Estimation" (p. 81). The medium, which is conceived of as having once been contiguous to the being it may no longer adequately represent, becomes the focus of attention and the reposi- tory of value.

Sterne's book is a compendium of arguments that may be used against Peters's conception of history. Without finding any personal animus against Peters and while still accepting Sterne's apparent hostility to Warburton, one can see in *Tristram Shandy* a notion of narrative configuration that denies the probable correspondence of simplicity of style and orderly presentation to the truth of event. *Tristram Shandy* in fact validates a fictional truth that shares characteristics with history, presenting a possible resolution of the problem addressed by the commentators on *Job*. Sterne's method, however, is to maintain his book's relationship to history by rejecting the naive valori- zation that a writer like Peters exhibits. The notion of a "plain and literal Meaning of common Words" (p. 8) that Peters relies on is obviously under- mined by *Tristram Shandy*: not only can no conversation between Walter and Toby proceed on the basis of plainness or literality (not to mention any of Tristram's own reported reflections), but the reader in the book is also defined as a perverse punster, or allegorizer, who must be beseeched "to believe it of me, that in the story of my father and his christen-names,—I had no thoughts of treading upon *Francis* the First—nor in the affair of the nose—upon *Francis* the Ninth—nor in the character of my uncle *Toby*—of characterizing the militiating spirits of my country" (IV, xxii, 360).[16] Peters's definition of history as an orderly relation of facts is persistently subverted by

---

[16] See Garrett Stewart, *Reading Voices: Literature and the Phonotext* (Berkeley: University of California Press, 1990), pp. 193–94, for a reading of some sentences from Slawkenbergius's tale that shows just how far from Sterne's practice is the view of language implied by Peters.

the temporal complexities of *Tristram Shandy* and by Tristram's demonstration that narrative is choice, and order is exclusion. Toby's difficulties in narrating his wounding question the authority that Peters grants to those who participate in the events they recount: Toby's view is limited and inarticulate until subsumed, distanced, and impersonalized by a map, when it becomes obsessive, leading him to disregard all other perspectives. The *Job* controversy, then, serves as a compendium of the historical thought (particularly as it attempts to adjudicate a largely untenable version of the opposition of the historical to the literary) that is the subject of Sterne's critique in *Tristram Shandy*.

Tristram Shandy also examines how veneration of an ancient object (such as Peters's *Job*) can become an attempt to transform it into a talisman. When interpreting the traces of the past that adhere to a document, Tristram often writes like a historian or editor, but his response then becomes not so much a matter of grounding his beliefs about the past as of stimulating his imagination:

> In a bundle of original papers and drawings which my father took care to roll up by themselves, there is a plan of Bouchain in perfect preservation (and shall be kept so, whilst I have power to preserve any thing) upon the lower corner of which, on the right hand side, there is still remaining the marks of a snuffy finger and thumb, which there is all the reason in the world to imagine, were Mrs. Wadman's; for the opposite side of the margin, which I suppose to have been my uncle Toby's, is absolutely clean: This seems an authenticated record of one of these attacks [of Mrs. Wadman on Toby]; for there are vestigia of the two punctures partly grown up, but still visible on the opposite corner of the map, which are unquestionably the very holes, through which it has been pricked up in the sentry-box. (VIII, xvii, 678–79)

Then acknowledging his apparent drift into religious and sexual imagination, Tristram concludes: "By all that is priestly! I value this precious relick, with it's *stigmata* and *pricks*, more than all the relicks of the *Romish* church."

Tristram's implicit mockery of Catholicism presumably leaves the foundations of his own religion intact, yet his secular imagination requires the support of the same kind of legendary materials that he mocks. His account of his visit to the tomb of the two lovers reflects this desire for a relic to stimulate as well as verify imagination. He recounts the story of the two lovers in a severely reductionist form and states his intention of seeing their tomb, on which he wishes to drop a tear; however, "When I came—there was no tomb to drop it upon. What would I have given for my uncle Toby to have whistled, Lillo bullero!" (VII, xl, 643). The absent tomb, its absence visible only to the consciousness already engaged by it, is a suitable icon for *Tristram Shandy*'s view of history. The historical is brought into being by the consciousness that is able to create it, and it is lost when imagination fails. Not only is Locke's *Essay*, as Tristram suggests, a history "of what passes in a man's own mind" (II, ii, 98), but so are all histories as well as all essays.

Nevertheless, Sterne permits no easy access to his characters' inner beings. Tristram celebrates the humane feelings and behavior of characters like Toby and Trim, but his representations of them emphasize their imprisonment in their private worlds. Only through an act of interpretation can the meaning of their conduct be made accessible to a larger world. Trim's catechism, for example, is conducted by Toby, who requests each of the ten commandments in the form of a military drill. The moral goodness that Trim demonstrates is articulated through the process of connecting an ancient text to his and Toby's obsessions with their previous lives as soldiers. This rote behavior through which Trim's catechism is elicited causes Walter Shandy to be skeptical of the Corporal's understanding. "Prythee, *Trim*," he asks, "What do'st thou mean, by '*honouring thy father and mother?*'" Trim answers: "Allowing them, an' please your honour, three halfpence a day out of my pay, when they grew old." After then ascertaining that Trim had indeed allowed his parents this sum, another listener, the parson Yorick, responds: "Thou art the best commentator upon that part of the *Decalogue*; and I honour thee more for it, corporal *Trim*, than if thou hadst had a hand in the *Talmud* itself" (V, xxxii, 470–71). Trim's remark is not, however, a comment on the biblical text but an absorption of it into the particulars of his life and society. Yet Yorick sees in Trim's too precisely specified response a desirable emphasis on the behavioral imperative of the text. He seizes on Trim's reduction of the commandment to the particular dimensions of his own conduct as an interpretable and thus once again generalizable emblem of the text's meaning. Trim's moral being is represented in the context of a rigidified form that causes it to be suspect; the truth of the text and of Trim's nature is then elicited only through interrogation and interpretation.

In *The Presence of the Word*, Walter Ong attempts to reconcile the rigidities of a medium with the presence that it is designed to convey. Pointing out the textual intricacies of the biblical presentation of the Word that is Christ, he argues more generally that those media which produce in us a sense of separation from a presence have also "brought history into being and opened the past to us, making it possible to discover the word with new explicitness, if less directness."[17] History is regarded as a way of recov-

---

[17] Walter Ong, S. J., *The Presence of the Word* (New Haven: Yale University Press, 1967), p. x.

ering presence, its documentations forming a guide to the apprehension of religious and secular truth. But Sterne often shows a less optimistic view of the possibilities of recovering presence through representations. His novel illustrates the process of representation taking on a life of its own, often alienated from what it is intended to convey.

Take, for example, the play on the *where* of Toby's wound, a wound exacerbated by Toby's difficulties in explaining in what part of Flanders it was received. The place of wounding is displaced from his groin to a "map of *Namur*," enabling him to "give his visitors as distinct a history of each of their attacks, as of that . . . where he had the honour to receive his wound" (II, iii, 101–2). When the mere map gives way to the models of the bowling green, Toby speedily recovers. The Widow Wadman, however, threatens to return the wound to his groin: "You shall lay your finger upon the place—said my Uncle Toby. —I will not touch it, however, quoth Mrs. Wadman to herself" (IX, xx, 773). Toby sends for his map, thus making his wound historical and documentable but not present.

Sterne's characters put the usual valorization of object over subject, history over fiction, into question, sometimes turning history into an appendage of the personal. Early in the story Tristram writes that "the history of a soldier's wound beguiles the pain of it" (I, xxv, 88), a statement that somewhat obliquely predicts the train of events by which the history of the War of the Spanish Succession is exfoliated from the history of Uncle Toby's wound in the groin during King William's War.[18] While trying to narrate even the small part of the war that he saw as a participant at Namur, Toby discovers that "he could neither get backwards or forwards to save his life" (II, i, 95). The expedient of a map then not only gives him relief by ordering his own history but begins to substitute for his history, and in its eventual concretization as model becomes part of his history. Toby and Trim return to the country "with plans . . . of almost every fortified town in *Italy* and *Flanders*" (VI, xxi, 534) and reconstruct on the bowling green each of Marlborough's battles, "regulating their approaches and attacks, by the accounts my uncle *Toby* received from the daily papers" (xxii, 536). Toby, however, takes his construction not as a representation of the daily papers' representation but as the very stuff of history. Warned by Walter that his modeling expenditures will ruin him, Toby replies: "What signifies it if they do, brother . . . so long as we know 'tis for the good of the nation" (III, xxii, 242).

[18] Theodore Baird, "The Time Scheme of *Tristram Shandy* and a Source," *PMLA* 51 (1936): 803–20, finds that Rapin's *History of England* as continued by Tindal is a major source for dates and allusions in *Tristram Shandy* and that historical events "exist in the consciousness of [Sterne's] characters in the same way that a contemporary historic event exists in our minds today" (p. 804).

For him the represented events are the presence that he denies in himself. Toby's mapping and modeling order and objectify experience, restraining its multiety and creating stasis. But Toby is reduced to unintelligibility or silence in response to the demand that he be the representative of his own history.

Tristram and Toby exemplify differing approaches to the perplexities entailed in narration. Tristram responds to the frustrations of self-narration by his persistence in pursuing the demands of his writing, being willing to include whatever temporal dimensions are required and insisting on his authority and responsibility as author, even if he has to use his entire life to write his life. When Toby's inarticulateness exacerbates his wound, he turns to a map for his representation. He is then able to locate his former self by sticking a pin in the very place where he was wounded. He expands this self-history to Marlborough's later campaigns, escaping from narrational difficulties by seeking an external representation that can at least rest in a series of temporary completions, in contrast to Tristram's fluid and temporally more complex narration. Toby appears to be diminishing, perhaps ultimately erasing, self—creating a counter reality out of a map and the later models that substitute for the self, extending self somehow without implicating it. Toby's reenactments of that soldier's life he can no longer live become a substitute reality and thus his own history as well as someone else's. For Tristram, in contrast, contemplation of Toby's plan of Bouchain erupts into personal meaning and private wit (VIII, xvii, 678–79). Tristram, however, also attempts to use Toby's story as a refuge from the burdens of self, as if he could evade through Toby the almost intolerable demands that his form of self-centered narration imposes: "Let us leave, if possible, *myself*" (VI, xx, 533–34). After entering into his account of Toby's bowling-green wars, Tristram promises to give a full account of these reenactments elsewhere in a number of volumes (xxi, 536). Such a refuge would be a parodic version of history, a repetition of repetitions, a verbal accretion deriving from a false concretization.

Tristram Shandy creates oppositions between conceptions of meaning as complete or exhaustible and conceptions of meaning as ever in progress, never fully comprehensible.[19] The genre of the anatomy, the attempt at exhaustive analysis of a subject as in Burton, is a literary model for much of Sterne's effort. The anatomy has a double aspect: its attempt at exhaustive-

---

[19] Melvyn New, *"Tristram Shandy": A Book for Free Spirits* (New York: Twayne, 1994), discusses both the seeming freedom of interpretation implied by Sterne's book (for example, draw your own version of the Widow Wadman) and the constraints on interpretation introduced at the same time (pp. 128–29).

ness implies potential completion even as the fecundity of its multiplying categories denies the possibility of closure. Tristram's narration exploits both aspects, protesting against the enclosure figured in attempts at finality but also acknowledging the attractions of rest. Tristram is aware of the multitemporal associations of all events, connected as each is to a multitude of others whose relevance depends on the intentions of a particular story, which will contain only a selection of those events. Such narration makes the very boundaries of event fluid and allows for almost continuous revisions of meaning. But this seeming expansion of meaning through narrative is regularly confronted with the conceptions of archive and institute, each of which purports to bound or complete meaning. The archive exists to make available all of the documentation for a defined institution, and the institute presents fully the principles of a branch of study.

Two not entirely compatible conceptions are at work in the efforts at comprehension implied by the archive and institute: the enclosure of all relevant *information* and the enclosure of all relevant *techniques of analysis* of whatever information might become available. These two conceptions may be defined in relation to Foucault's critique of the archive: he finds the complete archive not to be the documentation that supports a particular monument, but rather the conditions of meaning at a particular time that limit all assertions and validate particular kinds of assertions. Tristram's father finds Ernulphus's oath to be "an institute of swearing" in which were "collected together all the laws of it," and thus he can "defy a man to swear *out* of it" (III, xii, 215–16). Tristram on the other hand believes that the similarity of others' oaths comes merely from their copying Ernulphus because of their own lack of aptitude in swearing, their copying inevitably leaving them far short of the excellencies of an original (p. 215). From Walter's perspective, the oath defines the parameters of swearing without exhausting the possibilities of particularized instantiations, while Tristram envisions an ever-increasing archive of weaker derivatives of Ernulphus's supreme effort.

Tristram's father considers the *Tristrapaedia*, his system of education for Tristram, also to be an institute, thus able to encompass all eventualities of Tristram's minority (V, xvi); but that conception is rebuked by his slowness in writing, Tristram's development outpacing his father's institute. This same institute contains the theory of auxiliary verbs (attributed to the "elder *Pelegrini*"), allowing a "young gentleman to discourse with plausibility upon any subject, *pro* and *con*, and to say and write all that could be spoken or written concerning it" (V, xlii, 484). The succeeding chapter illustrates the use of the auxiliaries in exhausting all that might be said about a white bear without any knowledge or even sighting of the creature. Walter alone sees the triumph in this exercise and expands it into a system whereby Tristram "shall be made to conjugate every word in the dictionary, backwards and forwards the same way;—every word . . . is converted into a thesis or an hypothesis" (VI, ii, 492). No wonder Tristram flees these promises of totality, deriving as they do from enclosure and opposing his proclivity to flight. Yet he is not himself exempt from seeing the pleasures and promises of exhaustiveness; his archival researches in hot pursuit of his family's history demonstrate the predeliction later shown in such reportage as his listing of the Paris streets, a list he copies after being disoriented in that city at night. Tristram concedes, however, that there have been "considerable augmentations" since the 1716 survey that he uses as the basis for his list (VII, xviii, 602). The attractions of such compendia along with an acknowledgment of their insufficiency are shown in other discursive episodes, such as Tristram's listing of the characteristics of love by finding an adjective for each letter of the alphabet; Tristram skips several letters, breaks off before the end of the alphabet, and puts the *R* out of order, an exhibition of his and the alphabet's arbitrariness (VIII, xiii, 672–73). His mocking flirtations with compendious systematizations like those his father endorses are not, however, merely easy dismissals but also reflect a possibility that he foresees in narrative itself. His reduction of the story of the two lovers to the characters "Amandus———He" and "Amanda———she," and to the action "He———east and "She———west," followed by an almost equally bare paradigmatic sequence of additional events reflects the possibility of an "institute" of narratives, as well as of swearing (VII, xxxi, 627). His subsequent wish to drop a tear on these lovers' tomb is perhaps appropriately rewarded with the surprising discovery that there is no tomb there. The absent tomb may be Tristram's white bear: "What would I have given for my uncle Toby to have whistled, Lillo bullero!" (xl, 643).

Such implicit questioning of the very possibility of increasing knowledge as opposed to perpetually remaining within the boundaries of conventional knowledge returns us to issues pondered in Swift's *Tale*. One of Sterne's achievements is his extension of the critique of biblical and especially textual criticism to be found in Swift's *Tale of a Tub* to the whole range of historical studies.[20] Like many who had feared the potential destruction of canonical knowledge through the textual criticism of Bentley and his followers, Sterne regards historical interpretation as a force not only for the validation of meaning but also for its dissolution. It is possible that Sterne's linking of *A*

---

[20] Jay Arnold Levine, "The Design of *A Tale of a Tub* (with a Digression on a Mad Modern Critic)," *ELH* 33 (1966): 198–227, discusses many parallels between *A Tale of a Tub* and the issues of biblical criticism that were current in Swift's time.

Tale of a Tub and *The Divine Legation of Moses* with *Tristram Shandy* is his acknowledgment of the subversiveness of all three: "For what has this book done more than the Legation of Moses, or the Tale of a Tub, that it may not swim down the gutter of Time along with them?" (IX, viii, 754).

Consider, for example, Sterne's parody of the periodizing that had been so important to Christian historiography; its fixations of time are incongruent with his fixation on the inseparable layerings of time. Within the seemingly fixed chronological schemes, he shows the human being on whose imagination all meaning hinges. For example, in attempting to tell the story of the king of Bohemia, Trim identifies the time as shortly before "giants were beginning to leave off breeding" but, wanting a more specific time and encouraged by Toby to choose any date at all, he unfortunately specifies 1712. Tristram comments:

> Of every century, and of every year of that century, from the first creation of the world down to Noah's flood; and from Noah's flood to the birth of Abraham; through all the pilgrimages of the patriarchs, to the departure of the Israelites out of Egypt—and throughout all the Dynasties, Olympiads, Urbecondita's, and other memorable epochas of the different nations of the world, down to the coming of Christ, and from thence to the very moment in which the corporal was telling his story . . . the corporal contented himself with the very *worst year* of the whole bunch. (VIII, xix, 685)

Sterne here summarizes the kind of periodization found in a multitude of religious/historical treatises, including Bossuet's *Discourse on Universal History* (Sterne was perhaps most immediately motivated by Warburton's lengthy refutation of Newton's *Chronology* in *The Divine Legation of Moses*), and comically exploits the incongruity between such epochal history and the seemingly more empirically definable contemporary history. Toby objects to the year both because it is one in which England suffered a "sad stain upon our history" in Flanders and also because a story with giants needs "some seven or eight hundred years" to put it "out of harm's way, both of criticks and other people" (p. 686). Chronology either fades out of significance or merges with subjectivity.

Like Swift, Sterne is impressed by the factitiousness of fact and artifact, but he nevertheless conveys a keener sense of dependence on the artifact— whether manuscript or tomb—than Swift does. Tristram's narration is dependent not only on memory but also on other texts and artifacts that, like life itself, are mortal. Tristram's book is *himself dying* and his borrowings from other books often emphasize their deaths, too. Elizabeth W. Harries sees connections between Sterne's fiction and the eighteenth-century awareness of "antique and 'Gothick' fragments," including the excavations at Herculaneum and Pompeii.[21] However, she sees this eighteenth-century concern with fragments as very different from the "postmodern valorization of the fragment" (p. 9). I agree. Yet I also think that the question is incompletely posed if limited merely to "valorization" and the vagaries of "postmodern" thought. The eighteenth-century interest in these fragments is derived from their potentiality, their conceivable resurrection into wholes through intellectual, emotional, or physical completion. Nevertheless, as I have been arguing, the possibility that no such resurrection will occur, or that it will be of limited relevance, also haunts the eighteenth-century imagination and inhabits the eighteenth-century intellect. From all we know of Sterne, we are led to believe that he was far from skeptical of received religious truths, yet his writing nevertheless implies a deep skepticism about the possibility of definitive interpretation. Like the Bible revealed by textual criticism, the interpolated tales of *Tristram Shandy* disintegrate into damaged texts, poor translations, and dubious proveniences.

Tristram's accounts of his own writing point to the death implicit in the act of narration as much as to the continuance that it promises.[22] After narrating his own christening, Tristram (now author) sits awake alone: "All the curtains of the family are drawn—the candles put out—and no creature's eyes are open but a single one, for the other has been shut these twenty years, of my mother's nurse" (IV, xv, 345). Tristram here has closed the gap between past and present, keeping the family alive in his consciousness. Only his waking authorial eye keeps them asleep: they too have by now joined the then waking nurse in death. The burdensome poignancy of Tristram's position as sole recollector or memorializer of the dead eventually makes him cry for relief from consciousness: "Leave we my mother. . . . Leave we *Slop* likewise. . . . Leave we poor *Le Fever*. . . . Let us leave, if possible, *myself*— But 'tis impossible,—I must go along with you to the end of the work" (VI, xx, 533, 534).

Writing, like Tristram, is the product of sin and death, increasingly assimilated to frustration and decay rather than to transcendence. Fleeing Death, that "*son of a whore*," Tristram sets off for Europe, having "forty volumes to write, and forty thousand things to say and do" (VII, i, 576). He imagines fleeing from Vesuvius to Joppa, Jonah's port of departure when wishing to

---

[21] Elizabeth W. Harries, *The Unfinished Manner: Essays on the Fragment in the Later Eighteenth Century* (Charlottesville: University of Virginia Press, 1994), p. 42.

[22] Jean-Claude Sallé, "A State of Warfare: Some Aspects of Time and Chance in *Tristram Shandy*," in *Quick Springs of Sense: Studies in the Eighteenth Century*, ed. Larry S. Champion (Athens: University of Georgia Press, 1974), argues to the contrary that Sterne saw "the writer's creation making up, by its intensity, for the brevity of life" (p. 220).

escape from speaking God's message (p. 577).[23] The next chapter, describing Tristram's seasickness in a storm, points to his ambivalent sense of his fleeing and of his writing: *sic transit.*

Tristram's book, itself a monument to transcience, is informed with the sense of the mutability of what he represents in it and the triviality of much that is less transient. The reader of travels who wishes to know the "length, breadth, and perpendicular height" of a building is contemptuously dismissed, whereas Janatone (who "carriest the principles of change within thy frame") must be measured immediately (p. 589).[24] Tristram's very writing is a metaphor for mortality. Whereas a building may represent itself for "fifty years to come" (not, incidentally, a very long historical frame), "every letter I trace tells me with what rapidity Life follows my pen" (IX, viii, 754). The analogy of pen to life's frailty is elsewhere apparent. Having written about the crushing of his nose in childhood, Tristram remarks on his "sympathetic breast" that leads him to dip his pen with "sad composure and solemnity" while writing of his father's sorrows at his son's misadventure, contrasting this movement of the pen with his more usual one of "dropping thy pen,—spurting thy ink about thy table and thy books,—as if thy pen and thy ink, thy books and thy furniture cost thee nothing" (III, xxviii, 254). The involvement here would appear to be with his own body as well as sympathetically with his father—nose, pen, and spurting ink suggesting perhaps ejaculation but also bleeding, death counterpoised to generation and transience to creation.

Narrative becomes itself a figure of disintegration. Finding it increasingly difficult to keep his story "tight together" in anyone else's fancy, Tristram also admits to losing his own way (VI, xxiii, 557–58). Early in the book he promised an aid, "a map, now in the hands of the engraver . . . by way of commentary, scholium, illustration, and key to such passages, incidents, or inuendos as shall be thought to be either of private interpretation, or of dark or doubtful meaning after my life and my opinions shall have been read over" (I, xiii, 40). Derived from Swift's *Tale*, this passage promises a critical apparatus to recover the book even before it is well under way, a testimony to the sense of mortality that is woven into it.

Poised in opposing tension to the disintegrating narrative of *Tristram Shandy* is the book as object, the trace that remains when authors are gone. But while its palpability denies the metaphysical claims of its disintegration,

---

[23] The New edition of *Tristram Shandy* (III, 446) identifies the relevant biblical passages.

[24] Max Byrd, *Tristram Shandy* (London: George Allen & Unwin, 1985), p. 125, finds that the "major tension" in volume 7 is "between vitality and measurement"; into this tension Sterne introduces time, which "represents a deadly measurement, an implacable mathematical form that must be evaded."

its very bodily status allies it with the grave. The black page and the marbled page, comments on the book as body, claim the richness of emblem, revelatory of meanings more complex than the linearity of narrative allows. Both, however, express the dead end of narrative rather than an escape from it. The mystery they reveal even as they conceal is chaos and night. The black page expresses the incomprehension arising from the absolute incommensurability of death, and the "motly" marbled page expresses the encroaching chaos resisted by narrative. Tristram's mocking remarks to the reader hint at the inarticulateness of these chosen emblems: "For without *much reading*, by which your reverence knows, I mean *much knowledge*, you will no more be able to penetrate the moral of the next marbled page (motly emblem of my work!) than the world with all its sagacity has been able to unravel the many opinions, transactions, and truths which still lie mystically hid under the dark veil of the black one" (III, xxxvi, 268).

References to mystical and allegorical meanings occur frequently in *Tristram Shandy*, allusions to the (previously discussed) comprehensive interpretive scheme for the Bible that was devised by medieval Christianity and retained in part by Protestantism. Seventeenth-century Protestantism had kept and expanded one aspect of the allegorical tradition—typology, which had the function of connecting events and characters in the Old Testament to their fuller realization and more complete understanding in the New. This kind of typology was often extended to post-biblical history, and characters and events from the Bible represented a potential range of historical behavior that allowed all people to understand themselves in relation to biblical patterns. But in later eighteenth-century thought this expanded typology was increasingly restricted. In *The Divine Legation of Moses*, for example, William Warburton finds types only in the Old Testament, as their sole function is in his view to foretell the advent of Christ and the Christian dispensation (2:675–76). Although the extension of the Bible to contemporary history continued to have meaning to many in relation to apocalyptic thinking as found in the books of *Daniel* and *Revelation*, the easy personal connection between daily life and biblical pattern that one finds reflected in Bunyan, and to a lesser extent in Defoe, is suspect.

Walter Shandy's theory of names has an apparent affinity with typology. He sees names as passing on at least some of the powers of their own significance as acquired either from etymology or their former owners. This kind of typology has a hermeneutic as well as a prophetic function, for it connects a word to a tradition of language, history, or literature that implies a larger range of reference than the personal concerns of its author. It locates a book among other books, providing a meaningful structure in which private eccentricity may be corrected. This expansiveness, however, is frustrated in

Sterne's book. Walter Shandy's theories about names are at best the object of a smile, and they are vulnerable even to the ridicule of Trim and Toby: "Had my name been *Alexander*, I could have done no more at *Namur* than my duty" says Toby; "does a man think of his christian name when he goes upon the attack?" cries Trim (IV, xviii, 352). Walter's own associations with Job are mired in historical questions about the personage who is, or might have been, his prototype.

Sterne's book, then, dissolves the public claims of allegory, showing it to have its roots in that small world which is measured early in *Tristram Shandy*, "a small circle described upon the circle of the great world, of four *English* miles diameter" (I, vii, 10). Meanings are linked not to universal history but to this diminished "world" history. A direct quotation of the Bible may function appositely but not prophetically, for it is susceptible of as many meanings as are derivable from human psychology:

> '*Make them like unto a wheel*,' is a bitter sarcasm, as all the learned know, against the *grand tour*, and that restless spirit for making it, which David prophetically foresaw would haunt the children of men in the latter days; and therefore, as thinketh the great bishop Hall, 'tis one of the severest imprecations which David ever utter'd against the enemies of the Lord. . . . Now I (being very thin) think differently; and that so much of motion, is so much of life, and so much of joy—and that to stand still, or get on but slowly, is death and the devil. (VII, xiii, 592–93)

Like allegory, *Tristram Shandy* is a testament to the fecundity of language, yet the irrepressible possibilities in language that it celebrates are mutable, subject to decay and death. Language may keep alive what would be otherwise irretrievably lost, yet the forms of linguistic life are themselves constantly changing in analogy to, but not identically with, what they purport to represent. As Walter remarks apropos of the death of his son Bobby, "The fairest towns that ever the sun rose upon, are now no more: the names only are left, and those (for many of them are wrong spelt) are falling themselves by piecemeals to decay, and in length of time will be forgotten, and involved with every thing in a perpetual night" (V, iii, 422). Walter's reflections on mutability have sources in earlier literature,[25] yet this book's representations of the materiality of the text give the topos renewed force.

Sterne's novel, then, reflects for us that separation between presence and medium that was exacerbated by eighteenth-century historical and religious scholarship. Sterne exposes the processes of narrative representation, show-

---

[25] See the New edition, *Tristram Shandy*, III, 349–51.

ing us that his story is the product of the interaction of the narrator Tristram with the limited possibilities of his medium, as well as with the reality or being that the story purports to represent. Sterne exhibits the narrator/ author's struggle with a posited prior reality, producing a sense of an incomplete movement toward his chosen subject rather than a final representation of it. While enticing the reader sympathetically toward the subject matter, this treatment also qualifies the moral vision that is overtly communicated. The represented process of representing goodness allows for no easy uncritical overflow of emotions in sympathy with the characters. The sympathetic imagination is checked by the difficulties of interpretation.[26] What is purported to occur is past, mediated by an observer who is himself dependent on documents and hearsay, and whose account is mired in the intransigence of his narrative medium. *Tristram Shandy* conveys to us the power of an admirable moral vision, and also the limitations of viewpoint, the deficiencies of documents, and the impediments of narrative that in some repects often obscure that moral vision.

Sterne's relentless exposure of the weak foundations for many of the putative facts of *Tristram Shandy* and of the evanescence of the medium as well as of its creator reveals the analogous entanglement with death of other eighteenth-century novels.[27] The new fiction's robust attempts to ally itself with contemporaneous life frequently take the form of claiming the authenticity of history and paradoxically emphasizing the pastness of any narrative representation. What Ian Watt names "formal realism" calls attention to the need to verify and thus resuscitate a life and condition that are mutable and perhaps extinct.[28] Commonly recognized as a complex parody of conventional narrative procedures, *Tristram Shandy* is also an analysis of the mortality of our very representations of the mortal. Sterne's novel shows that by claiming the authenticity of history, the new fiction of the eighteenth century

[26] R. F. Brissenden, *Virtue in Distress: Studies in the Novel of Sentiment from Richardson to Sade* (New York: Barnes & Noble, 1974), suggests that "there appears to be a conflict between the inner life of the novel and its outer form. . . . Although Sterne's method of presenting the Shandys ultimately strengthens our sense of their reality it frustrates our attempt to involve ourselves with them" (pp. 190, 191).

[27] Robert Alter, *Partial Magic: The Novel as a Self-Conscious Genre* (Berkeley: University of California Press, 1975), remarks that the novel "concentrating on art and the artist" is "even in many of its characteristically comic embodiments, a long meditation on death" (p. 243). H. Porter Abbott, *Diary Fiction: Writing as Action* (Ithaca: Cornell University Press, 1984), chap. 10, "Samuel Beckett and the Death of the Book," discusses the paradoxical relationship of the material text and the spirit in Beckett, connecting this discussion to eighteenth-century fiction, especially Richardson. Garrett Stewart, *Death Sentences: Styles of Dying in British Fiction* (Cambridge: Harvard University Press, 1984), analyzes death scenes in fiction, primarily in later fiction but including analyses of Richardson and Sterne.

[28] Ian Watt, *The Rise of the Novel* (Berkeley: University of California Press, 1956), chap. 1.

also undermines the very claims of history on which it founds itself. His parody of narrative representation discloses the skull that lies beneath the flesh of history as well as of fiction.

II

The understanding of textual criticism as a struggle with time and death is not unusual in the late seventeenth and the eighteenth centuries. Swift's *Tale* plays unmercifully with the seeming modern abrogation of the past as exemplified in Wotton and Bentley but also acknowledges "the Restorers of Antient Learning from the Worms, and Graves, and Dust of Manuscripts."[29] Textual critics of the Bible such as Richard Simon and Bentley recognize the mutability even of the biblical text, seeing it as subject to the same vicissitudes as classical texts. Father Simon's *Critical History of the Old Testament*, published in 1678 and translated into English in 1682, was an attempt to defend the authority of the Roman Catholic Church by separating it from a too vulnerable reliance on a literal inerrant scripture.[30] Acknowledging the divine inspiration of the original documents and the importance of whatever remnants have come down to us, Simon nevertheless argues that the depredations of time have so degraded the text that without the traditions of the Church and the commentary of its fathers, religion can have no sound basis.

Simon's book raised considerable debate in England, not because of the importance it gives to the traditions of the Roman Catholic Church, a contention the English tended to dismiss as papist propaganda, but because of the learned attack on the textual integrity of a book whose literal meaning was becoming increasingly difficult to accept. The description given by Simon undermines the Bible's historicity as well as its religious authority and implies a skeptical view of secular history as well. Bossuet was impelled to answer with his remarkably different assumptions in the *Discourse of Uni-*

[29] Jonathan Swift, *A Tale of a Tub*, ed. A. C. Guthkelch and D. Nichol Smith, 2d ed. (Oxford: Clarendon Press, 1958), p. 93.

[30] Richard Simon, *A Critical History of the Old Testament*, trans. Richard Hampden [Henry Dickinson?] (London: Richard Davis, 1682), pp. 9–10. Subsequent references are to this text. Paul Hazard, *The European Mind, 1680–1715*, trans. J. Lewis May (Harmondsworth: Penguin, 1964), has a useful general chapter on Simon. Gerard Reedy, S.J., *The Bible and Reason: Anglicans and Scripture in Late Seventeenth-Century England* (Philadelphia: University of Pennsylvania Press, 1985), assesses Anglican responses to Simon's work (pp. 107–13). Phillip Harth, *Contexts of Dryden's Thought* (Chicago: University of Chicago Press, 1968), discusses the relationship of Dryden's *Religio Laici* to its occasion, Henry Dickinson's English translation of Simon's *Critical History*.

versal History.[31] Simon's work serves well as an analogy to, and predecessor of, the sense of textual frailty that invades the claims to historicity of the late-eighteenth-century novel.

For Simon, the historical parts of the Old Testament are mostly "but abridgements of the ancient Records" (bk. I, p. 5). Furthermore the "publick Writers" who kept the "Registeries . . . gave sometimes a new Form to the Acts themselves which had been collected by their Predecessours, by adding or diminishing according as they thought fit" (4). And even many of these truncated and reshaped records are missing: "We want at present whole Histories and Prophecies which the Scripture makes mention of" (5). In his "Author's Preface," Simon points out that the chronologies of the Bible cannot be consecutive because of the many abridgments. Furthermore, the material conditions of the biblical text have introduced confusions into even relatively sound records. Written on little scrolls rather than in books, the various portions of text have over the years fallen out of sequence. For example, Sarah, according to the narrative of Genesis, is loved in her old age by Abimelech: in Simon's view, the disorganization of scrolls is a more likely explanation of this unlikely event than that God "by a particular Providence had restored to Sarah the beauty of her youth" (Author's Preface). (We may imagine a book like *Clarissa* actually written as letters and subsequently spilled into disorder, thus requiring again a laborious reconstruction of the order that was created by Clarissa, Belford, and finally an editor.)

In attempting to keep this damaged biblical text relevant to religious truth, Simon endorses the soberer aspects of the allegorical interpretations of the Fathers: "It is much more easie to find out the Truth of Christianity by these Mystical Interpretations of the Fathers, than by the literal Explanations of the Grammarians, who indeed explain the History of the Old Testament, but they do not sufficiently make appear the Religion" (III, 42). He here raises an issue that appears in secular form in the sentimental fiction of Sterne and Mackenzie: these simulated damaged texts call attention to the decay of a medium that purports to represent the already somewhat attenuated meanings attached to an ethic of feeling. The material nature of the medium speaks of literality but also of silence and death, whereas the represented feelings allegorize the damaged text into a life putatively independent of the material.

Swift's *Tale of Tub*, avatar of the problematics of later fiction, comments on the perplexities involved in the contests of allegoresis and literality. The satiric reductionism characteristic of the *Tale* undercuts the claims of both.

---

[31] Hazard, *The European Mind*, has a chapter on Bossuet that includes discussion of his response to Simon.

The very vexation in defining their boundaries leads to the suspicion that the irreducible literal is those "Bales of Paper, which must needs have been employ'd in such Numbers of Books" ("Epistle Dedicatory," p. 35) and that the ultimate allegorical is the same paper burnt and turned to air, that is, kept pristine in a library and eventually put to the "tryal of Purgatory, in order *to ascend the sky*" (sec. 7; "Digression . . . on Digressions," p. 148). Of course both the allegorical and the literal here seem much the same, both figurative evaluations of certain kinds of books. This confounding of literal and allegorical is echoed in Jack's use of the Will when he had "Fits," burning "two Inches under his nose," his talent as an Aeolist enabling him to fix "Tropes and Allegories to the *Letter*, and [refine] what is literal into Figure and Mystery" (sec. 11). The *Tale*'s torturing of the categories of the literal and the allegorical suggests a possible reason for the irritated fascination it holds for the eighteenth-century novelists, who were trying to construct a fiction on the basis of a literal that tends to slide toward the meaninglessness of the material unless subjected to an allegoresis that threatens to leave the literal behind.

As an often-cited exemplar of the sentimental novel, Mackenzie's *Man of Feeling* (1771) might seem to be far removed from Swift's *Tale*, yet these seemingly opposed works are not irrelevant to each other. Although Mackenzie's central figure, Harley, illustrates abundantly the emotionality and passivity characteristic of the sentimental hero,[32] the fragmented form of *The Man of Feeling* looks back to Swift as Scriblerian satirist and from our perspective also forward to Scott as historical novelist.[33] As the connection to Scott suggests, *The Man of Feeling* is relevant to fiction's responsiveness to developments in historiography.

Henry Mackenzie's character Harley often demonstrates his claim to the title "man of feeling" by being responsive in ways that exceed any literal or

---

[32] G. A. Starr, " 'Only a Boy': Notes on Sentimental Novels," *Genre* 10 (1977), finds that "the sentimental novel deals sympathetically with the character who cannot grow up and find an active place in society. Its ideal is stasis or regression, which makes for episodic, cyclical narratives" (p. 501).

[33] Leo Braudy, "The Form of the Sentimental Novel," *Novel* 7 (1973), argues cogently that the sentimental novel shows "both a structural and a thematic continuity with earlier eighteenth-century novelists, and with the work of Pope and Swift" (p. 5). He adopts an allegorical view of the fragmented form of *The Man of Feeling*, which, in this view, asserts the "superiority of the inarticulate language of the heart to the artifice of literary and social forms." Braudy believes that the frame implies that "no sophisticated 'author' mediates between the reader and the work" (p. 6). As I argue below, this view elides from the book an ironic incongruency between Harley's sentimental characteristics and the book in which they are represented. G. A. Starr interprets the fragmentariness as a way of freeing the "hero from the ordinary effects of time . . . since narrative is always threatening to imply progress" (p. 502).

material context. When, for example, "old Edwards" describes his son's impressment into the army, Harley responds to the description as if to the event itself: "At these words Harley started with a convulsive sort of motion, and grasping Edwards's sword, drew it half out of the scabbard, with a look of the most frantic wildness."[34] Edwards's narrative creates for Harley what Mackenzie's older contemporary Henry Home, Lord Kames, called "ideal presence" in a discussion of the writing of history contained in his *Elements of Criticism*: "A lively and accurate description of an important event, raises in me ideas no less distinct than if I had been originally an eye-witness: I am insensibly transformed into a spectator; and have an impression that every incident is passing in my presence."[35]

The function that Kames envisages for ideal presence is consistent with sentiments expressed in Mackenzie's book. From ideal presence, Kames argues, "is derived that extensive influence which language hath over the heart; an influence, which, more than any other means, strengthens the bond of society, and attracts individuals from their private system to perform acts of generosity and benevolence" (p. 100). Harley is of course both eminently benevolent and receptive to words, and his fellow feeling character, the venerated Ben Silton, remarks that "there is a certain poetic ground, on which a man cannot tread without feelings that enlarge the heart" (p. 81). In keeping with this emphasis on responsiveness, Harley's principal function in the story is as listener rather than as actor. As a protagonist he is tentative and ineffectual, as an audience he is responsive and active, perhaps even a reproach to the reader who is less moved than the benevolent Harley by sad tales of human misery. This use of Harley, however, divides the reader's attention between Harley's experiences and his responsiveness. Attention is directed to Harley's sensibilities, thus placing the events to which he responds at a distance and undermining the "ideal presence" that Kames describes.

In an even more obvious respect Mackenzie's book violates Kames's prescriptions for achieving ideal presence in historical writings. Ideal presence is created by the reader's belief in the reality of events, a belief that is facilitated by a sense of their presentness. According to Kames, historians who wish to engage our emotions and secure our belief must write vividly enough to make us spectators of the events they describe: "A thing ill described is like an object seen at a distance, or through a mist; we doubt

---

[34] Henry Mackenzie, *The Man of Feeling,* ed. Brian Vickers (New York: Oxford University Press, 1970), p. 91.

[35] Henry Home, Lord Kames, *Elements of Criticism*, vol. 1, 6th ed. (Edinburgh: John Bell & William Creech, 1785; facsimile ed., New York: William Garland, 1972), p. 92. *Elements of Criticism* was first published in 1762.

whether it be a reality or a fiction" (p. 101). Our confidence in the truth of the narration is then weakened because "history cannot reach the heart, while we indulge any reflection upon the facts" (p. 96). Henry Mackenzie's narrative method in *The Man of Feeling* is aptly described in Kames's terminology as a "mist" through which we discern only dimly the objects that are set before us. Individual episodes are sharply etched, but they are fragments set within a disintegrated structure. Although the events of the story are not long past, the manuscript's putatively ruined condition emphasizes not only its pastness but also its evanescence, and the mental activity required to reconstruct details from the fragments evokes those reflections upon the facts that, according to Kames, keep the story from reaching the heart.

The "Introduction" identifies an editor who retrieves the manuscript from a fellow hunter, a curate who has mutilated it by tearing off pieces for gunwadding. This old device of the found manuscript is used by Mackenzie in all three of his novels.[36] Each novel dangles an "author" before the reader but then subordinates him to an editor or compiler. The found manuscript of *The Man of the World*, however, is not the narrative itself but only a source, and the "editor" of *Julia de Roubigné* is effaced throughout much of the book. The much shorter length and the obtrusive fragmentariness of *The Man of Feeling* make the editor more prominent and apparently more important to the reading experience.

The fiction of the mutilated manuscript is maintained by chapter numbering that is not consecutive and by the inclusion of several "fragments" that are less than chapters. The editor does not disappear as a presence in the story even after the various hiatuses have been explained by his introduction. He reannounces himself as "the Editor" in an initial footnote to the opening chapter, chapter 11, reiterating that the curate, not he, is responsible for the mutilations and that the chapter numbering and titling are being given exactly as they were in the manuscript (p. 7). He reappears in a footnote to chapter 21, where he takes a more vigorous editorial role, arguing that one section of the chapter is "the work of a later pen than the rest of this performance." Although the writer of this section seems "to have caught some portion of the spirit of the man he personates," the "hand is different and the ink whiter" (pp. 40–41). The editor speculates that this interpolation was made possible by a gap in the original manuscript. His next and last

---

[36] Mackenzie's responsiveness to the editorial fiction may have been stimulated by the furor over James Macpherson's "Ossianic" poems. Eventually Mackenzie chaired the committee that in 1804 finally declared that evidence of authentic originals for the poems was lacking. See Harold William Thompson, *A Scottish Man of Feeling* (New York: Oxford University Press, 1931), pp. 297–99.

appearance is a bracketed eruption into the text itself in which he justifies some suppressions, explaining that "even the partiality of an editor could not offer" to the reader the few scattered sentences left from the "depradations of the curate" (p. 125). From the fragments and from "some inquiries . . . in the country" he then presents several essential details not evident from the only two whole chapters still remaining (p. 126).

The continued emphasis on the fragmentary nature of the book and on the need for the reconstructive efforts of the editor suggest not the ideal presence that transcends the limitations of its medium but a manuscript that is subject to the same fate as the life it represents. Attention is drawn to the material medium (or what Roman Jakobson identifies as the "contact"), and the disintegration of the medium implies the tenuousness of the hold of Harley on posterity. The last chapter of the book that memorializes him is numbered 51, although the entire book contains only twenty chapters, which themselves include hiatuses and fragments not properly connected to the story line.

Mackenzie creates a narrative that must be reconstructed by the reader as well as by the editor. The focus of the story is sometimes not clear and the markers ostensibly given by the narrator to connect various parts of the story sometimes merely foreground the ruins of the narrative. The "Introduction" identifies Harley as the central figure of the book, but the opening chapter (chapter 11) breaks into an ongoing conversation in which the main speaker is finally identified as Ben Silton, who is "now forgotten and gone" (p. 8). The ending of this chapter introduces Harley abruptly and vaguely without locating him in relation to the opening conversation. Then in chapter 33 Ben Silton reappears as someone Harley first meets on a stagecoach, not "forgotten and gone" by any means. Although Ben Silton finally by this means achieves a relationship to the story line, the time scheme remains obscure.

As the story approaches Harley's end, and its own, the disruption increases. One of the more puzzling fragments, "The Pupil," occurs just before the editor acknowledges that much of the remaining manuscript is too disconnected to be included. The only ostensible connection of this fragment to the remainder of the narrative is that it is addressed to Harley. Although the characters of the fragment have not appeared before, they are nevertheless not formally introduced.[37]

Harley and the narrator also represent a different form of fragmentation in the book—its conflicting generic affinities, apologue against satire.

[37] See Dale Kramer, "The Structural Unity of 'The Man of Feeling,'" *Studies in Short Fiction* 1 (1964): 197–98, for a thematic analysis of this episode.

Harley's attitude to the world is that of the moralist who maintains his perspective no matter how inhospitable the world is to it. The world's tyrannies, says Harley, "teach us—to look beyond it" (p. 73). Faced with the possibility that his instinctive benevolence is misplaced, he cries out, "to calculate the chances of deception is too tedious a business for the life of man!" (p. 53). The narrator's voice, however, is predominantly satiric and does not always spare even the hero himself.[38] Harley's pride in his skill in physiognomy is repeatedly ridiculed, and even his esteem for Miss Walton's virtue is not above an ironic glance: "Not withstanding the laboured definitions which very wise men have given us of the inherent beauty of virtue, we are always inclined to think her handsomest when she condescends to smile upon ourselves" (p. 17).

The scene in Bedlam shows most fully the interaction of the two genres. Harley objects to the exposure of the mentally disturbed to idle curiosity, in his words an "inhuman practice" (p. 29). The episode ends with his appropriate tears of sympathy in response to the plaintive tale and touching behavior of a young lady whose lover has died (p. 35). But the other Bedlamite victims of the mind's frailty are used as satiric objects worthy of a place in Swift's *Tale of a Tub* or Hogarth's *Rake's Progress*. A "celebrated mathematician" goes mad when his table based "on the conjectures of Sir Isaac Newton" does not properly predict the return of a comet (pp. 30–31). A speculator in stocks loses his fortune and now spends his time tabulating columns marked "South-sea annuities, India-stock, and Three per cent. annuities consol" (p. 31). A schoolmaster tries "to be resolved of some doubts . . . concerning the genuine pronunciation of the Greek vowels" and now when subject to "fits . . . makes frequent mention of one Mr. Bentley" (p. 32). And Harley's conductor through the madhouse finally announces himself as the "Cham

---

[38] A number of critics have noted that Mackenzie's book does not present an entirely approving view of Harley. See, for example, David G. Spencer, "Henry Mackenzie, a Practical Sentimentalist," *Papers on Language and Literature* 3 (1967): 318, "The author's sympathy is tempered with common sense and worldliness and his hero's is not." John K. Sheriff, *The Good-Natured Man: The Evolution of a Moral Ideal, 1660–1800* (University: University of Alabama Press, 1982), goes so far as to argue that "all the episodes subtly ridicule Harley and show him to be triply a fool" (p. 90). Robert Markley, "Sentimentality as Performance: Shaftesbury, Sterne, and the Theatrics of Virtue," in *The New Eighteenth-Century*, ed. Felicity Nussbaum and Laura Brown (New York: Methuen, 1987), p. 230, finds that both "Sterne and Mackenzie can dramatize their heroes' benevolence but cannot convince either themselves or their readers that good nature is sufficient to correct the ways of a corrupt and unjust world." John Mullan, *Sentiment and Sociability: The Language of Feeling in the Eighteenth Century* (Oxford: Clarendon Press, 1988), identifies a source of potential ambiguity or misunderstanding in Mackenzie's fiction as follows: "From the centre of an urban culture usually taken to be, in the latter half of the eighteenth century, a nexus of progressive intellectual and commercial developments, is produced a type of fiction which finds value in reclusiveness" (pp. 126–27).

of Tartary" (p. 32). Although the exhibition of the mad is a revelation of the hardheartedness of the world in contrast to Harley's more appropriate sympathetic response, the stories of the inmates also show that they are perpetrators as well as victims of the madness of the world outside the madhouse.

A Man of Feeling is in several respects an extension of Swift's *Tale of a Tub*, the "Digression on Madness" in particular, with Mackenzie making use of the major insight of Swift's narrator—that the conventional ways of achieving worldly success are madness. Perhaps the most important affinity between the two works is their emphasis on the textual medium. The *Tale's* prefaces, digressions, notes, hiatuses, and progressive disintegration adumbrate the similar formal qualities of *The Man of Feeling*. Disintegration in the *Tale*, however, results from a willful constriction and perversion of consciousness, while the abandonment of the manuscript of *The Man of Feeling* and its casual mutilation by the curate signify the peripheral position that the man of feeling and his admirer the narrator have in their hostile world.

The final segment of *The Man of Feeling*, "The Conclusion," is a reflection on mutability, resembling the pastoral elegy generally and perhaps echoing Gray's *Elegy Written in a Country Churchyard* (1751). Unlike Gray's *Elegy*, however, Mackenzie's work makes little claim to preserve its putative author's identity through his memorialization of the lives of others. The narrator, the work's putative author, is himself a shadowy creature whose identity and purposes are never very clear. The "Introduction" identifies him as "The Ghost," a title as insubstantial as his apprehended characteristics: "a grave, oddish kind of man" who is recognized by "the slouch in his gait, and the length of his stride" (p. 4). Because "he left the parish, and went no body knows whither" (p. 5), he must remain in obscurity except for this mutilated "bundle of papers." Why he left the tale of Harley behind no one knows. It is written for an audience, not just for himself, as it has within it numerous markers for other readers: "We would conceal nothing" is his remark when he tells the reader of Harley's affection for Miss Walton (p. 14). Perhaps "The Ghost" rejects his own tale, just as the curate does. Even the editor has limited enthusiasm for this "bundle of little episodes, put together without art, and of no importance on the whole, with something of nature, and little else in them" (p. 5). As the editor recognizes, his judgments are tied to authorial identity, to questions of provenience, as well as to intrinsic merit: "One is ashamed to be pleased with the works of one knows not whom" (p. 5). Neither narrator nor editor is like the Shakespeare of Sonnet 55, the Pope of *The Rape of the Lock*, or even the less sanguine Gray of the *Elegy*, all of whom use a meditation on mortality in order to claim some version of immortality for others and themselves.

For Richard Bentley, editorial intervention is an act of cultural heroism. In his proposal for editing the New Testament, Bentley states that he "believes he may do good Service to common Christianity" and exults that his edition may last "when all the Antient MSS here quoted may be lost and extinguish'd."[39] In *The Man of Feeling*, however, the represented act of editorial reconstruction is given an equivocal value. Much of what remains is not fully coherent, and the editor's attitude is reserved.

This fictional evaluation of the act of editorial recovery comes after almost a century of nonfictional and occasionally hot debate about the significance of the new scholarly tools for understanding the past. Eventually it had become apparent that the flotsam and jetsam from the ancient world were susceptible to increasingly subtle interpretation that could lead to a reconstruction of literary contexts unimagined by the "ancients" of the ancients and moderns controversy. Joseph M. Levine describes the expanded interests of these modern antiquarians as they turned "from the classical literary texts to the other remains of antiquity, to the documents, coins, inscriptions, and monuments that could illuminate them."[40] But it was a long time before the full significance of these developments in scholarship was understood or accepted.[41]

The novel from Defoe onward is one of the signs of the equivocal triumph of this new historicism. To those techniques of "formal realism" that Ian Watt identifies as characteristic of the novel should be added "textual realism," a validation of the material transmission of the story. Richardson and Sterne in particular include within their narratives accounts of the proveniences of the fragments that make up their stories. This concern with a fictionalized provenience is not, of course, new. But Richardson and Sterne so elaborate the fictions leading to a realism of the document that the narrative itself is infused with the imitation or parody of scholarly procedures. Pamela's letters include accounts of the process of their writing and their transmission to a recipient. When Pamela presents someone else's note after it is no longer in her possession, she explains that she had previously

---

[39] *Dr. Bentley's Proposals For Printing a New Edition of the Greek New Testament and St. Hierom's Latin Version* (London: J. Knapton, 1721).

[40] Joseph M. Levine, *Dr. Woodward's Shield: History, Science, and Satire in Augustan England* (Berkeley: University of California Press, 1977), p. 115.

[41] Joseph M. Levine, *Humanism and History: Origins of Modern English Historiography* (Ithaca: Cornell University Press, 1987), states that "neither side won [in the battle of ancients and moderns]; the wits and men of the world were satisfied . . . that the ancients had been vindicated, and were able casually to brush aside Bentley's erudition. On the other hand, there were few scholars after 1699 to defend them. . . . The division between the two attitudes toward classical culture, with their corresponding views of history, became . . . increasingly impassible, at least until Gibbon tried to bridge them" (p. 164).

made a copy. *Pamela* claims not only the authority conferred by the moral character of its eponymous heroine but also that of being the authentic emanations of an identified character; they are her true thoughts and responses even if they are mistaken. But while Richardson firmly attaches narrator and narrative to each other, Sterne incorporates problematic documents that do not directly emanate from his narrator—Yorick's sermon, the curse of Ernulphus, Slawkenbergius's Tale. The narrative raises questions about the proveniences of these insertions, the search for their origins, like Tristram's search for his, sometimes ending in frustration or absurdity.

Sterne's skepticism about the efficacy of the search for provenience is suppressed in Richardson, whose letters are tightly and systematically linked to their originators and traced to their recipients. Richardson's effort is to achieve presence through the efficacy of the medium. As Leopold Damrosch Jr. points out, "Whereas a postmodern theorist would be particularly interested in the *absence* that presence conceals, Richardson is concerned with the *presence* that is possible even in absence."[42] Yet Richardson's obsession with the medium of transmission also betrays a less confident attitude about the powers of the pen. Each letter is, after all, a fragment that needs precise placement if expectations of coherence are to be met, and editorial intervention is needed to prevent the reader from failing to grasp the completeness of the arranged fragments. These editorial activities betray an anxiety about the possible encroaching chaos that may destroy the pattern that is intended to be found in these massive volumes of correspondence.

Laurence Sterne, the master of the fragmentary, intervenes between Richardson and Mackenzie. In Sterne, the fragment or the tendency to fragmentation is given full metaphorical force, representing both the instability of self as in Swift and the entropic tendency in narrative that is controlled by the anxious Richardsonian editor. Sterne extends the implications of the materiality of the text that the literary procedures of Swift and Richardson had emphasized, calling attention to the contingency and arbitrariness of the book as well as of the plot, conditions that are not merely willful but endemic to all books. And of course Yorick, Shakespeare's *memento mori*, is central to *A Sentimental Journey*, connecting the fragmentation of the book and plot to the inevitable disintegration of life itself.

The phases of disintegration in *A Sentimental Journey*, the single book lying most directly behind Mackenzie's *Man of Feeling*, include the evanescence of feeling; the impermanence of the "trace," the material object on

---

[42] Leopold Damrosch Jr., *God's Plot and Man's Stories: Studies in the Fictional Imagination from Milton to Fielding* (Chicago: University of Chicago Press, 1985), pp. 260–61.

which feeling attempts to found itself; and the ending that stops without resolution. To explain his imagining of the unseen face of a woman, Yorick chooses the image of recovering the head of a broken Roman statue of a goddess: "*Fancy* had finished the whole head, and pleased herself as much with its fitting her goddess, as if she had dived into the TIBER for it."[43] Yet this seemingly palpable certainty is immediately followed by a reversal that abandons imagination and leaves the statue an unreconstructed and, perhaps, traduced goddess: "Thou [Fancy] art a seduced, and a seducing slut" (p. 92). A manuscript fragment introduced later undergoes a more extended process of disintegration within the book. Served a pat of butter on a piece of paper containing writing in the French of Rabelais, Yorick reads the story of a notary who is about to record a story someone else is about to tell. The fragment then ends. The subsequent search for the manuscript's conclusion reveals the human inconstancy that is the metaphorical equivalent to the evanescence of the past. Having used the remainder of the paper to wrap a bouquet, the servant is sent to recover the ending, but his mistress has given the bouquet "to one of the Count's footmen—the footman to a young sempstress—and the sempstress to a fiddler, with my fragment at the end of it" (p. 256). And in its final fragmentation, perhaps its final faithlessness, Sterne's book stops when Yorick's hand, reaching in the darkness for a lady's hand, is interrupted by her fille de chambre's something or other—at which point the book's end intervenes.

The Richardsonian editor struggles against entropy and conveys a sense of the difficultly achieved completeness of his artifact, whereas Mackenzie's editor reconstructs a ruin, an inevitably diminished thing. A ruin, however, also makes a claim of its own, as Sterne's work suggests. Approaching the verge of extinction, it is particularly valuable because of the scarcity it implies: its represented life must be deciphered or lost. But however limited the decipherment that is possible, the object nevertheless retains its value as a relic, a talisman, connecting the present to the magic of the past. A ruin, a fragment, and an enigma may indeed convey a sense of the presence of the past more powerfully than more complete and completely known artifacts, because the undecipherability of their incompleteness suggests not so much communication from the past as the past itself. The disintegration represented by the fragment also suggests the ineluctability of death, and thus the fragment tantalizes with its unkept promise of being the key to that which is beyond our existence. The novel's sometimes ironic treatment of its fragments is then transformed into a claim for their value.

[43] Laurence Sterne, *A Sentimental Journey*, ed. Gardiner Stout Jr. (Berkeley: University of California Press, 1967), p. 92.

This concern with the mutability of the material transmitters of the past is by no means unique to Sterne and Mackenzie, nor to the later eighteenth century. It is however a concern that is given a new urgency by developments in eighteenth-century scholarship—textual scholarship, of course, but also geology and archeology, which hold out the possibility of recovering the history of civilization and even of the earth itself.[44] Such techniques for decoding the past make more poignant the demise of the artifacts, which are only on the verge of intelligibility.[45]

Although Mackenzie's man of feeling is isolated from all but a very small group of his contemporaries who share his values, the text that his life becomes holds out the promise of his continued influence. Nevertheless, that text is tattered and its mediation must be further mediated by an editor who is detached from many of Harley's values. Harley's movement is away from any engagement with history, but his text's fragmentation is also an acknowledgement of history.[46] Walter Scott's dedication of *Waverley* to Mackenzie as "the only man in Scotland who could have done . . . justice" to "the task of tracing the evanescent manners of his own country" is a tribute

[44] Stephen J. Gould, *Time's Arrow, Time's Cycle: Myth and Metaphor in the Discovery of Geological Time* (Cambridge: Harvard University Press, 1987), starts his discussion with Thomas Burnet's *Sacred Theory of the Earth* and shows that the conception of "deep time" developed well before Hutton and Lyell. For discussion of the controversies about fossils and their historiographical significance, see Paolo Rossi, *The Deep Abyss of Time: The History of the Earth and the History of Nations from Hooke to Vico*, trans. Lydia G. Cochrane (Chicago: University of Chicago Press, 1984). Lionel Gossman, "History as Decipherment: Romantic Historiography and the Discovery of the Other," *New Literary History* 18 (1986–87), finds that "the historical imagination of the nineteenth century was drawn to what was remote, hidden, or inaccessible: to beginnings and ends, to the archive, the tomb, the womb" (pp. 24–25). Something of this impulse was already present in the efforts of eighteenth-century English scholars and antiquaries. The rapidity with which even the recent past becomes remote is a source of consternation in Sterne and Mackenzie, as well as Scott.

[45] Two of Mackenzie's contemporaries, Samuel Johnson and Edward Gibbon, express with notable eloquence this sense of a past whose traces are vanishing more rapidly than they can be decoded. See Johnson's *Journey to the Western Islands of Scotland* (1775), passim, and especially his comments on the ruins of St. Andrews. In the concluding chapter of *The Decline and Fall of the Roman Empire* Gibbon compares Poggius's account of those ruins visible from the Capitoline in 1430 to an anonymous account of two-hundred years earlier in which many more ruins are noted. Frank Palmeri, "History as Monument: Gibbon's *Decline and Fall*," *Studies in Eighteenth-Century Culture* 19 (1989), studies the context and allusiveness of these remarks of Gibbon, seeing them as "consistent with his method of historical interpretation in the second half of the *Decline and Fall*, where he repeatedly juxtaposes . . . multiple frames of reference in order to construct a complex, many-sided, and ironic view of his subject" (pp. 241–42).

[46] See John Sitter, *Literary Loneliness in Mid-Eighteenth-Century England* (Ithaca: Cornell University Press, 1982), for a discussion of the movement away from history in the literature (especially in the poetry) written after 1740. Fredric V. Bogel, *Literature and Insubstantiality in Later Eighteenth-Century England* (Princeton: Princeton University Press, 1984), p. 114, discusses ambiguities in attitudes toward history in the later eighteenth century.

to Mackenzie's gift for literary representation, but it can also be taken as Scott's recognition of the relevance of Mackenzie's imagination to historical reconstruction.[47]

III

"History" is our construction of what happened. The documents and artifacts from which the past is reconstituted are themselves a part of the unreconstructed past, not representations but traces of it. Scott inserts the fiction of a private person into a relatively full context of acknowledged historical events, thus allowing us to follow the character's process of construing those events through the impediments of bias, accident, and limitation. Scott's fiction shows a clear continuity with the moderately skeptical historiographical tradition found in eighteenth-century fiction, the historicized fiction that is not necessarily historical fiction. *Waverley* and *Old Mortality*, for example, incorporate accounts of their own evidentiary basis that raise questions about the veracity of history. Yet Scott's novels also repair the theoretical boundary between the historical and non-historical which the novels of Richardson, Fielding, and Sterne had eroded.

In the "Postscript, which Should Have Been a Preface," Scott defines his purpose in *Waverley* as "preserving some idea of the ancient manners of which I have witnessed the almost total extinction" (p. 340). He has "embodied in imaginary scenes, and ascribed to fictitious characters, a part of the incidents which [he] then received from those who were actors in them." But coexisting with this serious concern with the preservation of the past is a less committed attitude toward his story, similar to that of a vaguely Scriblerian or Mackenzian editor. The "Postscript, which Should Have Been a Preface," for example, is reminiscent of Swift's *Tale*, an especially plausible connection in view of Scott's having published both *Waverley* and his edition of the works of Swift in 1814. Within Scott's narrative, various characters' highly emotional commitments to a version of history are counteracted by a notably detached representation of the excesses and perversions purveyed in the name of history. Outside the narrative, the emotional appeal of the story is checked, as in *The Man of Feeling*, by a representation of the process of reconstruction, a process foregrounded by the 1829 "Magnum Opus" edition.

[47] Walter Scott, *Waverley*, ed. Claire Lamont (Oxford: Clarendon Press, 1981), p. 341.

The version of *Waverley* that was produced by Scott for this collected edition bears an even greater resemblance to a scholarly, or perhaps mock-scholarly, text than the original edition did. A collage of prefatory material intended for the entire collection as well as for *Waverley* includes a "General Preface" followed by appendices of Scott's fragmentary juvenilia: for example, "Here the manuscript from which we have painfully transcribed . . . is so indistinct and defaced, that . . . we can pick out little that is intelligible" (p. 381). The text of the novel itself is given two sets of notes, one set at the bottom of the pages, longer notes at chapter ends. These notes most frequently explain the historical information, sources, and traditions from which Scott created a novel. On the one hand, this effort founds the novel more firmly on history; on the other hand it returns it to the fragmentariness that it had concealed. These fragments—the juvenilia, and the oral and written history with which Scott's mind was stocked—reach an unstable coalescence in the persona of their writer and compiler, who moves indefinitively between the roles of author and editor.[48]

Old Mortality, published in 1816, two years after *Waverley*, is a deeper exploration of historiography that makes explicit and extended use of what I call Mackenzian framing (thereby acknowledging Mackenzie as conduit although not necessarily as origin). The narrative is embedded inside framing material that identifies its source (Old Mortality), its narrator (Pattieson), and its editor (Cleishbotham), thus making the reader self-consciously search for the provenience of this obscurely introduced narrative with its multiplied mediators.[49]

The titular character of *Old Mortality* is not an actor in this novel but one of its putative sources, continuously present only in its title. Scott reemphasizes Old Mortality's importance by making him the subject of the introduc-

---

[48] Jane Millgate, *Walter Scott: The Making of the Novelist* (Toronto: University of Toronto Press, 1984), discusses Scott's appropriation of the editorial stance: "In the years that followed his first encounter with [Percy's] *Reliques* Scott made himself master of the apparatus of editorial possession by familiarizing himself with the full range of late eighteenth-century scholarship on ancient ballads and romances and with historical accounts of his own Border region" (p. 7).

[49] James Kerr, *Fiction against History: Scott as Storyteller* (Cambridge: Cambridge University Press, 1989), interprets Scott's historiographical skepticism as his way of putting "a good face on the ugly historical prospect of the British conquest of the Highlands" (p. 40). He regards Scott as undermining history in order to give himself the freedom to create a perspective that will "separate the reader from the terrors of the past" (p. 61). I am not persuaded that this imputation of a political intentionality to Scott entirely cancels his serious and laborious efforts at historical reconstruction and his "meditation on the process of making historical fictions" (p. 61).

tory essay added to the *Magnum Opus*. Old Mortality is the historian who figures death even as he fights it. He spends his life memorializing the dead Covenanters by "renewing with his chisel the half-defaced inscriptions [on their tombstones], and repairing the emblems of death with which these simple monuments are usually adorned."[50] It is he who narrates to the narrator the exploits of the now dead Covenanters: "One would almost have supposed he must have been their contemporary, and have actually beheld the passages which he related, so much had he identified his feelings and opinions with theirs, and so much had his narratives the circumstantiality of an eye-witness" (p. 66). His qualifications as "witness" are here extolled but also diminished, as his "circumstantiality" is a function of his rhetoric but not of his experience.

But rather than merely retelling the stories told by Old Mortality, the narrator strives for historical balance. The Covenanter-Whig bias of Old Mortality is corrected by other testimony, which will do justice to the Tories and the more moderate Whigs: "In embodying into one compressed narrative many of the anecdotes which I had the advantage of deriving from Old Mortality, I have been far from adopting either his style, his opinions, or even his facts, so far as they appear to have been distorted by party prejudice" (p. 68). The identity and character of Old Mortality's testimony disappears in the narrator's attempted objectivity, a disappearance that is forecast by the fate of his work. Although the respect in which he was held gave rise to the "fond imagination" that "the stones which he repaired will not again require the assistance of the chisel," in fact "the monuments which were the objects of his care are hastening, like all earthly memorials, into ruin or decay" (p. 68).

In the "Preface" to the *Magnum Opus*, Scott identifies the historical personage who became the Old Mortality of the fiction as Robert Paterson, a name resembling that of Peter Pattieson who narrates the story derived from Old Mortality. But this process of ostensibly locating the story more firmly in a factual world also emphasizes the indistinctness of that world. Scott quotes an account by Joseph Train of attempts to collect biographical information about Robert Paterson. According to Train, Old Mortality's work is still considerably more vivid than the novel suggests, but other evidence of his existence is sparse. An "account of his frugal expenses, found . . . in his pocket-book after his death" still remains, as does the "account of his funeral expenses," but his grave itself is lost and "his death is not registered in the session-book of any of the neighbouring parishes" (pp. 491–92). The search for nebulous traces and the authentication of only trivial

[50] Walter Scott, *Old Mortality*, ed. Angus Calder (Harmondsworth: Penguin, 1975), p. 64.

details conveys a diminishing confidence in the reality of Old Mortality, whose legendary status increases but whose historicity diminishes by virtue of our ignorance of his gravesite.

The incursions of time on this stonecutter, fighter of oblivion, are replicated in the life and death of the narrator, Peter Pattieson, who is informed by Old Mortality that "there is a colour in your cheek, that, like the bud of the rose, serveth oft to hide the worm of corruption" (p. 67). Although Old Mortality precedes Peter Pattieson to the grave, the reader has already met Jedidiah Cleishbotham in the frame of the frame (the "Introduction" preceding Old Mortality's appearance in chapter 1), the literary executor for the now-deceased Pattieson.

Cleishbotham is a comic figure into whose not very tender Scriblerian care Pattieson's manuscript has fallen. Cleishbotham's name appears on the title page and on the dedication to "His Loving Countrymen," although in the "Introduction," also his, he asserts that he is "*NOT* the writer, redactor, or compiler" (p. 52), a statement that he makes defensively for "the abashment and discomfiture of all who shall rashly take up a song against me" (p. 52). His amusing and self-serving "Introduction" states his claim to dispose of the manuscript because Pattieson's "papers had been left in my care" to defray death-bed and funeral expenses (p. 55). Cleishbotham has, however, scant respect for the manuscript, although he claims to have deferred to the author's request to submit it to the press "without diminution or alteration." In Cleishbotham's view Pattieson should have asked his executor "to have carefully revised, altered, and augmented" the manuscript, which gives signs of its author's having "more consulted his own fancy than the accuracy of the narrative" (p. 56).

Cleishbotham is a country Whiggish schoolmaster, who cares little about the historiographical niceties that had led Pattieson to seek multiple sources. The printed text gives evidence of Cleishbotham's considerable temptation to maul the manuscript. The opening chapter contains a number of his incursions by means of Scriblerian footnotes—unnecessary, minute, parochial, and self-regarding. The expectation that these incursions may turn into comic depredations of the main narrative is not, however, fulfilled, as Cleishbotham vanishes until his reappearance in a note to the last chapter. The narative here describes the death of John Balfour, portrayed as one of the most vindictive and treacherous of the Covenanters, whose grave is "still marked by a rude stone, and a ruder epitaph" (p. 476). The note to this remark is unsigned but identifiable as Cleishbotham's from its sentiments. It recounts Balfour's epitaph, "which I see no ground to discredit" (p. 476). The epitaph thus thrust into the book interprets favorably Balfour's brutal murder of Archbishop Sharp.

After the concluding chapter Cleishbotham appears as the writer of what with apparent self-regard he titles "Peroration." He informs us that only a part of the entire manuscript, *Tales of my Landlord*, has been accepted by the publisher, who apparently wishes to ascertain the success of the first four volumes before publishing any more. Although Cleishbotham professes himself "nothing doubting that they will be eagerly *devoured* [my emphasis], and the remainder anxiously demanded," Scott has represented the potential perils in the transmission of a text under the continuing care of this Whiggish Scriblerus.

The "Conclusion" may create even more trepidation about the future of this historical fiction under the pressure of readers like the one depicted there. The previous chapter brings two of the central figures of the novel to death, presenting a grim view of the intransigence and self-seeking of both Tories and Covenanters. In the "Conclusion" the narrator then submits this story to a neighbor, who will judge it by "the experience which she must have acquired in reading through the whole stock of three circulating libraries" (p. 478). She is responsive to the novel but desires a conclusion that satisfactorily defines the futures of all the characters, peripheral as well as central. This chapter, in which Pattieson responds to his critic, overtly warps the book into the shape necessary for romantic fiction, the historical succumbing to the novelistic.

As we have seen, the English novel replicates the developments of eighteenth-century historicism both in its valorization of "history" as the standard by which to judge truth and in its skepticism about the foundations of history. The authors of the early novel obsessively define the proveniences of the documents that make up their texts and also show the difficulties of ascertaining provenience. *The Man of Feeling*, with its decayed manuscript and unknown author, represents explicitly the anxiety about provenience and transmission often implied by earlier fiction. Mackenzie's admirer Walter Scott then achieves the most complete historicization of novelistic prose fiction up to his time, drawing on the traditions of eighteenth-century literature in order to explore the making of history both as writing and as event.

A brief consideration now of what was new in Scott may be useful in rounding off this treatment of history and the early novel. Georg Lukács's *Historical Novel* remains a stimulating guide to this topic. Lukács views the French Revolution as crucial to the creation of a new historical consciousness that profoundly affected literature, especially the historical novel. What is essential to this new historical consciousness is the comprehension of a past that constantly and significantly conditions the present. Among various innovations that encouraged such understanding, Lukács lists prominently the many revolutionary crises across Europe and the formation of mass armies. He argues that "the quick succession of these upheavals" made their "historical character far more visible" because the people's attention is insistently called to a process of change that is present but less obtrusive in seemingly more stable times.[51]

Despite this focus on the French Revolution, Lukács credits both the Enlightenment generally and the English realist novel specifically with a substantial measure of historical insight. Lukács sees Scott's achievement itself historically, as a definitive development of tendencies that preceded the French Revolution. English society had undergone two revolutions and was conscious of their consequences—the Puritan regicidal one, and the 1688 "Glorious" one to which was attributed significant economic consequence. While not the equivalents of the upheavals connected with the French Revolution, these revolutions produced a limited advance in historical consciousness among the British. In Lukács's view that advance is reflected in the achievements of the eighteenth-century novel.

Lukács credits the eighteenth-century novelists with "grasping the salient features of their world with a bold and penetrating realism" (p. 20), yet he believes they do not fully see these features historically (which I take to mean that they do not articulate the process of historical change embodied in the described events). Scott's salient advance in Lukács's view is to portray the process of historical change concretely: "Certain crises in the personal destinies of a number of human beings coincide and interweave within the determining context of an historical crisis" (p. 41). Scott thus portrays private life in connection with the historical events that shape it and are shaped by it.

What Lukács identifies as Scott's historical consciousness can be described in formalist terms as a method of structuring a novel to interconnect historical crises and the crises of private life. In this respect one might compare the treatments of the Jacobite invasion of 1745 in *Waverley* to that in *Tom Jones*. Waverley is a major actor in that rebellion, and a multitude of conflicting private relationships are entangled in it in some way, both directly and indirectly. The '45 in *Tom Jones* is a far more shadowy affair, although directly entering the plot on occasion and often the topic of conversation. Yet despite the many thematic interconnections of public and private life, the structure of the novel puts Tom and his search for Sophia at its center with the '45 on the periphery, important but without full interconnection to the private crises. Fielding would appear to be depicting a life that pursues its

---

[51] George Lukács, *The Historical Novel*, trans. Hannah Mitchell and Stanley Mitchell (Lincoln: University of Nebraska Press, 1983), p. 23.

internally compelling interests, while great but only partially understood, and partially attended to, events transpire sometimes in proximity, sometimes elsewhere.

Implicitly and explicitly eighteenth-century fiction deals with the understanding and the representation of events in the context provided by historiographical concerns. What Lukács provides is another, and relevant, question about the depth of the historical consciousness figured in these fictions. Historical consciousness is defined in Lukács's formulation as a sense of the past that is embodied in, or culminates in, an event. His focus is on the event's participation in change, as opposed to epistemological or hermeneutical questions about the evidentiary status of, or representational possibilities for, the event. There is much to be said about the historical consciousness of eighteenth-century fiction: for example, about the dying Whiggish past of *Tristram Shandy*; about the inexorability of the events of *Clarissa*, driven as they are by the rhetorical choices of its characters and the economic aspirations of the Harlowes; and also about the Stuart dynasty's impact on the world of *Tom Jones*. Yet these novels treat such matters implicitly, rather than representing a public crisis that is fully intertwined with the private events of the novel, as in Scott.

A treatment of questions of historical consciousness (in Lukács's sense) needs to take fuller account of the historians of seventeenth- and eighteenth-century England than it is possible to provide here. The novel constitutes itself from its interactions with history, and the voices of historians who wrote in and of this period must be heard before we can gauge the novel's historical consciousness, a consciousness formed in dialogue with history. My argument has been that the eighteenth-century novel is historicized fiction, not historical fiction. Raising questions that ally it with the moderate skepticism of contemporaneous historiographical thought, it is constituted as a new kind of writing through its differentiation of itself from conventional assumptions about poetry or imaginative literature and through its accommodations to assumptions about history. Scott, however, responds to the triumph of the novel not only by extending the skeptical scrutiny of history provided by the eighteenth-century novel but also by gesturing toward the fictional, as opposed to the historical, aspects of the now constituted novel. Thus Scott's historical fiction often assumes that the historical and the novelistic are independently categorizable and distinguishable despite their combination within a single book. Although Scott's combination of history and fiction continues the interrogation and emulation of history characteristic of eighteenth-century fiction, it also differentiates itself from history and from other realistic novels that merely simulate history and are thus to be allied with romance or poetry.

Foucault's assertion that literature appeared at the end of the Classical episteme, strange and contradictory as it appears, may also aid in describing the somewhat enigmatic separations being discussed here: "With the appearance of literature, with the return of exegesis and the concern for formalization, with the development of philology—in short, with the reappearance of language as a multiple profusion, the order of Classical thought can now be eclipsed."[52] Foundational to this assertion is the changed perception of language within the new episteme, where language needs no longer to be firmly linked to representation:

> For philologists, words are like so many objects formed and deposited by history; for those who wish to achieve a formalization, language must strip itself of its concrete content and leave nothing visible but those forms of discourse that are universally valid; if one's intent is to interpret, then words become a text to be broken down, so as to allow that other meaning hidden in them to emerge and become clearly visible; lastly, language may sometimes arise for its own sake in an act of writing that designates nothing other than itself. (p. 304)

This last form of language is what is quintessentially literature in Foucault's formulation. In a view attributed to Mallarmé, literature is ultimately "the word itself—not the meaning of the word, but its enigmatic and precarious being" (p. 305). While it would be absurd to regard the nineteenth-century realist novel as suddenly acquiring this Mallarmean indifference to what lies outside writing, it is not absurd to regard the nineteenth-century novelistic adaptations of the conventions (as distinguished from facts) of history as transparently and unambiguously fictional to an extent that eighteenth-century novels would have attempted to suppress.

In an important study of the relationship of history to literature, Lionel Gossman presents a more specific description of the process of separating historical from fictional writing.[53] Gossman describes the inclusion of history within the category of literature until the advent of ambitions for a scientific history. Early modern conceptions of history generally associated it with "presentation," not "scientific inquiry," and its "problems belonged therefore to rhetoric rather than to epistemology" (p. 4). But in "the final phase of neoclassicism . . . the long association of rhetoric and literature began to

---

[52] Michel Foucault, *The Order of Things: An Archeology of the Human Sciences* (New York: Random House, 1970), p. 303.

[53] Lionel Gossman, "History and Literature: Reproduction or Signification," in *The Writing of History: Literary Form and Historical Understanding*, ed. Robert H. Canary and Henry Kozicki (Madison: University of Wisconsin Press, 1978), pp. 3–39.

break down," with literature tending to be "associated with poetry" and even placed in opposition "to the empirical world of historical reality" (p. 5). History then became increasingly concerned with the "problems of historical knowledge" (p. 7), and the rhetorical concerns that had been common to both histories and poetry were submerged. Based on this explanation of a change in the categorization of literature, it is then plausible that the British novel succeeded in establishing itself through a contestation with history in which history is forced to defend its epistemology, with the novel subsequently afforded the apparent imaginative freedoms conventionally associated with poetry.

CHAPTER 6

Coda:
Epistemology, Rhetoric, and Narrative:
Historiography and the Fictional

The final fragment of this book represents an effort to place the historiographical critique mounted by eighteenth-century fiction more firmly in the context of the commonplaces of eighteenth-century historiography and, finally, in the context provided by the most powerful philosopher of history in the century, David Hume. Lucian, whose comments on history were widely known and admired in the eighteenth century, is my starting point, and I subsequently use three Enlightenment commentaries on history to present eighteenth-century concerns and commonplaces: [Peter Whalley], *An Essay on the Manner of Writing History*; [René Rapin], *The Modest Critic; or, Remarks Upon the most Eminent Historians, Antient and Modern*; and Nicholas Lenglet-Dufresnoy, *A New Method of Studying History, Geography, and Chronology.*[1] Hume shares some concerns and presuppositions with these earlier writers, yet he also devises resolutions for some of their characteristic problems.

Whalley, Lenglet-Dufresnoy, and Rapin specifically claim to be restating earlier views rather than inaugurating their own unique views, and each includes Lucian prominently, along with Cicero and Quintilian. But each

---

[1] [Peter Whalley], *An Essay on the Manner of Writing History* (1746), ed. Keith Stewart (Los Angeles: William Andrews Clark Memorial Library, 1960). Keith Stewart thinks Whalley's may have been the first essay on the writing of history published in English. The following works by Langlet-Dufresnoy and Rapin are translated from French. Nicholas Lenglet-Dufresnoy, *A New Method of Studying History, Geography, and Chronology ... by M. Languet Du Fresnoy, Librarian to Prince Eugene To which is added A Dissertation by Count Scipio Maffei of Verona, concerning the Use of Inscriptions and Medals by Way of Parallel*, 2 vols., trans. Richard Rawlinson (London: Charles Davis, 1730); [René Rapin], *The Modest Critick; or, Remarks Upon the Most Eminent Historians, Antient and Modern* (London: John Barnes, 1689).

also has his own emphases and approach to the contested issues in eighteenth-century historiography. A common denominator of these discussions is the seeming impasse between an epistemological and a rhetorical emphasis in historiography—essentially the distinction between knowing and being persuaded.[2] The two should in some sense be synonymous, yet persuasiveness in historical writing is often suspected of not necessarily reflecting an authoritative evidentiary base. History seeks to understand what truly happened, not just what might plausibly have happened. Furthermore, none of these writers accepts a bare listing of events as acceptable history without some form of meaningfulness being claimed for the represented events. Yet when commentary is merely superadded, its assertions appear to be external to the recital of events. While truth is regarded as persuasive, it must be represented in a manner that insinuates its immanence in the described events. These writers find a potential resolution in narrative; in their view narrative maintains the structural integrity of events while also implying meanings through interconnections. Yet the suspicion remains that narrative too may create the meaning it does not find. One of Hume's signal contributions is his recognition that the meanings of past events can only be understood in a present and cannot simply be immanent in a past. Narrative understanding creates meanings not available at any single point within events, but is not, therefore, to be invalidated.[3]

These historiographical texts share a great many of the concerns we have already uncovered in the conflicts between eighteenth-century fiction and the novel. If, for example, we think back to the controversies about *Job* that are alluded to in *Tristram Shandy*, we see a similar uneasiness about attempts to combine literary patterning and historical truth: the more visible the literary patterning of *Job*, the less likely its historical truth. Yet Sterne shows that any writing must inhere in a chosen viewpoint, make choices about inclusion and exclusion, and respond to an audience. The view that historical writing should have no character of its own is not a plausible one. History obviously needs its own rhetoric to give a persuasive account of events no longer present. Furthermore, persuasion entails some kind of

---

[2] Dominick LaCapra, *History and Criticism* (Ithaca: Cornell University Press, 1985), analyzes the tendency to disregard rhetoric in recent investigations and productions of history, asking: "How may the necessary components of a documentary model without which historiography would be unrecognizable be conjoined with rhetorical features in a broader, 'interactive' understanding of historical discourse?" (p. 35).

[3] Avrom Fleishman, *The English Historical Novel: Walter Scott to Virginia Woolf* (Baltimore: Johns Hopkins University Press, 1971), argues a similar point: "The historical novelist writes trans-temporally: he is rooted in the history of his own time and yet can conceive another. In ranging back into history he discovers not merely his own origins but his historicity, his existence as a historical being" (p. 15).

meaningfulness, a "bare" recital being impossible or at least unsatisfactory. What historiography desires at this time is some way of presenting an immanent meaning through language without having the meaning be *in* the language. Yet the effacement of language achieves no significance in itself; the resources of writing are required to give a persuasive and meaningful account.

The novel establishes itself in its eighteenth-century form between these twin demands of effacement before an external reality and the creation of persuasiveness and meaningfulness through a rhetorically effective emplotment. If history attempts a retreat toward some potentially bare recital of past events, it loses significance. As the novel creates its plausible world out of the linguistic and rhetorical resources that history has reluctantly abandoned, it acquires the persuasiveness and even significance that history loses. In a sense the goal of the struggle is for one of the categories— history or the novel—to absorb the other. When Hume accepts the present as the standpoint from which a never before fully construed meaning is to be constructed, he makes an implicit claim that the resources of the novel, the literary form that respects probability, be absorbed by history for the construal of past actuality. The remainder of this chapter, which consists of a rehearsal of conflicts mainly within history, needs to be read with this struggle against the fictional in mind.

Lucian was frequently cited in eighteenth-century discussions of history, his emphasis on truth-telling in style as well as content apparently continuing to appear cogent. When Lucian gives explicit advice to the historian in "How to Write History," he insists on the need to separate history from poetry. In poetry there is "one law—the will of the poet"; whereas the "historian's sole task is to tell the tale as it happened."[4] Lucian advises the historian to avoid even "poetic words," words connected to the traditions established by Homer, Hesiod, and other poets, as the Loeb translator suggests (p. 33). Yet Lucian recognizes that mere avoidance of the poetical is an insufficient recommendation, for the historian must have some positive presentational manner: "What historians have to relate is fact and will speak for itself, for it has already happened: what is required is arrangement and exposition. So they must look not for what to say but how to say it" (pp. 64–65). The historian must somehow achieve fidelity to event alone, despite the intervening language, a task that entails the avoidance of extraneous commitments and ambitions; when writing history, the historian needs to be "a stranger and a man without a country" (p. 57). Lucian conflates the two senses of

[4] Lucian, "How to Write History," trans. K. Kilburn, in *Lucian* 6, Loeb Classical Library (1959), pp. 13, 55.

history, history as event and history as construction or reconstruction, granting validity only to that history in which some apparent identity has been forged between the two. Yet even this goal of a transparent medium cannot eliminate considerations of language and rhetoric; the historian must be prepared "to give a fine arrangement to events and illuminate them as vividly as possible" (p. 65).

Lucian hovers over Peter Whalley's *Essay on the Manner of Writing History* as its most important influence, enjoining the qualities of truthfulness and impartiality that Whalley agrees must be regarded as essential. History's appeal is to improvement and instruction, not entertainment, which is the province of poetry (pp. 4–5). But if the qualities of being "*easy, elegant*, and *agreeable*" are also added to the historian's achievement, "there will overflow a Satisfaction that will contribute greatly to the Delight, if not to the real Use of his Readers" (p. 11). These seemingly extraneous qualities have a significant role in Whalley's instructions on writing history, and his essay reveals an implicit conception of the role of rhetoric in historical writing that is substantially more complicated than the dichotomized categories of entertainment and truth will allow to appear explicitly.

Early in the essay, Whalley remarks favorably on the annalists' having "cut off" the "Luxuriance and Superfluity" so common but undesirable in later historians. Nevertheless, the annalist is deficient as historian because the true historian must also explain "Motives and Consequence" to us (pp. 3–4). The implications of Whalley's distinction between the bare annalist and the valorized historian can be seen in his summary of the requirements for the task of historian, a summary that moves from the fundamental demand for truthfulness, through additional requirements for adequate commentary and appropriate emphasis, and finally to various emotive desiderata that seem to be largely removed from the initial demand for unadorned truth. Even the Longinian sublime is eventually recognized as appropriately sought in history.

As we follow the series of requirements for the historian given by Whalley, the difficulty of halting at any point in the series becomes apparent (pp. 15–27). If interpretations of motives and consequences and judgments on characters are demanded, the boundary of a simple factual truthfulness is blurred. How much commentary needs to be introduced as a supplement to the recital of events? For Whalley the ordering or arranging of the account becomes of major importance as a way to avoid apparently extraneous commentary. He states that interpretations going beyond annalistic citing need to be recognizable as part of a purposeful structure: "As the Field to be laid out increases, great Judgment is required, the better to dispose the Whole in such a manner, as that a certain *Uniformity* and *Design* may be conspicuous throughout it" (p. 16). Such an implicit purposeful organization can be usefully assisted by "apt and graceful *Transitions*," which "connect the distinct Members to each other." "Reflections" are obviously needed to inculcate the desired perspective on various parts of this structure, but they must not appear to be extraneous: they "should seem to be *inlaid*, not *embossed* upon the Work" (p. 17).

Having derived the need for a purposeful structure from the requirement that the proper historian interpret events and people, Whalley engages in the process of defining how that structure can be made persuasive. He does not accept the view that historical truth is only a question of persuasiveness, exclusively a rhetorical issue, but continues to defend the view that the fundamental requirement of history is to define what actually happened in a full and meaningful way; no method can, nevertheless, be found to meet the responsibilities of historical writing to truth without engaging rhetorical concerns, including questions of appropriate and appealing style.

Delight is gradually reintroduced into Whalley's analysis as a necessary appeal to the reader, who must be persuaded to accept the value and appropriateness of the narrative structure in which the embedded events of history are made meaningful. Such a consideration then also reintroduces the relationship between history and poetry that had earlier been rejected. They were said to differ because the demand on history is purely that of an austere Lucianic version of truth, whereas poetry's less rigorous instruction must be enhanced by delight. But when the rhetorical nature of history demands delight to support its interpretive aspect, the difference between history and poetry becomes not primarily a matter of their different truths but of their different decorums—the ornaments and metaphors of history ought to be more restrained than those of poetry. If "realistic novel" were to be substituted for "poetry" in this scheme, even the decorums would have similarities, and the discrimination of these two categories would then be obscured because their epistemological differences would not then be engaged by the rhetorical criteria used to define the two forms.

Lenglet-Dufresnoy in his preface to *A New Method of Studying History* recommends René Rapin's "Institutions of History" (a version of which appeared in English under the title *The Modest Historian*), which "ought to be termed the rhetoric of Historians" (p. x).[5] Rapin urges the devotion of

---

[5] I have summarily compared the following versions of *Instructions pour l'histoire*, as several library catalogs treat *The Modest Critick* as if it were less authentically connected to Rapin than are other translated titles. This work by Rapin appears in English translation as *Instructions for History*, translated by J. Davies, 1680; as *The Modest Critick*, without authorial or translator's attribution other than "by one of the Society of the Port Royal," in 1689; and as *Reflections upon History* in several editions of the works of Rapin by Basil Kennett in the early eighteenth century. The translations differ markedly and the prefatory apparatus is omitted in Kennett; however, each of these texts contains roughly the same material content.

history to truth and its opposition to fictions with as much fervor as Whalley: "*Romance* only pleases, *History* instructs"; "*Truth* being its greatest Ornament, an *Historian* that will please, ought to speak true" (pp. 29, 33). He suggests that the historian who would achieve this pleasure of truth must be devoted to research: "seeking [truth] in its purest original, by searching the Closets of the Learned and curious, and by consulting the Instructions of those who had a share in businesses, to unravel what has been most mysterious in the most private intrigues" (p. 34). Yet Rapin's view is that truth is insufficient by itself; the historian "must give it also a fine turn" (p. 38). This "fine turn" appears to be related to a writer's desire to have a work survive, as in the recommendation (following Cicero) to write "purely," observing the "propriety of words . . . the natural ordering of the phrases . . . and moderate use of figures,"for "without that advantage [of writing purely], an *Historian* will be but short liv'd" (pp. 12, 11).

Yet the writing must also persuade its reader of truthfulness: "But the fittest Style for *History* is that which has most of the Character of Truth, and wherein that natural light of Sincerity, which commonly accompanies the Truth, shines most: for, people easily believe things digested thus" (p. 39). History-likeness implies history for Rapin, and there are techniques for achieving such likeness: "Truth, which is the Soul of *History*, becomes suspicious, as soon as it is too much adorned; and Carelessness has more an Air of Sincerity" (p. 47). But it would be a misinterpretation to say that Rapin is counseling hypocrisy; rather, he is attempting to give body to the belief that events can in some way be fully represented by writing—put another way, that writing can be made transparent to events. But in this context it is appropriate to note that Rapin's objection to the lengthy speeches reported of the great figures of history is not so much to the weaknesses of their evidentiary foundations as it is to their failure to give pleasure to the reader. He agrees that such speeches have a "false look" because of the absence of any appropriate "Memoires" that could provide such detailed information (p. 82), but he places his emphasis on other deficiencies:

> A small Discourse made on purpose in an *History*, by one that bears a Character fit to make it, being also well suited to the Person and Subject under hand, may please, being put in its due place. But those formal Speeches at the Head of an Army ready to engage, and those Deliberations of a tedious prolixity . . . are almost out of fashion in good *Histories*: And the wisest chuse to make their *Heroe* speak things in few words, without engaging themselves to say set speeches. (pp. 83–84)

Much in Whalley and Rapin overlaps, and, of course, neither makes any pretensions to be doing something substantially original; their aim is rather to provide a more systematic and contemporary formulation and application of what has already been written. Rapin has, however, a more explicit formulation of the functions of narrative than can be found in Whalley, although some of Rapin's views of narrative appear to be implicit in Whalley's statements about the historian's need for a purposive organization. Through his remarks on narrative, Rapin is able to satisfy his conception of a cooperative relationship between the representational and rhetorical aspects of history. He regards narration as mimetic of the temporal order of history: "*History* being . . . nothing but a *Rehearsal* of things past, and in the same order as they came to pass, ought also to be a continued *Narration*" (p. 47). But then he opposes to the "order of Times" an "order of *Reason*" that "ought particularly to be the study of an *Historian*" (p. 51), a somewhat enigmatic formulation that corresponds, however, to Whalley's definition of the interpretation that is the historian's responsibility, as opposed to the mere annalist's easier task. For Rapin, narrative (or emplotment) enables the historian to insinuate a range of evaluations and interpretations into a history as seemingly an integral part of the rehearsal of past events in order of occurrence: "It is only by that secret Order that you may endear your Reader, so as to imprint your own Sentiments on his Mind, when you shew him Men acting naturally as they ought: and when you shew him their Manners, their Thoughts, their Designs and their Motives, as they are in a kind of dependency upon each other in the same natural order, which joyns them well together" (p. 51). Thus, the orders of reason and of time are joined in the narrative or plot, with events represented in a way that persuades the reader of the inherent connection of the realms of time and reason, representation and rhetoric seemingly become one.

Rapin goes on to warn the historian of the potential dangers in this function of narrative. If unsuccesfully joined to plot or narration, the order of reason is visible as mere private opinion, which has ruined the reputations of historians who have capitulated to the "itch of mingling their Conjectures with all Events, and imposing their own Conceits upon the *Publick* instead of *History*" (p. 69). Reflections on events must be made sparingly and as "natural as may be . . . such as arise from the Subject it self" (p. 95). Eloquence must be restrained, for that writer "persuades best, who explains himself in the easiest manner; it is persuasion only which gives to things that colour of Truth" (p. 106).[6]

---

[6] Hayden White, *The Content of the Form: Narrative Discourse and Historical Representation* (Baltimore: Johns Hopkins University Press, 1987), gives an excellent analysis of contemporary views of historical narrative, including an elegant account of Ricoeur's "metaphysics of narrativity" ("The Question of Narrative in Contemporary Historical Theory," pp. 26–57). These varying recent attitudes to narrative will also be found to be relevant to the questions that

Turning to Lenglet-Dufresnoy's *New Method of Studying History*, we see an increased concern with specifically evidentiary issues in history; but just as epistemological concerns cannot be eliminated from the primarily rhetorical concerns of Whalley and Rapin, so rhetoric is also included in Lenglet-Dufresnoy's conception of history. In addition to recommending Rapin's work, Lenglet-Dufresnoy gives the crucial rationale for a rhetorical view of history, its instructional burden. He disparages the accumulation of details such as "Years, Ages, Olympiads, or Epochs," or "Kings, Emperours, Councils, and Heresies," and instead defines a knowledge of history as being "acquainted with men the subjects of it" and judging "rationally of them" (p. 25). Like Bolingbroke, he further recommends that such historians be studied "who have somewhat in relation to our own circumstances, or those we have in common with the rest of mankind" (pp. 25–26). His concern here is to maximize history's usefulness and also to prevent readers from becoming discontented through reading histories inappropriate to their social stations.

As the title implies, the emphasis of *A New Method of Studying History* is on the reading of history in a critical and more than cursory way. It thus deals at some length with what should be accepted as persuasive in history— specificially with the kind of knowledge that an intelligent reader needs in order to apply appropriate factual and methodological tests to historical representations. The recommendations are a curious mixture of the old and new, a combination of views that would have been acceptable throughout early modern history with, however, increasing deference to antiquarian concerns. In "Of Inscriptions and Medals" he remarks, for example, on the undesirable separation of antiquarians from the tradition of humanist history: "It has been a Misfortune hitherto, that the most learned and famous Criticks had not the Knowledge of Medals, and that the greatest Part of the Medallists and Antiquaries have not been Men of Learning" (p. 242). Yet despite hints of the outlook of a "modern," he also recommends Bossuet's *Discourse on Universal History* as a good starting point for acquiring the great outline of history.

Lenglet-Dufresnoy devotes considerable attention to conflicts between

---

worried eighteenth-century theorists of history. Dominick LaCapra, *History and Criticism*, regards this essay of White's as a departure from the "genetic structuralism that appeared in his earlier writing" (p. 35n). See Wulf Kantsteiner, "Hayden White's Critique of the Writing of History," *History and Theory* 32 (1993): 273–95, for an analysis of the difficulties of analyzing White's position(s). Kantsteiner suggests that in providing answers to criticisms of his work, White has on occasion destabilized his own position.

testimony and probability, the issue that Hume later handled so brilliantly in
"Of Miracles" and that vexes Fielding's narrator in *Tom Jones*. Lenglet-
Dufresnoy's kind of skepticism acknowledges that "certain Histories easy to
be believed were false" but urges that we not, on the other hand, reject a
"Fact, which by the Weakness of our Imagination and Want of Capacity we
cannot comprehend" (pp. 261, 262). He determines that we ought to accept
strong testimony that is "related by judicious Authors, although there may be
something in it beyond Probability, yet ought it rather be believed than
rejected" (p. 262). But he immediately follows this rather generous acceptance of testimony by a series of critical comments: we should not always
credit even "Cotemporary Authors" until we have examined the "Causes and
Interests, which may have induced them to relate such Facts" (p. 263). And
in concert with Bolingbroke's later *Letters*, he suggests that we read the
critics of historians in combination with the historian: "Wherefore in reading
Herodotus, we may unite *Plutarch*'s piece against this Historian, nor read
Thucydides without the Notes of Dionysius *Halicarnessensis* upon him" (pp.
270–71).

Reports of miracles are a severe test of the eighteenth-century historian's
views of probability and testimony. To reject all miracles is to rely on
a probabilistic historiography above religion, but to set aside a probabilistic
historiography to save religion implies that religion is perhaps not verifiable
through historical means. Lenglet-Dufresnoy takes a conventionally moderate course in allowing testimony to take precedence over probability, but
also in requiring testimony to be subject to critical interrogation. Thus
pious people need not believe all accounts of miracles, but the freethinker
cannot dismiss all miracles because of deficiencies in the accounts of
some.

This evidentiary focus is continued and directed toward ostensibly anti-
quarian concerns in the work included with Lenglet-Dufresnoy's *New
Method*, the "Letter from Count Scipio Maffei, of *Verona*, to the Right
Honorable, the Countess Adelais Felix Canossa Tering of *Seefeld*. Being a
Comparison of the *Use* of *Inscriptions* and *Medals*." Such materials had been
studied for many years and thus cannot be seen as unusual in scholarship.
But what gives a slightly different cast here is that this material appears in a
book that supports the rhetorical view of the practical exemplary function of
history and is not written for an audience of scholars. It is here assumed that
at least some nontechnical, typically antiquarian questions may be profitably
considered by a general audience. Hardly as momentous as Bentley's action
in writing his *Dissertation upon the Epistles of Phalaris* in English, this letter
on medals and inscriptions may nevertheless be seen as a later exemplar of

the implication of Bentley's earlier action—that a nonscholarly audience might have a legitimate interest in the problems and controversies associated with scholarly historical research.[7] The letter's treatment of the material remains of the past moves from a concern for their evidentiary status to a valorizing of the material itself, a valuing of even an inexplicable trace for its contiguity to a past. We have already examined both scholarly and novelistic explorations and exemplification of this materializing tendency, this final resort to the object itself.

This letter is organized as a debate about the relative values of coins and monumental inscriptions, both having long been demonstrated to be an important supplement to other discursive records. Inscriptions in marble or brass are found to be more valuable mainly because they are longer: "These discourse not in a few maimed Words, but often in long Periods, full Diction, and sometimes give us at Length Letters, Harangues, Relations, Records, Acts, entire and Prolix Instruments" (p. 330). The subject of the letter is not, however, so much this announced debate as a justification of the systematic collection and display of the ruins of antiquity already begun: "the design of my new *Musaeum*" (p. 359).

This activity is most ostensibly motivated by the need to preserve valuable artifacts for historical scholarship, yet there are profoundly affective aspects to the count's conception of the project. Indeed the technical concerns alluded to seem far less urgent than the talismanic conception of antiquity that enlivens the letter. Monuments are perishing through the "Injuries of Time, Neglect, and the base Use made of them in our Buildings," and, in addition, Italy is "daily pillaged" by foreigners (p. 349). What gradually emerges is a changed focus, a turning from the evidentiary superiority of these monuments toward a view of the ontological superiority of brass and marble to books. If these monuments are lost, he first argues, we will be reduced to the uncertainties of books, which may be mere transcripts needing existing monuments for correction (p. 351). But to him the monuments *are* the past of Verona, not just a medium for its purveyance. He sees the writing on the monuments as in some sense originary in contrast to the derivations of books, a formulation that is perhaps glossed by his remarking on the use of marble by God himself: "as with his Eternal Hand he wrote on Marble the Conditions of the *Old Law*" (p. 324). He regards the very materials of marble and stone as themselves approaching transcendence: "One would imagine, that the Providence of God had directed Nature her

[7] Rudolf Pfeiffer, *History of Classical Scholarship from 1300 to 1850* (Oxford: Clarendon Press, 1976), finds that Bentley's writing of his *Dissertation* in English instead of Latin was "an innovation that marks an epoch in classical scholarship" (p. 150).

Work of Marble and Stone in the Bowels of the Earth for this End chiefly, that by them might be handed down to the last Posterity some Certainties of the remotest Ages, and the rather were these important Memoirs committed to them, as most likely to be preserved by the durableness of the Materials" (p. 324). These materials are of course conventional for memorializing the dead, and perhaps his own desperate hopes for immortality mingle in this account of the scholarly superiority of inscriptions to coins and of the founding of a museum to order the vanishing monuments of antiquity.

That transparency of language to event that Lucian and his Enlightenment admirers urged as a standard for written history appears less achievable as it is increasingly interrogated by the evidentiary concerns of the antiquarians, textual scholars, and the novel, which exposes not only the textuality of representation but also the textuality of much seeming reference and verification, allowing no mystification of writing through references to the durability of marble and brass. The research of the historian, the dependence on documents and inscriptions, is part of its rhetorical persuasiveness but nevertheless does not lead to a world of things wholly visible and comprehensible through the text. The fraudulent trace had long been a staple of satire. Lucian's narrator in *A True Story* claims to have received a new Homeric poem on his visit to the underworld (unfortunately he lost it), and Gulliver brings back little sheep from Lilliput (now propagating and producing an unusually fine wool), and wasp stings from Brobdingnag (now on display in Gresham College). Conventionally such claims in history have the status of verification (until the wasp stings can't be found) and in realistic fiction as signs that disbelief is to be suspended. Their satiric function, however, is to show that textuality has no necessary external reference even if it is layered as narrative and metanarrative. The force of the eighteenth-century novelists' exposure of the layerings of textuality is both more and less skeptical than those of history and satire. It is more skeptical in that there is less assurance of a world in which textuality might possibly be evaded by the right-minded search for reference; it is less skeptical in that truth is not exclusively conceived of as dependent on external reference.

The retreat from text to monument and, finally, to the refuge in marble and brass of the Count Scipio Maffei's letter is analogous to patterns in the fiction of the eighteenth century. The eighteenth-century novel allies itself to history by constituting itself as trace but then recognizes that this movement toward trace entails a loss of articulation. Of considerable relevance to this topic are, again, Paul Ricoeur's reflections on the trace in *Time and Narrative*, where Ricoeur shows the double character of the trace as a mark and a passage.[8] The paradox of the trace is that "the passage no longer is but the trace [or mark] remains" (p. 119). In its character as mark the trace appears more durable than the transitory human beings to which it bears witness, but this durability is achieved at the cost of becoming a thing among other things. As a "product" of people of the past, the trace has both a dynamic and a static aspect: as "mark," as present witness to past existence, it is static, but as product it enters into a cause-and-effect relationship to the past that is dynamic, speaking of "passage," movement, by connecting the marking thing to that which produced it (p. 120). Yet as the novel often shows, the search for the connection of the trace to its cause keeps turning up other traces, eventually narratives of narratives.

History's claim to the verifiable is placed under stress by the novel's claim of historicity, not because history cannot be distinguished from the novel, but because the traces on which history founds itself are often only with difficulty characterizable in terms different from those that the novel putatively assumes. The trace is a claim to presence that under scrutiny threatens to undermine the notion of reference. In its self-constitution as trace and as mediated through an editor, the novel sometimes resembles an assemblage of documentation, a "mark" that raises questions of evidentiary validity while at the same time claiming to be a talismanic bearer of the past. The editor who attempts to authenticate the documents that have been contiguous to a former presence is to some extent a realistic but disquieting replacement for the seer.

Eighteenth-century fiction's preoccupation with the trace brings its own attempts at verisimilitude to the point of collapse and can thus not leave history itself entirely ignorant of the meaning and dangers of its own practice. The identification of narrative with the trace implies either the collapse of narrative into the material mark, or into a sign of passage, the something which *was* but *is* not there. The novel's pursuit of the materiality of the trace leads to the silences of black pages and of paper itself, all of which figure death, despite their attempted alliance with the mark that outlives human transience. The careful placement in time that is a feature of formal realism is also a reminder of the incommensurability of this public time with the existential time that is always too short in comparison to the vastness of time figured by planetary movements.

David Hume addresses the problem of narrative, of emplotment, that lies behind the novel's paradoxical search both for less limited articulation than that available to history and for a seemingly more secure grounding *in* or

[8] Paul Ricoeur, *Time and Narrative*, vol. 3, trans. Kathleen Blamey and David Pellauer (Chicago: University of chicago Press, 1988), chap. 2.

even *as* the materials that history articulates. What Hume shows is that history's emplotment is both the very source of its meaningfulness and also the construction of a historian in the present, not something entirely immanent in events. Hume justifies by implication the efforts not only of the historian to understand the past but also of the novelist to create knowledge, narrative fiction serving for the creation as well as the conveyance of knowledge for both the historian and the novelist. The perceived differences between the novelist and historian derive then from debates about whether the knowledge produced is authentic knowledge of an actual past or probable knowledge of a possible past. In addition to his consideration of emplotment, Hume deals with the thorny issue of the constancy of human nature: if human nature is inconstant we are deprived of much probabilistic and inferential knowledge of the past such as both history and the novel rely on, yet if human nature is constant all history becomes to a certain degree contemporary and even fiction becomes a prey to repetitiousness, as Fielding and Johnson recognized. These and other considerations in Hume work to reconcile the evidentiary and rhetorical features of history, as his questions are often about the grounds of our persuasions in everyday life. Such concerns foreground questions about the nature of the organizing fictions of our everyday life and thus also about the fictions of our novels. The following analysis is heavily indebted to a study by Donald W. Livingston, *Hume's Philosophy of Common Life* (1984), which makes Hume's historical outlook central to all of his major work, showing persuasively the importance of the categories of the historical and the narrative for Hume's views generally.[9] I use Livingston's analysis to connect salient writings by Hume on the topic of history and narrative to an exploration of the interactions of history and fiction.

The novel claims a relationship with history that covertly acknowledges the superiority of history but, nevertheless, attempts to aggrandize fiction by insisting on its potential similarity to history. The success of eighteenth-century fiction in sustaining this similarity, however, leads not to the merely parasitical relationship that its sometimes implausible claims to referentiality imply, but to a position that implicitly threatens history's claims to truth by enacting those limits of textuality that history conceals. The eighteenth-century novel constitutes itself as historicist inquiry into its fictional subject

[9] Donald W. Livingston, *Hume's Philosophy of Common Life* (Chicago: University of Chicago Press, 1984). Many of the references here, although not all, are drawn from chapter 8, "Historical Understanding." I have adapted Livingston's argument to issues relevant to the novel and have, thus, used his analysis of Hume selectively. Readers interested in the full implications of these arguments for Hume need to consult Livingston's book, reading at very least chapter 8 in its entirety.

matter, thus including in its scope not only the depiction of a social world through the invention of realistic characters and events, but also those concerns about epistemology and the adequacy of representation that it shares with history. This fiction exposes its own fragmentariness and its difficulties in finding plausible, let alone true, foundations, yet creates a compelling and complex version of past human experience despite these apparent difficulties. History is made vulnerable to fiction when the traces on which it founds its narrative are shown to be hard to distinguish from the traces created in fictional narrative. The question then becomes, "How can history justify its fictionality?" not just, "How can fiction claim historicity?"[10]

Among Hume's various and major contributions to this discussion, perhaps the salient one is his understanding of the fictional (in the sense of constructed) element of history. History cannot in some mysterious way bring the past itself before us without acknowledging its own standpoint in a present, and thus it creates for us an understanding that could not exist in that past seemingly being recreated. Hume's historian attempts to be internal to what is described, both trying to understand events as they appeared to contemporary spectators and trying, as well, to grasp the less public motives of participants in historical events. These dual perspectives must, however, also be supplemented by one external to this past, seeing it and understanding it according to consequences, values, and concepts outside it.

For Hume history is a "moral science," a category that is constituted by connecting consciousness to what lies outside it. The moral sciences are not for this reason suspect: Hume recognizes that the various conventions of social existence are arrived at over periods of time—in Livingston's words, they are "the unintended result of man's involvement with the world and with his fellows" (*Common Life*, p. 4)—and thus can be understood only through their history. Hume does not accept the invidious distinction implied by the division between primary and secondary qualities, in which qualities that are thought to be *in* objects, like weight, are regarded as primary and those that result from human interaction, like color, as secondary. For Hume, the assumptions of common life inevitably constitute the arena within which true philosophical thought operates, and they cannot be discarded in the interests of a reason that disregards apprehended life.

---

[10] LaCapra, *History and Theory*, suggests that the "most telling question posed by the novel to historiography may be whether contemporary historical writing can learn something of a self-critical nature from a mode of discourse it has often tried to use or explain in overly reductive fashion. A different way of reading novels may alert us not only to the contestatory voices and counter-discourses of the past but to the ways in which historiography itself may become a more critical voice in the 'human sciences'" (p. 132).

Consequently, for Hume, history rather than, for example, mathematics, becomes the paradigm for human understanding. This situating of history at the very center of our attempts to understand the human world, and the concomitant and related acknowledgment that historical understanding is a constitution of events in relation to a present—a construction as opposed to a recreation—defines history as the inclusive fiction that constitutes our social world and enables our understanding of it. Its very acknowledgment of fictiveness incorporates fiction's analytical powers into its own.

The principal connection between fiction and history in Hume occurs through narrative, which is a factor obviously common to both. The human bondage to presentness introduces an element of narrative into all reflections on the past: "The imagination can never totally forget the points of space and time, in which we are existent; but receives such frequent advertisements of them from the passions and senses, that however it may turn its attention to foreign and remote objects, it is necessitated every moment to reflect on the present."[11] This present-referring propensity of the imagination suggests that for Hume human beings are involved in an ongoing process of creating narrative webs between past and present, these narrative webs constituting experience as meaningful: in Livingston's words, "Events in a story gain meaning by being viewed from the perspective of later events, and later events are narratively unintelligible unless seen in the light of earlier events" (*Common Life*, p. 130). The activity of the historian is an extension of the same narrative activity by which people attempt to understand their own existences. Again in Livingston's words: "History, then, is not a structure in the world to be discovered by the historian . . . it is a point of view written into the very idea of history" (p. 234).

The third section of *An Enquiry concerning Human Understanding*, "Of the Association of Ideas," reveals Hume's understanding of the related emplotments of both history and acknowledged fictions. Hume designates three categories of association by which we connect ideas to each other— resemblance, contiguity in time or space, and cause and effect—suggesting that even the "loosest and freest conversation" has a connection "in all its transitions" (p. 22).[12] In all editions of the *Enquiry* in his lifetime except for the last one Hume followed this discussion with an analysis of how literature,

[11] David Hume, *Treatise of Human Nature*, ed. L. A. Selby-Bigge and P. H. Nidditch (Oxford: Clarendon Press, 1978), II, iii, vii, 427–28 (cited here and in the text by book, part, section, and page number).

[12] The entire third section, "Of the Association of Ideas," including the portion that was omitted from the last edition of Hume's lifetime and rarely appears in modern editions, is here quoted from *The Philosophical Works of David Hume*, vol. 4 (Boston: Little, Brown, 1854), pp. 22–29. Hume presumably canceled the earlier discussion of association in literary texts because it overbalances his more general discussion in the remainder of the section. There is no reason to believe that he repudiated it.

including history, derives its unity from these categories of association. Ovid's *Metamorphoses*, for example, connects all its episodes by resemblance, the only similarity demanded is that of a "fabulous transformation" (p. 24). The "historian, who should undertake to write the history of Europe during any century" would include events contiguous in time and space "though in other respects different and unconnected." But a more powerful connective is cause and effect, which "while the historian traces the series of actions according to their natural order," enables also the discovery of "their secret springs and principles, and delineates their most remote consequences" (pp. 24–25). Hume implies that the unity Aristotle required for poetry is also achievable in the writing of history. He envisages the possibility of a history with the meticulous order that Aristotle found possible only through the constructedness of poetry and optimally successful only in a temporally confined form like drama. In contradiction to Aristotle, Hume argues that a unity of cause and effect is possible even in a dispersed form like biography: "Nor only in any limited portion of life, a man's actions have a dependence on each other, but also during the whole period of his duration from the cradle to the grave. . . . The unity of action, therefore, which is to be found in biography or history, differs from that of epic poetry, not in kind, but in degree" (p. 25). This greater degree of unity required in poetry results from its need of "passions more inflamed" than those needed in narration confined "to strict truth and reality." The stimulated reader needs "minute circumstances, which, though to the historian they seem superfluous, serve mightily to enliven the imagery and gratify the fancy" (p. 26). Such an emotional demand can be sustained for only a relatively short time, however, and thus the epic must be shorter than history and have a more focused unity than history or biography, for example, the wrath of Achilles, not the life of Achilles.

This connectedness that Hume makes so central to both history and narrative poetry is one that is to varying degrees existent but also constructed. In the realm of moral philosophy, which deals with the social and personal world, there is a connectedness that derives from the intentionality of human activity: "As man is a reasonable being, and is continually in pursuit of happiness, which he hopes to find in the gratification of some passion or affection, he seldom acts, or speaks, or thinks, without a purpose and intention" (p. 24). Such intentionality then also characterizes the writing of epics and histories, which reveal their own constructedness as well as their replication of the connectedness they find elsewhere: "A production without a design would resemble more the ravings of a madman, than the sober efforts of genius and learning." Hume does not, however, finally separate the structure of the narration from the structure of knowledge, although the narration will have a form that is not identical to the events that it uses as its basis. In history, a cause-and-effect narrative imposed on the associative pattern of contiguity in time and space will create the most stringent unity and also the "most instructive" narrative, "since it is by [knowledge of causes] alone we are enabled to control events and govern futurity" (p. 25). The historian's ordering and narration of events create an understanding that does not exist prior to this narrative ordering, yet that understanding has a validity outside the ordering consciousness. Hume relates this understanding to a rather strong formulation of the usefulness of causal thinking in controlling events and governing the future, although in practice, as Hume shows elsewhere, cause-and-effect relationships usually take the form of probabilities, sometimes rather weak ones, rather than of absolutes.

These formulations show a rather different picture of narrative thinking from that characterized as the "eclipse of narrative," which was the drift of much explicit eighteenth-century thought about the interpretation of narrative. Rather than reducing narrative to reference (as Frei suggests was the case in much interpretation of history-like biblical narrative), Hume makes reference dependent on narrative for meaningfulness. He thus finds history and epic poetry to verge on theoretical inseparability: "As the difference . . . consists only in the degrees of connection, which bind together those several events of which their subject is composed, it will be difficult, if not impossible, by words, to determine exactly the bounds which separate them from each other" (p. 28).

Despite Hume's almost insouciant near-conflation of the fictional and the historical, he is finally deeply concerned with the validation of veridical history as opposed to the limitations of fictionality. He does not wish to deprive history of either the benefits of narrative complexity that it shares with fiction or the persuasiveness of referentiality that enables its triumph over fiction. Elsewhere, Hume deals with the ambiguities of history and fiction in terms of the conditions that bring about belief: "Truth, however necessary it may seem in all works of genius, has no other effect than to procure an easy reception for the ideas, and to make the mind acquiesce in them with satisfaction, or at least without reluctance" (*Treatise*, I, iii, x, 121). This truth-effect explains why tragedians borrow from "some well known passage in history." Hume refers to the difference between reading a "romance" and a "history" as one between two levels of affect:

> If one person sits down to read a book as a romance, and another as a true history, they plainly receive the same ideas and in the same order . . . tho' [the author's] testimony has not the same influence on them. The latter [the one reading as if reading history] has a more lively conception of all

the incidents. . . . While the former, who gives no credit to the testimony of the author, has a more faint and languid conception of all these particulars. (vii, 97–98)

It seems plausible that Hume here has in mind a prose story with features of history, something like the novel. This comment might indeed be read as if explicating Richardson's unwillingness to give up the term *history* for *Clarissa*. Hume's "history" is in many respects like fiction, having the same potentialities for generating meaning through elaborate emplotment, but it has in addition the power over the imagination that is derived from the assumption of its identification with reality, a power that fictional works can generate only through their rhetoric and ornament:

> What more agreeable entertainment to the mind, than to be transported into the remotest ages of the world . . . to see all the human race, from the beginning of time, pass, as it were, in review before us; appearing in their true colours, without any of those disguises, which, during their life-time, so much perplexed the judgment of the beholders. What spectacle can be imagined, so magnificent, so various, so interesting?[13]

Hume's acceptance of the possible formal similarities between history and the novel, as well as his view of the emplotment of history, may possibly be construed as a historical skepticism that regards history not as a form of knowledge but, nevertheless, as a more persuasive story than that usually told by novelists. Such an interpretation can be supported by reference to Hume's view that consciousness is insistently present-referring, allowing us no access to the past that does not also entail a view of ourselves in a present. Furthermore, his rather too optimistic statement that we see the past "without any of those disguises" that "perplexed the judgment of the beholders" may be construed as meaning not that we now see truth, but that we now construct a scenario that is presently persuasive but reconstructs no actual past. The view just described here is not, however, Hume's. Hume's discussions of history and fiction usually take place in the context of his definition of the factors that lead us toward belief, discussions Hume pursues not in order to cast doubt on the validity of history but in order to explain the importance of exploring our conventions of belief, which provide the parameters within which philosophy must seek its sometimes conflicting truths: in Livingston's words, "No custom or belief of common life however 'methodized and corrected' can satisfy this demand of thought to know the real, and

[13] David Hume, "Of the Study of History," in *Essays, Moral, Political, and Literary*, ed. Eugene Miller (Indianapolis: Liberty Classics, rev. ed., 1987), pp. 565–66.

yet it is only *through* these customs and prejudices that we can think about the real" (*Common Life*, p. 3). And, as suggested earlier, the basis of much of Hume's philosophy is historical: in his view, an understanding of the moral world is possible only through an understanding of the historical process by which its conventions were formed.

Hume does not underestimate the difficulties of establishing the provenience of documents and, however genuine, of validating the testimony contained in them. But ultimately the critical judgment of sources is dependent on the reader's experience of people and events as well as of writings. It is this experience that places the historian outside the documents, able to criticize them, yet also inside the represented actors, able to understand them: "It is universally acknowledged that there is a great uniformity among the actions of men, in all nations and ages, and that human nature remains still the same, in its principles and operations. . . . Would you know the sentiments, inclinations, and course of life of the Greeks and Romans? Study well the temper and actions of the French and English."[14] Consequently to "explode any forgery in history, we cannot make use of a more convincing argument, than to prove, that the actions ascribed to any person are directly contrary to the course of nature, and that no human motives, in such circumstances, could ever induce him to such a conduct" (p. 84).

Hume's uniformitarianism, his belief in the constancy of human nature, has been regarded as a disqualification of his historical thought. How would someone who *a priori* does not accept one era as distinct from another discern the existence of even blatant difference? Is not the assimilation of the past to the present a trivialization of history? And more important, perhaps, is not uniformitarianism inconsistent with Hume's sense that human conventions are formed slowly and insensibly over time and can be understood only through uncovering their historical development? In what sense can there be a constant human nature that inheres in a constantly altering moral world?

Hume's exposition of the tenets of his particular kind of uniformitarianism shows it to be markedly less vulnerable to these criticisms than it at first appears to be.[15] Hume questions the possibility of any knowledge of the past

[14] David Hume, *Enquiry concerning Human Understanding*, in *Enquiries*, ed. L. A. Selby-Bigge and P. H. Nidditch (Oxford: Clarendon Press, 1975), sec. 8, part 1, p. 83.

[15] Despite Ricoeur's dismissal of Hume on history, there appears to be common ground. Ricoeur proposes a dialectic in dealing with the past: sameness to the past; difference from the past; and the analogy of past to present. Sameness produces rethinking (reenacting) of the past; difference returns otherness to the past; and the analogous then produces a resemblance between relations in the past and relations in the present, rather than a direct relationship between terms in the past and in the present (*Time and Narrative*, 3:142–54).

if there is no derivable pattern, only uniqueness. He shifts the question to those who assert that human behavior is utterly unpredictable, asking what then would be the point of attempting to understand the moral world (*Enquiry*, sec. 8, part 1, p. 85). He cautions that, on the other hand, no complete uniformity can be expected, thus taking the debate out of the realm of absolutes and into that of probabilities. Hume's conception of human consistency is intelligible if not always itself perfectly consistent: outward behavior, manners, can vary greatly and can be mysterious unless connected to motives. Such diversities of manners can, however, be made intelligible because they are formed through circumstances that if understood will make apparent the constancy of the human motivations that are reflected in them. Although, "men *always* seek society" (*Treatise*, II, iii, i, 402), their manner of seeking it and the kind of society formed may differ markedly depending on the constraints of an incalculable number of variables. The constancy of human nature cannot be discerned except through the historical study that acknowledges differences of manners and circumstances.[16]

How far Hume is from the reductive uniformitarianism sometimes attributed to him can be readily seen in "A Dialogue," a work in which one character narrates his experiences of a strange land, arousing the listener's contempt for the immoral behavior described, which is then identified as that of ancient and venerable Greeks: "And I think I have fairly made it appear, that an Athenian man of merit might be such a one as with us might pass for incestuous, a parracide, an assassin, an ungrateful, perjured traitor, and something else too abominable to be named; not to mention his rusticity and ill-manners" (*Enquiries*, p. 329). But the initially appalled listener then goes on to show that these activities although repugnant to him in themselves grow out of the assumption that in particular circumstances they are "*useful*, or *agreeable* to a man *himself*, or to *others*," which are the reasons for assigning approbation in any society (p. 336). If a context is described in addition to the bare recital first presented, it is then possible to see a coincidence between those values revered in modern society and those aimed at in the seemingly reprehensible activities of a different society: "The principles upon which men reason in morals are always the same; though the conclusions which they draw are often very different" (pp. 335–36).

For Hume history is internal, external, and narrative. The external perspective yields the atemporal truths of human behavior, but is derivable only

---

[16] See Livingston, *Common Life*, pp. 214–25, for a sustained analysis of Hume's historical uniformitarianism that demonstrates its imperviousness to many frequent criticisms of it.

from an internal understanding of the agents and their particularized circumstances. These two perspectives provide both knowledge and understanding, but must be connected also to the temporal position of the historian, whose comprehension is enhanced through "viewing [past events] by the light of later events where both sets of events are in the spectator's past" (Livingston, *Common Life*, p. 234). Narrative brings the internal and external perspectives together with a present from which the historian can look back over a series of former events, thus allowing the construal of a past through these mutually illuminating perspectives.

History is for Hume linked to a master narrative, although not the providential one; for Hume, this master narrative is the story of the improvements of the human mind, and it constitutes society. The various smaller narrative sequences combine into large sequences that bring, in Livingston's words, "historical unity into common life" (pp. 234–35). Hume's point is not that all histories will in fact agree anymore than that all that is taken for knowledge will cohere, but rather that the disagreements can be worked out only within the frame of the larger story that constitutes the community. Hume exposes a contradiction in history—its need to achieve a completed narrative ordering in order to acquire its full complexity of meaning, yet its need also to maintain a constantly shifting relationship to the always-in-revision master narrative that constitutes the community.[17]

David Wootton suggests that Hume as historian saw himself as competing with the novelists, recommending history as a replacement for novel reading.[18] In fact, much that Hume incorporates into history is what the

[17] Louis O. Mink, "Narrative Form as a Cognitive Instrument," in *Historical Understanding*, ed. Brian Fay, Eugene O. Golub, and Richard T. Vann (Ithaca: Cornell University Press, 1987), pp. 182–203, analyzes the often unstated assumptions that experience is narrative and that all historical narratives should cohere, assumptions that survive despite our apparent rejection of the possibility of a universal history. He sees narrative and history as concepts that interfere with each other: "Narrative histories should be aggregative, insofar as they are histories, but cannot be, insofar as they are narratives. Narrative history borrows from fictional narrative the convention by which a story generates its own imaginative space ... but it presupposes that past actuality is a single and determinate realm, a presupposition which, once it is made explicit, is at odds with the incomparability of imaginative stories" (p. 197). A different formulation of a doubleness in history is that by Paul Hernadi, "Clio's Cousins: Historiography as Translation, Fiction, Criticism," *New Literary History: A Journal of Theory and Interpretation* 7 (1976): 247–57, who conceives of history as a translation "from the idiom of events, forever past, into the idiom of continually present discourse" (p. 247). Hernadi divides the historian's translations into two kinds that either order experience into patterns of cause or into patterns of purpose—one scientific, the other mythic. The historian thus "labors under two sometimes conflicting jurisdictions" (p. 249).

[18] David Wootton, "David Hume, 'the historian,'" in *The Cambridge Companion to Hume*, ed. David Fate Norton (Cambridge: Cambridge University Press, 1993), pp. 281–82.

eighteenth-century, as well as the later, novel performs with distinction.[19] The rendering of the private world of the historical agent, as well as the demonstration of that private world's frequent opaqueness, is what fiction performs superlatively well, thus revealing the motivations for, or the mysteriousness of, public actions. The combining of this internal view and an external one, with both then brought into significant relationship to later events and the still later position of the narrator, can be taken to be a description of the telos of the narrative experiments of eighteenth-century fiction. Fiction thus critically engages history through their common connection with narrative. The narrator's present is not only a neutral vantage on the past but also a force in its construal and narration. The novel, despite Hume's suspicions of this competitor to history, has provided an important critique of our master narratives, both expanding and analyzing the narrative possibilities that constitute our communities.

[19] Carol Kay, *Political Constructions: Defoe, Richardson, and Sterne in Relation to Hobbes, Hume, and Burke* (Ithaca: Cornell University Press, 1988), analyzes eighteenth-century fiction in relation to political and social issues of the kind Hume is here exemplifying. For her, "Hume and Burke emerge . . . as socially oriented theorists and historians of society, inspired by their perceptions of the organizing power of customary, natural-seeming social systems" (p. 7). She suggests that "readers of novels should be alert to the political interconnection between characterization and plot, the link between modes of understanding other people and the social narrative, the consolidation of a stable society or its disintegration" (p. 26).

INDEX